China's Rising Foreign Ministry

Studies in Asian Security

SERIES EDITORS

Amitav Acharya, American University   David Leheny, Waseda University

*For a complete listing of titles in this series, visit
the Stanford University Press website, www.sup.org.*

China's Rising Foreign Ministry

Practices and Representations
of Assertive Diplomacy

Dylan M.H Loh

STANFORD UNIVERSITY PRESS
Stanford, California

Stanford University Press
Stanford, California

Printed in the United States of America on acid-free, archival-quality paper

Library of Congress Cataloging-in-Publication Data
Names: Loh, Dylan M. H., author.
Title: China's rising Foreign Ministry : practices and representations of assertive diplomacy
    / Dylan M.H Loh.
Other titles: Studies in Asian security.
Description: Stanford, California : Stanford University Press, 2024. | Series: Studies in
    Asian security | Includes bibliographical references and index.
Identifiers: LCCN 2023041890 (print) | LCCN 2023041891 (ebook) | ISBN 9781503638204
    (cloth) | ISBN 9781503638679 (ebook)
Subjects: LCSH: China. Wai jiao bu. | China—Foreign relations—21st century. | China—
    Foreign relations—Southeast Asia. | Southeast Asia—Foreign relations—China.
Classification: LCC JZ1734 .L65 2024 (print) | LCC JZ1734 (ebook) | DDC 327.51—dc23/
    eng/20231213
LC record available at https://lccn.loc.gov/2023041890
LC ebook record available at https://lccn.loc.gov/2023041891

Cover photograph: Max12Max, CC BY-SA 4.0, via Wikimedia Commons, https://commons
.wikimedia.org/wiki/File:Ministry_of_Foreign_Affairs,_Beijing.jpg

Contents

Acknowledgments

This book is the result of eight years of research, writing, and editing. More importantly, it is a product of the friendship, support, and counsel of my peers and family that have nurtured it to completion.

Ayse Zarakol provided invaluable guidance and mentorship. She believed in me and my project, and this served as a vital source of continuous support. I thank K. C. Lin, who was a constant sounding board for my work. I am grateful to the Department of Politics and International Studies at Cambridge University for shaping me to be the scholar that I am today. I am indebted to St Catharine's College at Cambridge for giving me a home during those wonderful years. My time at Cambridge are some of the best times of my life. Friends like Yingfeng Ji, Wenyu Wang, Yasu Okazawa, Ryo Koblitz, Lifan Li, Marie Prum, Hakan Sandal, Liang Ce, Jonny Mak, Frances Hyslop, Danilo Cardim, Terry Wu, Leonard Ng, Yuan, Dev Anand, Laure Giuliano, Jimmy Xu, Maggie Zhou, Janis Atelbauers, Heqing Huang, Christian Schultheiss, Jose Velazquez, and Aulia Beg made time spent away from home far too enjoyable.

My research would not have been possible if not for the generous Singapore Teaching and Academic Research Talent scholarship funded by Nanyang Technological University (NTU) and the Ministry of Education. The Public Policy and Global Affairs Programme at NTU keeps me gainfully employed, enabling me to pursue this book's publication. To readers of earlier drafts of the book, either in part or in whole, I am thankful for your time and effort. In alphabetical order, I thank Chen Hao, Christian Bueger, Hoo Tiang Boon, Jaakko Heiskanen, Jérémie Cornut, Kei Koga, Kerry Brown, Max Lesch, Pascal Vennesson, Paul Beaumont, Rebecca Adler-Nissen, and Vincent Pouliot. The book also benefited from conversations with Aarie Glas, Deepak Nair, Xiaoyu Pu, Lucas de Oliveira Paes, Stéphanie Martel, Sean Fleming, Andrea Ghiselli, and Babak Mohammadzadeh.

My deep gratitude goes out to the expert team at Stanford University Press (SUP), including Alan Harvey, Daniel LoPreto, Cat Ng Pavel, Caroline McKusick, Chris Peterson, and Elisabeth Magnus. Daniel was a reassuring and positive presence throughout the entire process, and his expertise was critical to the book's publication. I also thank the series editor Amitav Acharya and David Leheny for their counsel and feedback. I am especially thankful to David for his wisdom and encouragement as he went over and beyond the necessary to carefully guide me at every stage of the manuscript. Thank you for seeing the potential in the manuscript and for your patience with me! Suffice it to say, this book could not have found a better home than the Studies in Asian Security series at SUP.

My time as a student and, subsequently, as a research analyst at the S. Rajaratnam School of International Studies (RSIS) was instrumental in kicking off my academic career. I am thankful for the friendship and mentoring I received there. I am most grateful to Mr. Barry Desker, who, fortunately, "hijacked" my job application at RSIS. His encouragement and mentorship gave me the space and time to grow as a scholar. I also thank Ambassador Ong Keng Yong, Alan Chong, Kwa Chong Guan, Joseph Liow, Tan See Seng, Ralf Emmers, Kyaw, Farish Noor, Bhubhindar Singh, Mingjiang Li, Sarah Teo, Khong Yuen Foong, Ang Cheng Guan, Benjamin Ho, David Han, Harry Sa, Fitri Bintang Timur, Mely Caballero Anthony, Joel Ng, Henrick Tsjeng, and Tan Ming Hui for their advice, support, banter, and jokes during my time at RSIS. I further wish to thank Tan Joo Ean, who was my professor when I was a sociology undergraduate at NTU. The imprint of my undergraduate training as a sociologist (credit to the wonderful faculty at the Sociology Department) at NTU is evident in the book's social-theoretical approach.

I would like to express my appreciation to my extremely capable research assistants who aided me in editing the manuscript: Lim Ziqian, Jocelyn Wong, Lim Jia Ying, Ian Seow, and Chng Chun Kang. To my interviewees—I am forever in your debt for your openness and willingness to speak with me. Thank you for your hospitality, fantastic meals, Tsingtao beers, and Moutai liquor. This project would not have been possible without you. Finally, I would like to thank my family. My late father, Loh Boon Aun, left far too soon and is dearly missed. My mom, Loh Poh Lin and my uncle, Eric Loh, both silently supported me in their own little ways. My wife, Mabel, has been a constant and stable presence throughout this eight-year writing journey. Thank you for putting up with me, reading my manuscript, and trying to understand what I do! My daughters are my fuel and my lodestars. I never knew I could love someone the way I love both of you. I dedicate this book to my daughters—Calla Loh and Cassia Loh.

Dylan M.H Loh
SINGAPORE
MARCH 23, 2023

List of Abbreviations

1MDB1	Malaysia Development Berhad
ANT	actor-network theory
ASEAN	Association of Southeast Asian Nations
BFSU	Beijing Foreign Studies University
BP	bureaucratic politics [approach]
BRI	Belt and Road Initiative
CCP	Chinese Communist Party
CFAC	Central Foreign Affairs Commission
CFAU	China Foreign Affairs University
CIIS	China Institute for International Strategic Studies
CMC	Central Military Commission
CNOOC	China National Offshore Oil Corporation
CoC	Code of Conduct
CoP	Community of Practice
IR	international relations
MCA	multiple correspondence analysis
MND	Ministry of National Defense
MOFA	Ministry of Foreign Affairs (PRC)
MOFCOM	Ministry of Commerce (PRC)
NDRC	National Development and Reform Commission
PCA	Permanent Court of Arbitration
PLA	People's Liberation Army
PLAN	People's Liberation Army Navy
PRC	People's Republic of China
PSC	Politburo Standing Committee

PT	practice theory
SCS	South China Sea
SIIS	Shanghai Institutes for International Studies
SOEs	state-owned enterprises
THAAD	Terminal High Altitude Area Defense

China's Rising Foreign Ministry

Why China's Foreign Ministry and Diplomats Matter (More Than We Think)

Quotidian, routine, and, perhaps, somewhat boring. These are qualities not typically associated with diplomacy and diplomats (e.g., Sharp, 1999, pp. 41–42; Kleiner, 2008). Indeed, diplomacy, viewed popularly, tends to play out as public spectacles: Donald Trump's Singapore summit with Kim Jong Un in 2018 and Xi Jinping's meeting with Ma Ying-jeou in 2015 are a couple of examples. Whether one understands diplomacy as the "application of tact and intelligence to the conduct of official relations between governments" (Satow, 1979, p. 3), the mediation of estrangement (Der Derian, 1987), or the "management of frontlines between different political entities" (Cooper & Cornut, 2018, p. 300), diplomacy does not usually evoke images of mundanity. Yet diplomats often associate it with tedium, as one Chinese diplomat says plainly: "Actually, this involves a lot of hard work. This is a tough job. What we do every day consists of repeated meetings and paperwork. Most things and times are unexciting, even boring" (Interviewee 1, personal communication, November 20, 2016). In contrast, international relations (IR) as a discipline is often fixated on visible and major events of international life such as wars, crises, and revolutions that serve as "benchmark dates" (Buzan & Lawson, 2012). What is more, IR sometimes underestimates diplomacy's relevance in that states and structures become "unproblematic and unproblematized entities" that "play out their games in ways that admit little attention to diplomats and diplomacy" (Sharp, 1999, p. 34). Thus diplomacy has been observed as being "epiphenomenal or redundant" to IR theory (Pouliot & Cornut, 2015, p. 298), despite being the "engine room" of international affairs (R. Cohen, 1998, p. 1).

Addressing this issue head on, scholarship motivated by the "practice turn"—analytical inquiry focusing on human/institutional "doings and sayings"—has made important inroads in highlighting diplomacy's importance to a wide range of IR phenomena such as international hierarchy (Pouliot, 2016), power in multilateral arenas (Adler-Nissen & Pouliot, 2014), politics of knowledge production (Neumann, 2012), and international humanitarian interventions (Autesserre, 2014). Even as diplomatic studies have made important progress in studying diplomats and foreign ministries in the West (e.g., Neumann, 2012; Cornut, 2015; Bicchi & Bremberg, 2016), little has been said regarding Chinese diplomacy. This presents a gap in our understanding of international diplomacy, particularly as Chinese diplomats and diplomacy become more consequential in world politics. Running parallel to this gap is IR's tendency to theoretically minimize China's rise, which, despite its importance, "has yet to systematically appeal to the core IR theoretical community" as "a potentially theory generating event" (Pan & Kavalski, 2018, p. 291). How do we make sense of China's consul-general in Brazil insulting the Canadian prime minister by calling him a "running dog of the US" (Ceco, 2021), People's Republic of China (PRC) diplomats allegedly beating up Taiwanese representatives during a reception for Taiwan's national day in Fiji (Hille, 2020b), or the Chinese Ministry of Foreign Affairs (MOFA) insisting that the US deputy secretary of state meet with China's foreign minister under the downgraded diplomatic nomenclature of *huijian* (diplomatic meeting 会见) instead of *huitan* (diplomatic talk 会谈) (Xinhua, 2021)? In words and in deeds, a more assertive "wolf warrior" shift has been observed in Chinese diplomacy (D. Loh, 2020b). Even so, relatively little is known about how MOFA and its diplomats contribute to foreign policy and the reasons for, and effects of, this more muscular diplomacy.

Against this backdrop, this research seeks to extend the insights of the practice turn in IR to investigate Chinese diplomacy—particularly its assertive diplomatic shift from 2009 to 2020.[1] Prevailing interpretations of China's assertiveness often describe this phenomenon in terms of China's military rise (J. Zhang, 2013), ascendant nationalism (Carlson, 2009), President Xi's strategic intent (Mastro, 2015, pp. 155–156), or a combination of these factors (see Friedberg, 2014). I argue instead that Chinese assertiveness has increasingly come to be represented by Chinese diplomats and MOFA—so much so that MOFA is now the central driver and representation of the "assertive China" meme.

China's Rising Foreign Ministry and Its Representational Role

The research questions motivating this book include: How is China's assertiveness (defined as the tendency to use its power and influence to impose costs on others to extract compliance and/or police behavior) represented, and what are its concrete manifestations? Why is Chinese behavior on the international stage increasingly *evaluated* by different international actors and publics as assertive? How do other state actors construct and understand Chinese foreign policy behavior? As I will demonstrate, these questions can be answered only by investigating MOFA's representational role (acting/speaking on behalf of the state/Party and expressing its interests, values, and ideologies) and its diplomatic practices. Indeed, President Xi asserts that China's diplomacy now "represents the will of the state" (Xinhua, 2018), underlining MOFA's representational significance. What is more, China has "bolstered the political clout" of MOFA and further invested in its diplomacy since 2008 (Thomas, 2021, para. 14). This is evinced in the promotion of foreign minister Wang Yi, in 2018, to one of only five state councillor positions and the elevation of former foreign minister Yang Jiechi to the Politburo in 2017—the apex of political power, which "restores the top diplomat's status to the level once enjoyed by his former mentor Qian Qichen" (Y. Wang, 2017, p. 11). Wang Yi himself was, subsequently, promoted to the twenty-four-member Politburo in October 2022 (Kaneko, 2022).

Besides, China's assertiveness is one of the biggest foreign policy debates in recent times, so it needs to be more accurately assessed. Currently, much of this discussion centers on China's purportedly assertive behavior since 2009 and the factors that gave rise to this phenomenon (e.g., Y. Shi, 2013; I. Chen & Hao 2013). Some argue that it is a result of competition between China and the US due to America's rebalance to Asia (Buszynski, 2012). Others maintain that China is practicing "proactive assertiveness," like the staging of maneuvers in the South China Sea to reinforce future claims (J. Zhang, 2013). The popular charge of "creeping assertiveness" describes China as making slow and seemingly harmless advances to score consolidated gains over time (Storey, 1999). Finally, some scholars claim that China's foreign policy assertiveness is "new" and denotes greater willingness to flex its military and diplomatic muscle, especially over its territorial claims (Yahuda, 2013; Thayer, 2011). Conversely, others have identified the post-2008 period as one in which China has become more cooperative and responsible (Zheng et al., 2010). Through an analysis of seven major foreign policy events in 2010—often touted as cases of Chinese assertiveness—Johnston argues that extant literature on China's assertiveness has not properly accounted for assertive behavior before 2010, while also suffering from flawed "selection on the dependent variable; ahistoricism; and poor causal specification" (2013, p. 31). Jerdén (2014) questions the assertive characterization itself and insists that there has been no change in China's foreign policy behavior. G. Chan et al. add that China has "adopted an increasingly cooperative approach to working with major international institutions" and that it has played a bigger regional role in the wake of the 2007–2009 economic crisis (2012, p. 61). Others acknowledge China's assertiveness but also explain how Beijing is positively contributing to the international order (Godement, 2012, pp. 231–

232). Finally, some scholars aver that the most obvious feature of Chinese foreign policy is its fluidity and inconsistency (M. Li & Loh, 2015; Shambaugh, 2013, p. 14; Goldstein, 2012, pp. 55–57).

Intervening in this debate, I assess Chinese foreign policy in Southeast Asia from 2009 to 2020 and catalog "assertive" and "cooperative" behavior (Appendix A). The data indeed shows that assertive practices can be empirically documented across the military, diplomatic, and economic realms. Nevertheless, cooperative and "positive" Chinese practices are also regularly identified, underlining the sometimes contradictory character of China's foreign policy (see Rühlig, 2022). While the presence of assertiveness or inconsistencies in foreign policy is not unique to China, what is more interesting is to understand why international actors are increasingly making such appraisals of China and to flesh out specific instances of assertive practices. It is not an understatement to stress that perceptions matter in international politics because they elicit significant political (re)actions (see Jervis, 1976). In the context of China's rise, this is all the more important because countries' China policies are informed by their evaluations and perceptions of the PRC. As Shambaugh reminds us, mischaracterizations of China will "contribute to an inexorable action-reaction cycle" that will make it "increasingly difficult to cooperate with China internationally" (2011, p. 25).

Relatedly, IR theorists of different persuasions have engaged in discussions on China's rise anchored in its assertive behavior. Realists contend that China's forceful international behavior mostly derives from its burgeoning might (e.g., Bisley, 2011; S. Zhao, 2013a). Nevertheless, they cannot satisfactorily explain why this assertiveness is seen now, given that the growth of China's economic and military prowess precedes it. Liberal institutionalism, like constructivism, underlines Beijing's dissatisfaction with the existing normative world order and points out how the government is harnessing China's economic vitality to advance national interests. This, they argue, will take place not through conflict but through jostling for international leadership positions and bargaining power (Ikenberry 2011, p. 57). Growing international trade, according to institutional liberalism, will make China's rise peaceful since its economy has become inextricably embedded in global trade relations (Ikenberry, 2011, p. 62). Furthermore, it is claimed that participation in international life will curb the PRC's worst impulses (Qin, 2010, p. 247). Indeed, China's limited role in shaping global norms and rules and its reputed role as a "price taker" are often presented, by constructivist and liberalist scholars (e.g., Breslin, 2010; Christiansen, 2016), as key reasons for China's global push for the Belt and Road Initiative. Still, it is important to note that China has emerged as a staunch defender of multilateralism, free trade, and climate mitigation efforts (Guo, 2019)—normative packages that it played only a modest role in shaping. China has also proven that it can conduct assertive and even belligerent activities while deepening economic integration with other nations and partaking meaningfully in international life (see Appendix A). He and Feng (2013, p. 215) pointedly observe how, "like liberals, constructivists also face difficulties when accounting for China's 'assertive turn' of foreign policy since 2009." In short, liberalist and constructivist IR scholars offer few explanations for China's truculent diplomacy. Revealingly, they have also shown little interest in understanding China's diplomacy within the context of China's emergence. By contrast, this book underlines how *diplomatic assertiveness* is, in fact, integral to the trope of China's assertiveness more broadly because of MOFA's representational role. Getting a more accurate grip on Chinese foreign policy and how assertiveness is "made" will give us better indications as to the course China will take. Why has China's diplomacy experienced an emphatic uptick in assertiveness? Why do international actors, across different geographies, increasingly perceive Chinese practices as such?

With the above in mind, this book identifies three main gaps in the current literature on China's foreign policy. First, dominant analyses remain rooted in state-centric epistemologies (Nathan & Scobell, 2012, p. xvi) that largely disregard the lived experiences of actors.[2] China's foreign policy has, for example, been studied through the lens of global governance (Chin & Thakur, 2010); intergovernmental organizations and institutions (Ikenberry, 2008); China's relationships with major powers (C. W. Hughes, 2009; J. Wang, 2011; Coker, 2015); its security and territorial interests (Nathan & Scobell, 2012; Holslag, 2010); nationalism (Carlson, 2009; Zhao, 2013b); and soft power (Breslin, 2009; Shambaugh, 2015). The lack of attention to lived realities and practices is surprising when one considers how diplomacy is "an everyday activity that has been an aspect of social life wherever there have been distinct political entities" (Neumann, 2013, p. 14). If we believe that the social world is constituted in and through the doings of people who populate it, we must pay greater attention to the actual "doings" themselves. As Pouliot warns, if we disregard this, "dominant IR theory cuts itself short from a key generative force" (2016, p. 12).

This parallels the problem of traditional foreign policy analysis, where "most accounts . . . take for granted the existence of the state and see foreign policy as its actions" (Laffey, 2000, p. 430). Furthermore, since 2008, China has seen an increase in the number and variety of its foreign policy voices (Lanteigne, 2017, pp. 1–3). This development, according to Lequesne (2020, p. 2), has exacerbated neglect in the study of foreign ministries, as "the demonopolisation of the MFAs' role leads scholars to consider too quickly that they have become marginal institutions in the making of diplomacy." Such neglect is further compounded by confidentiality safeguards inherent in foreign ministries, which create an "accessibility problem" for academics studying Chinese politics: gaining access to policymakers for interviews or observation is difficult because of secrecy and the opacity of the Chinese policy apparatus. Nonetheless, scholars working on Chinese politics have relied, fruitfully and extensively, on interview data for their analyses (e.g., A. Barnett, 1985; Lu, 2000; Goldstein, 2001; Weiss, 2014; Ding, 2022; Rühlig, 2022) despite increasing difficulties in conducting academic research under Xi (Taber, 2018). This study adds on to this body of work by adopting an ethnographically sensitive approach in its investigation of Chinese diplomacy.

Another gap in the literature's interpretations of Chinese foreign policy is a tendency to study either agents (e.g., key leaders, People's Liberation Army [PLA]) or structures (e.g., nationalism, domestic politics), independently. The distinction creates the problem of empirical separation: existing explanations of China tend to examine, in isolation, either the structure or the agents. My investigative approach, leaning on practice theory, is conscious of structural constraints but also attuned to the game-playing potential of agents. In other words, the practice-theoretical approach gives us the tools to examine the agents involved in producing diplomacy and assertiveness while also accounting for structural limits present in the diplomatic field.

Finally, accounts of Chinese international politics often consider MOFA briefly and superficially in their analyses (see Sutter, 2012, p. 27; L. Jones & Zeng, 2019, p. 1416). The literature tends to sideline MOFA in favor of other foreign policy actors and forces (such as nationalism or domestic politics). As a result, the empirical and theoretical importance of MOFA and Chinese diplomacy is not precisely captured. Thus, there is a need for systematic analyses of MOFA considering its increasing visibility and its growing representational role for the Chinese state and the Party (Chhabra & Haas, 2019). Indeed, MOFA has occupied a leading role in China's foreign policy and diplomacy across a range of issues big and small, from successfully weakening and hampering the issuance of statements by the Association of Southeast Asian Nations (ASEAN) on the South China Sea to managing the release of detained Singaporean armored vehicles. Seen in this light, mainstream accounts of MOFA's weakness do not correspond with the evidence that points to its role in contributing to and intervening in assertive evaluations of contemporary Chinese behavior. A sociologically sensitive analysis of China's diplomatic practices can provide better explanations for the "how" and the "why" of China's contemporary foreign policy behavior and can better document, in concrete terms, Chinese assertiveness and the process through which other international actors view it.

Directly addressing the aforementioned gaps, this book advances four interrelated arguments. First, I suggest that China's assertiveness is progressively guided by and represented through MOFA and its diplomats rather than military actors, though the latter have traditionally been considered the key component of Chinese assertiveness (cf. Zhao, 2013a; Pugliese, 2015). Diplomatic assertiveness accelerated under Xi Jinping in 2013 as incentives in the field of diplomacy shifted to reward and discipline particular diplomatic practices and became the main route through which China *pre-*

sented itself to others. It is telling that the label "wolf warriors"—inspired by the eponymous film featuring a fictitious Chinese military hero—is used to signify diplomats rather than soldiers. A critical analysis of Chinese diplomatic practices illustrates the rapidity with which MOFA took on a representational role, and the expansion of its prominence that gave rise to assertive diplomacy. As I will detail in subsequent chapters, MOFA is consistently speaking on behalf of other Chinese actors (such as the PLA, the Chinese Communist Party [CCP], and the Ministry of Commerce), and as an attendant effect, it generates acts of assertiveness directly and vicariously for the state.

Second, I nuance claims made by some scholars about the limited role that PRC diplomats and MOFA allegedly play. For example, Stenslie and Gang note that MOFA holds a "relatively low rank" (2016, p. 130) and that they have had to occupy a "middle position" in foreign affairs (2016, p. 129). Brown writes how MOFA "has very little power to articulate fresh positions on foreign-policy issues" (2017, p. 44). And others have claimed that MOFA's top diplomats are relatively powerless (e.g., Breslin, 2013, p. 1280; Jakobson, 2016, pp. 141–143). Some Southeast Asian diplomats also point to MOFA's weak domestic position and claim that it translates into weakness internationally (Interviewee 2, personal communication, May 9, 2014; Interviewee 3, personal communication, February 10, 2015). In contrast, this book argues that MOFA's influence has expanded considerably since 2009, as evinced by two main factors: top political leaders' increased reliance and confidence in diplomacy, indicated by an increase in the apportionment of material resources to MOFA, and MOFA's higher profile domestically and internationally. Indeed, Chinese leaders today are relying much more than previous ones on the nation's diplomatic apparatus by investing heavily in MOFA and its diplomats (e.g., W. Hu, 2019; B. Smith, 2019). As the main interface of China's foreign policy, MOFA often communicates Chinese positions in various domains such as foreign policy, security, finance, and even domestic politics. As the only official institution that holds daily press conferences,[3] it is the main vehicle through which "China" is articulated and (re)presented to international audiences. Taken together, all of this elevates MOFA's capacities since it now has both the official mandate and the appetite to do more by showing "fighting spirit" and "attack[ing]" any affronts to China (J. Shi, 2020). To be clear, this does not mean it has the power to operate independently or the wherewithal to resist and overturn Party leaders or the president's wishes. My more modest claim, vis-à-vis MOFA's influence, is that Chinese envoys (compared to diplomats before 2009) are more *incentivized and entrusted* to practice and represent assertiveness.

The leadership's endorsement of MOFA is also supported by concrete and symbolic support. For instance, there has been a significant material increase to MOFA, with its diplomatic budget doubling to RMB $60 billion in 2018 from RMB $30 billion in

2011 (Clover & Ju, 2018). Additionally, the Lowy Institute's 2019 Global Diplomacy Index revealed that China overtook the United States, for the first time, in having the largest diplomatic presence in the world—276 diplomatic missions compared to America's 273 (Meredith, 2019). The reorganization and renaming of China's Leading Small Group on Foreign Affairs to the institutionally more important Central Foreign Affairs Commission (CFAC) in 2018 (Xinhua, 2018) is another politically consequential move, as a "commission" (*zhongyang waishi gongzuo weiyuanhui* 中央外事工作委员会) ranks higher than a "leading small group" (*Zhongyang waishi gongzuo lingdao xiaozu* 中央外事工作领导小组). Notably, MOFA is now able to extend its purview to areas outside diplomacy. For example, in a press conference during China's "two sessions" (*Lianghui* 两会) in 2020,[4] China's foreign minister enumerated how MOFA had helped Hubei and Wuhan weather the crisis when the Covid-19 pandemic first emerged. Strikingly, he added that MOFA would take on a critical role in supporting Hubei's economic recovery efforts and would coordinate with other national agencies to help the province rebuild and renew itself (CGTN, 2020). This demonstrates how the coordinating and facilitating functions and work duties of MOFA have extended, in a substantive manner, into other areas. To be clear, I am not proposing that MOFA has policymaking powers in those fields; I am simply stating that MOFA is *representing various domains of China to international audiences*. That is to say, MOFA is discursively and practically speaking on and intervening in a myriad of issues that it previously did not. This suggests that MOFA's domestic and international profiles have risen, with significant effects in terms of how other international actors view China and how other domestic institutional actors relate to MOFA.

Thus the second reason behind MOFA's growing influence lies in its higher profile. Since 2019, the proliferation of Twitter accounts and the diplomatic activities there have raised public awareness of MOFA. Interviews with Chinese diplomats indicate how their online presence and activities, specifically through Twitter, are now part of performance appraisals. In a direct way, Chinese envoys are compelled to spend time on Twitter to react, respond, and critique as they often try to outdo each other (Brandt and Schafer, 2020). It must also be underlined that China's Twitter diplomacy has produced counterintuitive results, costing Beijing some reputational points. For instance, in November 2020, MOFA's spokesperson tweeted a falsified image of an Australian soldier smiling while slitting the throat of an Afghan child (British Broadcasting Corporation, 2020). The doctored photo sparked outrage and prompted demands by Canberra for Beijing to apologize. France, the United States, and New Zealand swiftly joined Australia in condemning China (Reuters, 2020). Nevertheless, MOFA's spokesperson Hua Chunying defended her colleague, questioning Australia's (over)reaction (Chappell, 2020, para. 2). As China increasingly takes to Twitter for its forceful brand of diplomacy, perceptions of diplomatic assertiveness and intransigence form and deepen.

Segueing to the third argument in this book, I submit that the Chinese example provides key insights into how power manifests as functional capacities, complicating what constitutes "power" in international politics. I highlight three functional abilities of MOFA at play: advising, implementing, and facilitating/coordinating. None of these processes, exclusive to MOFA in China, have been theorized, even though they have important political repercussions. For logistical and practical purposes, MOFA provides expert advice on matters big and small in leaders' foreign policymaking. Despite MOFA's limited policymaking powers, it can, in the words of a Chinese diplomat, *influence policies*, as its advice is often taken as authoritative. Often the "diplomats-as-implementers" meme is invoked in the literature to highlight the limited role PRC envoys perform. In contrast, I found that envoys could exercise considerable influence through the process of implementation. For instance, in multilateral events and conferences, Chinese diplomats' extension of courtesies to visiting dignitaries (e.g., the type of meals, the hotels, the rank of Chinese politicians receiving guests) signifies their "importance." On the flip side, withholding or downgrading these courtesies, which PRC diplomats gate-keep as implementers, sends important political messages. Such was the case with one Filipino contact, who told me that MOFA had disinvited him at the last minute from an ASEAN-China event because of the arbitral case that the Philippines brought against China. Bode and Kalsrud correctly observe that practitioners' implementation is not purely "technical or apolitical," as practitioners can introduce "meaningful instances of agency" (2019, p. 461). As for MOFA's facilitating functions, these foreground its representational role explicitly. In my investigations, I found PLA personnel—traditionally seen as one of the most important foreign policy institutions in China—ceding facilitating powers to MOFA in specific security domains. Thus, in the South China Sea, MOFA is increasingly coordinating and facilitating Beijing's response (Qi, 2019). MOFA was also playing the leading role in managing disputes, delivering threats, and articulating Chinese positions in the 2017 Doklam standoff[5] and the 2020 Galwan Valley clash with India, rather than the PLA (Ministry of Foreign Affairs, 2017).

Last but not least, I illuminate how China's diplomats construct perceptions of China for external audiences. I explain how China's foreign ministry and its officials generate significant identity effects. Indeed, a key task for foreign diplomats stationed abroad is to produce reports and briefs for political leaders back home (Yun, 2014, pp. 20–21), and a considerable part of their analyses derives from their interactions with Chinese diplomats and MOFA-endorsed texts (D. Loh, 2020b). Through these exchanges, PRC envoys mediate and construct "China" for consumption at others' national capitals.[6] Phrased differently, MOFA and its personnel are indispensable purveyors of China's image in international politics, highlighting its representational roles.

These arguments are advanced through a multiyear and multisited fieldwork study of MOFA, involving extensive interviews, participant observation, and artifact analysis, to investigate the practices and politics of diplomacy. This research is, therefore, the first study of contemporary Chinese diplomacy and its foreign ministry (2009–2020). Specifically, I conducted a mixed-qualitative investigation through 102 interviews with eighty-four Chinese diplomats/secondary diplomatic actors and non-Chinese diplomats from 2016 to 2020, together with case studies and primary text analysis. Adding to that, I made use of participation observation data drawn from my experience working in a Singaporean think tank from 2013 to 2015, principally through involvement in track-1.5 and track-2 diplomatic forums involving Chinese interlocutors. I elaborate my research design in greater detail in chapter 1. Additionally, through field analysis, I mapped out the relationships between key foreign policy actors within China. This mapping produced a topographical visualization of the most significant local diplomatic players.

The Practice-Theoretical Approach and Chinese Diplomacy

This project draws on Bourdieu-inspired practice theory (PT), an approach that devotes full analytical regard to *practices*—understood as the doings and sayings of actors in the world. I promote the methodological and theoretical claim that PT is best suited to study China's diplomacy, as it pays attention to (micro) practices and processes that are overlooked in traditional analysis of China's IR in at least three specific ways. First, PT pays attention to the lived realities of diplomats and grounds its analysis in these experiences and practices. As mentioned, existing Chinese studies do not take diplomats and MOFA seriously enough in their scholarship, let alone their lived realities. Yet these practices are important if we are to accurately understand the representational role MOFA has assumed. On a theoretical level, it further implies that we train our analysis of international relations through a *logic of practicality*. As Pouliot explains: "World politics as in any other social field, does not derive from conscious deliberation or thoughtful reflection—instrumental, rule-based, communicative, or otherwise. Instead, practices are the result of inarticulate, practical knowledge that makes what is to be done appear 'self-evident' or commonsensical. This is the logic of practicality" (2008, p. 258). A logic of practicality insists that "commonsensical" and everyday practices are key drivers of diplomacy and foreign policy.

Second, PT's sensitivity to practices and its constituent role in constructing structures mean that analysis is not ontologically determined prior to analysis at either the individual, state, or systemic level. Instead, the notion of *practices* (by diplomats, the foreign ministry, or the state) dissolves these distinctions, since there is no inherent quality or unique significance attached to larger international phenomena. Thus, for PT, global phenomena are the same as local ones, as they are all rooted in social practices (Schatzki, 2011, p. 2). In other words, for PT, small/micro political practices are constitutive of large international political phenomena. This theoretical commitment, in turn, requires us to refocus our analysis on the processes and practices that traditional paradigms such as realism and liberalism consider irrelevant or epiphenomenal. While the literature on the performative nature of diplomacy is rich (see McConnell, 2018; Visoka, 2018; A. Jones & Clark, 2019), it often omits the role of objects and technologies in enabling diplomatic performances. I show how material objects and arrangements (such as books and MOFA's architecture) and technological tools (such as WeChat and Twitter) are constitutive of and fundamental to contemporary Chinese diplomacy and its representational role.

Finally, the Bourdieusian approach to research demands that concepts unfold only in the course of one's research—"a permanent reminder that concepts have no definition other than systemic ones, and are designed to be *put to work empirically in systemic fashion*" (Bourdieu & Wacquant, 1992, pp. 95–96). This openness gives us flexibility in selecting the method that best suits the question at hand, rather than adjusting the puzzle to suit one's methodological conviction (Bourdieu & Wacquant, 1992, p. 28). The upshot of this is that the researcher is less inhibited by theoretical strictures—in which empirics serves merely to either validate, refine, or reject a theory—and can instead focus on uncovering what is interesting and unseen. Hence, seriously engaging with practice theory for the analysis here is not a methodological whim but an analytical requirement.

Beyond the empirical and theoretical advantages, this research is important because of the sheer political, economic, and cultural weight of China. As its heft increases, so too will its impact on the region and the world. How and in what way it chooses to wield its diplomatic influence will prove instructive, especially as claims multiply regarding China's more activist leadership role in the face of purported decline in the liberal international order (Pillsbury, 2015). The PRC has grown more confident and has both the desire and the capacity to play a larger role in the world: the establishment of the Asian Infrastructure Investment Bank in 2016, the Belt and Road Initiative," and the articulation of the "Major Power Diplomacy" discourse are manifestations of this ambition and self-belief. Furthermore, with Xi Jinping taking the helm in 2013, China has one of its most powerful leaders since Mao Zedong (Campbell, 2017). The full effects of his power consolidation and demands for the realization of the "China Dream" and the "Twin Centenaries"[7] have yet to be understood. Most significantly, little is known about MOFA's role in China's rise or the extent to which MOFA intervenes in contemporary Chinese foreign policy behavior. This research therefore examines Chinese diplomatic practices from 2009 to 2020 to understand MOFA's evolution and its contemporary function in instigating and representing China's foreign policy and its assertive dimensions.

Research Scope

The geographical focus on Southeast Asia in this research is meant to provide empirical grounds for the theoretical application. Hence, while the empirical analyses are frequently nested within Southeast Asia, the empirical findings are designed to go beyond the region as Chinese diplomacy's effects are felt globally. At any rate, from the period identified (2009–2020), Southeast Asia is, and continues to be, the space where Chinese diplomacy is most visible and active as part of Beijing's renewed focus on its periphery diplomacy (*zhou bian wai jiao* 周边外交) (Swaine, 2010). Furthermore, Southeast Asia is where the change from a passive to a more robust diplomacy is clearest (I. Chen & Hao, 2013; see also Appendix A). The year 2009 was chosen as the starting point for this analysis, as it is the year that scholars generally demarcate as reflecting "greater" or "increased" assertiveness (Swaine, 2010; Yahuda, 2013; Kao, 2014; Rozman, 2012, p. 157). It is also from 2009 that academic works and media reports on China's assertiveness saw a spike compared to previous years (Johnston, 2013, pp. 10–12). The next key touchstone date that anchors this analysis is 2013 because this is the year that Xi Jinping formally took over as president. Finally, 2019 saw a flurry of official Chinese diplomatic Twitter accounts established, which paved the way for diplomats' very active and robust presence online. In that way, the period spanning 2013–2019 showed significant impact on MOFA as a result of Xi's assumption of power, while the period before that (2009–2013) serves as an important prelude to point out that significant changes in MOFA and Chinese foreign policy were a result of evolution (rather than a sudden break with established diplomatic practices), instigated by greater control from the top leadership.

Organization of the Book

The book is organized into six chapters. In chapter 1, I delve into the literature on Chinese foreign policy and unpack it thematically. By doing so, I elaborate in greater detail important gaps in the scholarship, while carving out a space where this research locates itself. The chapter also explains my methodological approach and how the empirics will be performed. This entails a short review of PT and how this approach offers an alternative and updated view of China's assertiveness, its foreign policy, and MOFA's representational role. Moving to the data collected, chapter 2 zooms in on an analysis of MOFA and the practices of diplomats. Here, I argue against traditionalist views in the scholarship that relegate MOFA to the sidelines. In contrast, I show how Chinese diplomats and MOFA have been increasingly empowered as their representational function has been given prominence, particularly since Xi Jinping assumed the presidency. From this perspective, I identify how diplomatic assertiveness is constructed through MOFA's communicative and embodied practices.

Suturing habitus to the field and vice versa, chapter 3 pans out to the international level to give an account of how diplomatic influence is brought to bear in transnational fields, creating conditions for change and disruption. In that connection, I offer a field-theoretic account of change in the bilateral and multilateral spaces where Chinese actors operate, while providing the first visual charting of the diplomatic field in China. Through an examination of Chinese multilateralism, I specify how Chinese interlocutors modified both the formal and informal field rules according to their own operative logic and how non-Chinese actors viewed such practices. In chapter 4, I use the concept of *institutional habitus* as a heuristic tool to study China's foreign ministry by examining how institutional scripts, dispositions, and history impel diplomats to adopt, internalize, and perform assertive diplomatic practices. I empirically document how non-Chinese diplomats construct China's identity and behavior from these diplomatic practices, hence underlining MOFA's role in generating identity effects in international relations. Through this interrogation of contemporary Chinese foreign policy, the book complicates commonly held notions of Beijing's foreign policy and diplomacy as being completely procedural and rigid. In contrast, my investigation shows that while the top leaders hold undisputed authority over foreign policy, MOFA has significant say over foreign policy knowledge production, policy implementation, and coordination.[8] Significantly, I contend that MOFA is critical in forming perceptions of China among other diplomats and their countries.

In chapter 5, I examine the effects of China's "Twitter diplomacy." This relatively new form of diplomatic practice emerged in the early 2010s but only truly caught on from 2019 onwards in China. My findings suggest that leveraging social-technological tools for diplomatic signaling is now a key prong of Chinese diplomacy and an increasingly important work activity for diplomats. Concretely, I outline how Chinese diplomats use Twitter to advance bureaucratic interests and delegitimize non-Chinese diplomatic actors. I argue that this form of diplomacy is critical to our understanding of China's bid to increase discourse power, while illustrating how this can also prove detrimental to PRC's standing. The book ends with a chapter where I summarize my findings while underlining the role of material objects and arrangements in enabling assertive diplomatic practices.

ONE

Chinese Foreign Policy, MOFA's Role, and the "Practice Turn"

> Well, you can just stop and think of what could happen if anybody with a decent system of government got control of that main land. Good God. There'd be no power in the world that could even—I mean, you put 800 million Chinese to work under a decent system . . . and they will be the leaders of the world. The Indians—you could put 200 billion Indians to work, and they wouldn't amount to a goddamn. . . . But the Chinese, they're all over Asia. I know. They've got what it takes.
>
> RICHARD NIXON, conversation with the
> US ambassador to the PRC, 1971[1]

In surveying the contemporary scholarship on Chinese foreign policy and diplomacy,[2] one easily spots the preponderance of neorealism in the literature (see also Buzan, 2010, p. 23).[3] Neorealists generally believe that geopolitical competition and struggles over scarce energy resources will become more acute (Klare, 2001), even as they differ in opinions over whether conflict involving China is inevitable. While offensive realists are quite clear that it is (Mearsheimer, 2006), defensive realists are more optimistic that war can be avoided through deterrence or alliances (Kirshner, 2010).

Liberalist scholars contend that economic cooperation and integration will prevent war by increasing its costs (Findlay & Watson, 1997). Thus the rise of China need not inescapably lead to conflict with status quo powers such as the United States, due to their economic intertwining (Keohane, 1998, pp. 85–86; Ikenberry, 2008). Meanwhile, constructivist scholars argue that China's political norms, culture of pacifism, and nonhegemonic behavior will result in a peaceful rise (Kang, 2003). States, Acharya (2006) adds, are social actors that can be transformed through interactions, the internationalization of norms, and so forth. Callahan highlights how ideas, projects, and institutions—such as the China Dream discourse and the Belt and Road Initiative (BRI)—interconnect to form Chinese diplomatic behavior and to propagate a "new grand strategy as a norm-maker" (2016, p. 238). Yet in seeing states as either socializers or the socialized, a constructivist understanding of China treats the state as a coherent entity, possessing inherent qualities (e.g., Buzan, 2010; Han, 2017). In this way, current scholarship typically views the Chinese state as a rational and monolithic actor (Goldstein, 2003). What is more, these analyses do not *think from* and *think about* MOFA to explain broader IR phenomena. This presents a gap in our understanding of Chinese foreign policy as PRC diplomats and their practices take on a global significance. Indeed, MOFA often remains a marginal analytical figure, existing as a mere by-product or tool of Chinese foreign policy—like a ghost in the background, present but hidden and unacknowledged.

Beyond the sketch above of the main IR paradigms used to evaluate China, in the following sections I categorize the literature that describes Chinese foreign policy as voicing five broad themes: "assertive China"; "elite actors and bureaucratic politics"; "history, tradition, and culture"; "domestic politics and nationalism"; and "inconsistent foreign policy practices." Through this exercise, I expand upon the three principal gaps in the IR literature that I broached in the introductory chapter—its state-centric focus, its tendency to stress the role of security actors in driving perceptions of Chinese foreign policy behavior as "assertive," and its analytical inattention to MOFA. Finally, I will demonstrate how practice theory is best suited to fill the gaps identified.

An "Assertive" China

As the "assertive China" discourse dominates discussions on contemporary Chinese foreign policy, it is important to address it from the outset. S. Zhao (2013a) contends that China has been increasingly assertive since 2008 and observes that this is apparent in its interactions with the United States, Europe, and countries in Asia-Pacific. One reason the author gives is that China is attempting to restore itself from a self-perceived state of "victimhood" in world affairs (2013a, p. 110). Meanwhile, for Åberg, assertiveness means "standing up for one's needs, wants and rights" (2016, p. 1127). In contrast, Johnston (2013, p. 10) sees assertiveness as a form of foreign policy that threatens to impose costs on others. Yahuda perceives China's "new" assertiveness as a result of "the growth of its military power, its 'triumphalism' in the wake of the Western financial crisis and its heightened nationalism" (2013, p. 446), and having a sense that China's achievements across various domains are on par or nearing parity with those of its global peers such as the US. To Friedberg, it is clear that the "root cause of China's recent assertiveness can thus be found in the mindset and perceptions of its leaders. As their country has grown stronger, they have felt empowered to move back toward the position of centrality and influence to which they believe history entitles them" (2014, p. 136).

As evinced here, "assertiveness" is used frequently as a dependent variable in the existing literature of Chinese foreign policy behavior (e.g., Bisley, 2011; Pugliese, 2015).[4] It is also important to state that depictions of "assertiveness" are mostly from analyses by Western-based scholars. Swaine's (2010) "Perceptions of an Assertive China" is an exception in that it provides as well a meticulous explication of how Chinese scholars view Chinese "assertiveness" (see also Zeng et al., 2015). As my own analysis of Chinese foreign policy practices in Southeast Asia from 2009 to 2020 tells us (Appendix A), the PRC is indeed displaying assertive behavior but also demonstrating a willingness to cooperate and engage in "good neighborliness" in the region. Against this backdrop and following Johnston's (2013) interpretation of assertiveness as the imposition of costs, I define *assertiveness* as the tendency to leverage one's resources to impose costs on others to extract compliance and/or police behavior. By the same token, *diplomatic assertiveness* refers to using various diplomatic levers to extract concessions, police behavior, and impose costs.

Elite Actors and Bureaucratic Politics

Several scholars attempt to describe China's "character" or account for its foreign policy by examining the views of Chinese elites—broadly understood in the literature as educated and politically significant groups such as academics, policymakers, and officials (see Harding, 1981). Glaser, for instance, discusses the role of elite Chinese think tanks and how they contribute to foreign policy (2012, pp. 99–100). Indeed, government ministries, including MOFA, do solicit ideas from think tanks and intellectuals as foreign policy becomes more pluralistic (C. Li, 2017). Thus public intellectuals' influence on foreign policy projects—such as Wang Jisi's articulation of the BRI—should not be understated (Wuthnow, 2017, p. 12). Lynch, in an analysis of sixty-three Chinese "internal" (*neibu* 内部) journal articles, classifies Chinese elites into three groups—realist empiricists, defensive realists, and offensive realists. He argues that China sees the world in realist terms: "inherently conflict ridden culturally, with the ideational fault lines reinforcing the lines of military and economic conflict" (2013, p. 650).

Looking at the importance of "bargaining" among elites in Chinese politics, Lampton alerts us to domestic competition over resources: "One bargains over what is scarce: in the PRC, financial resources, power and position in the hierarchy, high-quality goods and services, and access to the international system and to highly skilled personnel are among those things most sought" (1992, p. 40). He mentions how "only *proximate leaders* bargain—that is, equals in the hierarchy, and entities (persons, organizations, factions, localities) one step above and one step below that level" (1992, pp. 51–52). A. D. Barnett reveals that in the 1980s, while top leadership played key roles in foreign policymaking, there was a significant shift of duties to the State Council[5] (1985, pp. 9–11). Hence, he demonstrates how policymaking moved from Mao Zedong's "imposition-by-fiat" to Deng Xiaoping's garnering of support through Party coalition building. This meant a move from individual to collective decision-making within the regime. In contemporary China, Callahan establishes how the work of so-called nonelite citizen intellectuals[6] "challenges Beijing's official foreign policy" and "is evidence of expanded space in the PRC's civil society" (2012, p. 641).

Lieberthal and Oksenberg also ascertain that, while organizational hierarchies and the perceptions people have of bureaucracies in China give the impression that top leaders are in control, "the reality diverges sharply from the policies proclaimed in Beijing, and orders are not scrupulously implemented in the provinces" (1988, p. 32). Importantly, they insist that "lower level units have important resources they can bring to bear" (1988, p. 23). What is true, at least in contemporary Chinese foreign policy, is that political elites clearly matter but so do the "street-level bureaucrats" that Lipsky famously speaks of (1980). As Stern and O'Brien (2012, p. 190) clarify, a strange mixture of centrally and provincially led policy processes contributes to the complexity of bureaucratic dynamics in domestic institutions. Indeed, "The Chinese state, even at its most repressive, is not as single-minded as it is sometimes portrayed" but instead consists of a "hodgepodge of disparate actors" (O'Brien & Li, 2006, p. 66). Policy outcomes can be construed as a result of "bargaining . . . horizontally between government ministries, agencies and state enterprises, as well as vertically, between different levels of government" (Andrews-Speed, 2012, p. 27).

Zhu (2011) alleges that there is an inconsistent quality in Chinese diplomacy, where different views send "mixed messages to the outside world." He adds that "the Foreign Ministry is now perceived as just one of many government agencies, and not necessarily a very powerful one" (2011, p. 189). The People's Liberation Army (PLA) is traditionally touted, more than MOFA, as the elite player in China's international politics, which is unsurprising given the PLA's decisive foreign policy role during the formative years of the PRC (A. D. Barnett, 1985, p. 96). Barnett also points to the existence of a "foreign policy community," analogous to Bourdieu's *field*, writing: "One feature of the Chinese bureaucratic system that most impresses foreign observers is the degree to which Chinese organizations tend to function as 'independent kingdoms.' It is true that, in the field of foreign affairs, as in other fields, the primary orientation and loyalty of most individuals is to their own 'unit'" (1985, p. 135).

More recently, Mastro identifies one of the key drivers of an uptick in China's assertiveness as none other than the president: "Xi Jinping himself has articulated more hardline policies concerning territorial disputes, and Chinese assertiveness has noticeably increased under his watch" (2015, p. 153). An approach that shares some affinities with practice theory (PT) is "bureaucratic politics" (BP) in that it takes seriously some practices of substate actors, specifically organizations and organizational inhabitants, in political outcomes. This approach sees policy outcomes as a consequence of negotiation and bargaining by key actors in governmental institutions. As Allison and Halperin put it, the "Bureaucratic Politics Model sees no unitary actor but rather many actors as players—players who focus not on a single strategic issue but on many diverse intra-national problems as well" (1972, p. 43; see also Allison & Zelikow, 1999). Drawing on BP, Lieberthal and Oksenberg argue that "the fragmented, segmented, and stratified structure of the state promotes a system of negotiations, bargaining, and the seeking of consensus among affected bureaucracies. The policy process in this sphere is disjointed, protracted, and incremental" (1988, p. 3). Thus the authors reveal the splintered nature of the Chinese bureaucracy through inconsistent and messy policy processes (1988, p. 22).

Recent scholarship shows how bureaucratic distortions of policy implementation are a persistent feature in Chinese governance. Indeed, A. H. Zhang, in her study of BP and antimonopoly laws, concludes that policy results in China obtain from politicking and struggles over who decides which antitrust issue is most important for their power and bureaucratic stature (2014, pp. 674, 705). Works by Lieberthal, Oksenberg, and others are valuable in understanding how policy is made and in revealing the warping effects of bureaucracies, yet they frequently erase the practices of individual actors within the organizations.

In contrast, PT is more attentive to the experiences and practices of agents while still properly considering macro-level effects beyond the bureaucracy, through the broader notion of *fields*. This approach enables analysis to expand by tracking agents as they move within (and across) fields in the same bureaucratic structure (such as MOFA diplomats in local diplomatic fields versus international diplomatic fields) or across bureaucracies. Besides, BP places individual and organizational interests at the heart of bargaining, negotiating, and policy results (Allison & Halperin, 1972) with little regard for social and practical logics in motivating agents. Indeed, that approach is silent on how individuals, groups, and bureaucracies decide on rule following/ breaking and on how normative orders are implemented. In this respect, Bourdieu and PT provide us with unparalleled insights into the habitual and practical dimensions of rule following and order implementation in social life (see Raymond, 2019) that can help us trace how assertiveness is implemented, represented, and performed in Chinese diplomacy.

On a related note, scholars often emphasize the challenge, for Beijing, in controlling local governments and their bureaucrats (Shirk, 1990). According to Saich, "Top level policy often amounts to little more than a rhetorical flourish that is ignored or blunted in the middle and lower reaches of officialdom" (2001, p. 136), and the central government "does not command automatic allegiance" (2001, p. 152). With specific reference to the defense and foreign affairs institutions, A. D. Barnett observes how "the defense establishment and civilian agencies involved in foreign affairs operate fairly autonomously, for the most part, below the very top level of the leadership" (1985, p. 68). Lieberthal and Oksenberg go as far as to claim that lower-level entities are "capable of thwarting and subverting Beijing's demands" (1988, p. 135). All of these authors show instances where local institutions and bureaucrats have provided the basis for national implementation and adoption of policies, in a "bottom-up" rather than "top-down" direction.

Undoubtedly, much in the Chinese society and state has changed in the decades since the Deng era. It is correct that in contemporary China the Party Politburo Standing Committee (PSC), especially the general secretary, retains overwhelming control. China's BRI, Xi's massive anticorruption campaign, and the Asian Infrastructure Investment Bank projects are prime examples of how leaders' programs and policies are executed with impressive speed. Yet at the same time, there is evidence of attempts by the rank and file to resist. This is clear from Xi's ongoing fight to outlaw internal dissent by stifling discussions critical of government policy, and from the "passive resistance" of Party insiders who, "in terms of execution, just go through the motions" (Denyer, 2015, para. 15). Former Premier Li Keqiang displayed frustration that policies were not being carried out, chiding the bureaucracy for being "too slow" in policy implementation and rhetorically asking, "Why is it so difficult for ordinary people to get things done?" and "Why does the government put up so many obstacles that stop people getting things done?" (Hewitt, 2015, para. 4).

Contemporaneously, Hameiri and Jones push the "resistance" argument furthest. They claim that "multiple state and quasi-private agencies, having become somewhat autonomous foreign policy actors, are pursuing uncoordinated and sometimes contradictory agendas overseas, notwithstanding efforts to coordinate them" (2016, p. 85). Lieberthal and Oksenberg (1988, p. 28) also observed (almost three decades earlier) that political leaders "must employ tactics that permit them to retain the resources they consider necessary over the long run, often at the cost of advancing their preferred choice on a particular policy issue." To be sure, top leadership holds undisputed power over its agencies. Provincial governments, state bureaucracies, and ministries are not alternative autonomous power centers. Yet what is equally clear is that lower-level bureaucrats (be it in the provincial governments or at MOFA) do have some space to maneuver and exert influence. Finding out to what degree and in what ways this can happen in practice is a key task of this book. As Lipsky urges, since "policy implementation in the end comes down to the people who actually implement it," so too must these street-level bureaucrats be recognized as policymakers (1980, p. 8). Indeed, Chinese bureaucracies and ministries are not helpless. They can sometimes "force an issue onto the agenda of the highest leaders" (Lieberthal & Oksenberg, 1988, p. 30).

History, Tradition, and Culture

Fairbank (1983) underlines how interpretations of Chinese politics ought to be grounded in an understanding of its intellectual and cultural beginnings. To that end, scholars have looked for the key drivers of Chinese foreign policy in its history, its traditions, and its accumulated culture of governance (e.g., Kissinger, 2012; Dreyer, 2006). In *Autocratic Tradition and Chinese Politics*, Z. Fu argues for the endurance of the autocratic tradition and its continuing influence on Chinese politics. He reiterates how important "political culture" is in sustaining the political order and emphasizes the durability of political processes such as infighting and jockeying for position (1993, pp. 9–11). Relatedly, traditional client-patron ties or *guan xi* (关系) feature strongly in domestic Chinese politics (Pye, 1995; Nathan & Tsai, 1995). Thus their effect on domestic politics and the intricacies of factional formation within the top echelons of leadership cannot be disregarded. Yet the link between factional politics and diplomacy is unclear and not fully worked out within the scholarship.

Dreyer, like Fu, emphasizes how Chinese foreign policy is guided by tradition and history (2006, pp. 12–13). She stresses how leaders' belief in the superiority of their culture and expectations of obeisance, paying tributes, and so forth continue to direct Chinese foreign policy. The author says that in the past Marxism and Leninism provided prisms through which Chinese leaders viewed the world and guided their actions but that these were progressively replaced by nationalism. Finally, she opines, "The responsibility for foreign policy decision making rests with the supreme leader: Mao, then Deng and, after them, Jiang Zemin and Hu Jintao" (2006, p. 309). Likewise, Johnston found that the principles in the "Seven Military Classics" (*wu jing qi shu* 武经七书) have been a recurrent feature of Chinese strategic thinking. To him, this provides historical evidence of a Chinese Realpolitik similar to Western notions of Realpolitik (Johnston, 1995; A. Loh, 2008, pp. 282–283).

In reviewing scholarship that takes history as the basis for China's foreign policy, S. Zhao (2015, p. 981) recognizes how understanding the past can help us apprehend China's future, but he also warns us that "Chinese intellectuals and political leaders [have] not only selectively remembered but also often reconstructed history to advance the current political agenda of the Chinese government and justify their concept of justice and their view of China's rightful place in the world" (see also Dreyer,

2015). The historical anchoring of China's behavior in international life is valuable, but such accounts remain fairly static and ineffective in accounting for change. They also fail to identify the emergent conditions that enable transformation to take place. Furthermore, analyses drawing on tradition, history, and culture do not provide adequate explanations for the uptick in assertiveness since 2009 and how it appeared when it did. A practice-focused inquiry, combined with field analysis, as I demonstrate, is more sensitive to changes in Chinese diplomacy.

Domestic Politics and Nationalism

China's former foreign minister Qian Qichen once said, "Diplomacy is the extension of internal affairs" (as cited in Q. Zhao, 1992, p. 159). It is no surprise, then, that there are numerous attempts to look at domestic sources of Chinese foreign policy, among which nationalism is frequently invoked. Indeed, throughout modern China's history, leaders have been quick to seize on the discourse of nationalism to achieve national and personal objectives. Mao, for instance, used the Taiwan Strait Crisis of 1958 to garner support for his "Great Leap Forward" campaign and later to draw attention away from its disastrous results (C. R. Hughes, 2005, p. 3).

Rosecrance defines nationalism as the " 'we-feeling' among members of a nation to the point where national loyalties take precedence over most other obligations" (1973, p. 16). It is recognized that external events can create "grassroots" nationalism and swell nationalist sentiments (Gries, 2001). For instance, external factors can propel hypernationalist feelings, which, in turn, apply pressure on the government to act or to be seen to act. J. Zhang contends that "the recent rise of nationalistic sentiments in China is both domestically driven and externally invoked" (2003, p. 109). Likewise, nationalism can be promoted by ruling elites for diplomatic aims. For instance, Weiss's (2014) research on Chinese nationalism demonstrates how political elites can govern nationalist forces to send foreign policy signals—such as indicating resolve by enabling antiforeign mobilization or signaling reassurance by stopping nationalist protests.

In terms of ideology, S. Zhao (1998) suggests that the demise of communist ideology led the CCP to turn to nationalism to legitimize its rule. Echoes of this can be seen in China today as Xi blends nationalism with some elements of socialism, producing an amalgamated "Xi Jinping Thought on Socialism with Chinese Characteristics" (Y. Wang, n.d.). Whiting (1995) uses the idea of "Mandate of Heaven"[7] to underline the role of ideology, beliefs, and assumptions held by Beijing in driving foreign policy. Along comparable lines, Qin, studying the lack of Chinese IR theories, contends that the "traditional Chinese intellectual mind had no room for something similar to the concept of 'international-ness' " (2007, p. 322), adding that the tributary system and the *tianxia* perspective[8] continue to shape the Chinese psyche with regard to a foreign policy worldview. Challenging realist perspectives on foreign policy, Ross explains that assertive diplomacy by China in 2009 was a result of greater nationalist sentiments in Chinese society. At that time, "Nationalism emerged as a more pervasive political force" and "contentious Chinese diplomacy and the corresponding instability in regional affairs reflected the insecurity of the Chinese leadership arising from China's deteriorating economic and social conditions and its appeasement of strident nationalism" (2013, pp. 79, 87).

Yet current indicators point to China's pursuit of an increasingly assertive bilateral and multilateral diplomacy in Southeast Asia (Appendix A). Nationalism fails, in this regard, to account for cooperative behavior in Chinese foreign policy, especially in view of increasingly strident nationalistic voices (Mastro, 2015, p. 152). Indeed, the literature on nationalism and foreign policy does not show that foreign policy is directly influenced by domestic nationalism in an unfiltered way. While Chinese foreign policy is undeniably influenced in part by domestic pressure, nationalism cannot convincingly account for its fluctuations or for why Chinese diplomats have come to increasingly play a decisive representational role.

Inconsistent Foreign Policy Practices

It is important to note that scholars studying the IR of China have sometimes noted inconsistency and ambiguity in Chinese foreign policy practices, a subject in itself worthy of academic inquiry. To begin with, X. Wu's (2001) study of the underlying reasons for China's mercurial foreign policy behavior identifies "four contradictions." First, China is a great but poor power. Second, China has an economic "open-door" policy toward foreign investment but does not want to lose control. Third, China tries to follow "guiding principles" but also aspires to be pragmatic. Finally, there is an ongoing tension between bilateralism and multilateralism. Shambaugh writes how the multiplicity of voices involved in foreign policy creates a situation where the PRC "exhibits diverse and contradictory emphases" (2011, p. 7). Rühlig also observes that competing tendencies in the CCP's goals mean that "the sources of legitimacy, economic performance, and national pride contribute to its contradictory foreign policy" (2022, p. 18). What is more, each of these aforementioned factors has competing propensities. For instance, "national pride" fuels a form of aggressive nationalism that emphasizes an uncompromising foreign policy stance but also drives a desire to be seen as a respectable, responsible global power, which "requires China to cooperate with international rules to reassure the international community of its good intentions—even if it comes at a cost to the national interest, including on state control" (2022, p. 18). Drawing on social psychological theories, Pu contends that competing legitimacy and status demands at home and abroad create a situation where "China sends contradictory signals about its status and role in the twenty-first century" (2019, p. 5). Y. Chen lists multiple foreign policy attitudes and characteristics inherent in the Chinese state—including deep suspicion of the enemy; adherence to dogmatic "principles" by leaders past and present; poor diplomatic skills resulting in inaccurate grasp of diplomatic reality; insularity and faulty intelligence; and an inflated sense of ego—and claims that these produce foreign policy outcomes that are "inconsistent with reality and mutually contradictory" (2003, p. 716).

Y. Zhang, in turn, observes that "China has exhibited a pattern of international behavior that is often seemingly contradictory to its own declared principles and certainly much more complex than in previous decades" (2008, p. 149). He notes that contentious discourses "sustain the pattern of China's international behavior," essentially interpreting China's inconsistent foreign policy as a result of paradoxical narratives in official and academic discourses. He explains that broadening discourses in the post–Cold War era meant an "intellectual disorientation" that brought to bear "competing images of global politics, contradictory assessments of the changing power configuration, differing interpretations of economic globalization, and diverse policy prescriptions" (2008, p. 161). Hameiri and Jones (2016) also intervene in the discussion of policy "inconsistency" by invoking the Gramscian notion of "state transformation."[9] They claim that state state/governmental authority in China has become fragmented, decentralized, and internationalized (2016, p. 9). While their arguments are not completely persuasive,[10] they are useful in underlining how policy implementation is uneven and even unpredictable under Xi Jinping.

Gaps in the Literature

There are several principal gaps in this literature on China's foreign policy. First, there is a conspicuous lack of attention pertaining to the role of diplomatic actors (MOFA and PRC diplomats) and diplomacy in China's international politics. Some analyses focus on actors such as the PLA, the core leadership group, "public opinion," or the president to explain China's foreign policy and its international behavior. Others focus on structural variables such as "nationalism," "Chinese political culture," and domestic factionalism. Similarly, in discussions of Chinese assertiveness, scant attention is paid to how exactly assertiveness is constructed and perceived by others, and which actors are key in this representation. In this regard, there is little mention or systematic analysis of MOFA. Even when it is considered, it is usually mentioned in passing, or is used as an example of how ineffectual it is (see G. Smith 2014, para. 3).

Current empirical data suggest the opposite—MOFA's diplomatic budget doubled to RMB $60 billion in 2018 from RMB $30 billion in 2011 (Clover & Ju, 2018). There is also a conscious turn to professionalizing its diplomatic corps by improving its quality and importance (C. Wang, 2022). I hasten to add that the importance of MOFA has ebbed and flowed throughout its history, as Liu's tracing of the evolution of MOFA makes clear[11] (see also Jakobson & Knox, 2010, pp. 8–10). In her work, Liu showed how in the early 1990s MOFA "moved from its early insistence on ideological orientation and political loyalty to a charismatic leader to more professionalized and bureaucratic criteria based on rules and rationality" (2001, xv). As I shall argue, under Xi Jinping we are seeing a return of ideological control and political loyalty, moving in lockstep with increased professionalism. As noted in the Introduction, studies on Chinese assertiveness do not properly locate MOFA in its analytic configuration (see D. Chen et al., 2014). Instead, familiar themes, such as nationalism, territorial disputes, Sino-American relations, and national resources are raised by scholars to explain China's assertiveness (see also Yeo, 2019, p. 459–478). Besides, the scholarship seems to suggest implicitly and explicitly that security actors and strategic processes are the main or sole drivers of contemporary Chinese assertiveness (e.g., Yahuda, 2013; Yeo, 2019; Feng, 2020). In contrast, the research here shows how MOFA is increasingly complementing but also displacing other actors (such as the PLA) in certain domains to become the main interface of Chinese assertiveness. Thus the importance of MOFA, its diplomats, and its representational responsibilities—as keys to unlocking explanations of China's assertiveness—cannot be overstated.

Second, existing approaches are unsatisfactory because of their inclination toward state-centrism (in realism and liberalism) or culturalist arguments (in constructivism). State-centrism overlooks the manifold diplomatic actors and the practices they engender, cutting off an important generative force in international politics and, even in the most sympathetic reading, reducing them to insignificant by-processes or epiphenomena. This asymmetric view hides the dynamic, relational, and conflictual nature of diplomacy. Culturalist explanations, for their part, do pay greater attention to nonmaterial elements by attributing social action to rule- and norm-following behavior. Nevertheless, such interpretations generally dissolve practices in which "norm based actions stem from a process of reflexive cognition based either on instrumental calculations, reasoned persuasion, or the psychology of compliance" rather than on the unspoken, prereflective, and contingent nature of practices (Pouliot, 2008, p. 262).

In deriving China's international action from culturalist arguments such as "tradition," "culture," and "nationalism," constructivism essentializes these concepts either as forces that are always being exerted on individuals from the outside or as internalized mental schemas guiding them toward appropriate behavior. Such representations conceal how social action is motivated not purely by externalist or internalist motivations but by an amalgamation of both, expressed in practices where "it is a matter of instantiating structures, old or new, in and through practice. Without practice, intersubjective realities would falter" (Pouliot, 2008, p. 264). Furthermore, in resuscitating the agency of individuals and in privileging ideational elements, constructivism displaces materiality. Ba, for instance, writes how constructivists believe that "ideas underlie definitions of material interests and are thus prior to material" (2009, p. 24). Yet materiality, in manifestations of material structures and objects, is fundamental to social life. Indeed, in this book, objects and material arrangements like WeChat accounts, books, and press conferences enable diplomatic practices and its representational role to emerge. Without properly grasping the material world, and by prioritizing the ideational plane, constructivism cedes analytic capacity and control over entire categories such as "rationality," "self-interest," and "material power" to neorealism and neoliberalism. In any case, constructivists have yet to adequately explain China's escalatory activities in the South China Sea (SCS) and in the multiple high-profile cases of its influence campaigns across Asia, despite attempts by international actors to socialize and shame it into moderating its practices.

Finally, the literature on contemporary Chinese international politics generally suffers from a lack of work that takes the lived experiences and practices of actors as its starting point. This is problematic considering how micro-level processes "emphasize key factors that escape macro-level theories yet are the very elements through which macro-forces are often filtered" (Solomon & Steele, 2017, p. 268). The value of approaches to IR that are sensitive to processes, practices, and individuals is well documented (e.g., O'Tuathail, 2003; Neumann, 2002; Dufort, 2013; Autesserre, 2014). Johnston laments how "constructivism has tended to leave the microprocesses of socialization underexplained. It tends to assume that agents at the systemic level have relatively unobstructed access to states and substate actors from which to diffuse new normative understandings" (2008, p. 16). Thus a turn to the micro "enables the *grounding* of macropolitics within micropolitical spaces" (Solomon & Steele, 2017, p. 271). Certainly, Pouliot sees how "the unfolding of everyday practices" creates "the bigger phenomena and social realities that we know of. By implication, empirical granularity is not a methodological caprice but an analytical necessity" (2016, p. 50). To be sure, works such as X. Wang's novel *The Civil Servant's Notebook* (2012), Weiss's work on nationalism (2014), Ding's scholarship on performative governance (2022), and Pieke's (2009) investigation of the Party cadre system represent such endeavors. However, because of issues with access and transparency, any systematic study of Chinese bureaucracies, such as MOFA, remains challenging.

Where there has been a turn to microanalyses in China, these works typically concentrate on a few key elites. Such analyses are commonly undergirded by psychology- or personality-based approaches, such as He and Feng's (2013) attempt to "bring the leaders back in." In their analysis of President Xi Jinping (2013, p. 218), they conclude that Xi's belief system is similar to that of his predecessor and "signifies that Xi's foreign policy will not depart significantly from Hu's" (2013, p. 229). The fact that their predictions have proven inaccurate shows how, in devising their analysis from a psychological standpoint, they miss out key structural dynamics while inflating the influence and agency of individuals in such a way as to overlook diplomatic practices. In that regard, Brown provides a more nuanced account of Xi's power and points out how his authority obtains from "the institutional, tangible and material (the Party, central ministries and their executive authority and the PLA) and the abstract, intangible and ideological (control of narratives, new ideas, ways of speaking and emotional appeal)" (2016, p. 273).

In sum, by privileging state, structural, or culturalist arguments, important microprocesses, materials, and actors are often erased. On the other hand, micro-focused research on China commonly expunges structural dynamics. Against this background, this research seeks to "identify, inventory and specify the consequences of innovative micro-practices," a hallmark of "transformational research" in constructivism (Ruggie, 1998, p. 27) that seems to have been overlooked by constructivists. All in all, this study hopes to be catalytic in proving how a focus on practices that demands a turn to the micro-macro nexus can shed light on important empirical questions pertaining to China's international relations.

China's Diplomacy and Practice Theory

The Chinese bureaucratic landscape is vast and labyrinthine. Problems of bureaucratic coordination in China have led to Schurmann's observations (1968, pp. 188–193) that the Chinese system uses "dual and vertical" rule to exert control. This is analogous to the Chinese terms of *kuai* (area 块) and *tiao* (branches 条) within the bureaucracy. *Tiao* "indicates that a ministry at the central level has control over all the units at the lower levels," while *kuai* "indicates that the party committee at each level would be the primary point of authority coordinating the activities of the organizations" (Saich, 2001, p. 109). Conceptually, the hierarchical structure and domains of control of both *tiao* and *kuai* are akin to Bourdieu's notion of *fields*. In this regard, the coming together of *tiao* and *kuai* and the struggle over authority and resources can be understood as the struggles within a field.

The relationship between central and provincial governments is also illuminating in pointing to how the concept of *field* can be deployed fruitfully. Saich explains how, in the province of Guangdong (where the Party is historically weak and seen as less important than the local government), senior officials sent from Beijing to seize control felt disillusioned as they were "shut out from informal politics" and "longed to return to Beijing" (2001, p. 147). The politics of the local-central relation tells us the importance of lived realities and practices of actors in informing broader structural dynamics. In their discussion of foreign policy, Lieberthal and Oksenberg remark that "the past experiences of the official" can be a major influence on his perspective on a policy, "as these may have led him to some basic conclusions about risk taking, the reliability of certain kinds of information, the efficacy of various types of initiatives, and so forth that can play a major role in shaping his views on the matter at hand. This is the effect of background" (1988, p. 28).

This "background" effect is analogous to the "background stock of knowledge" (Stein, 2011, p. 88) and is a core analytical focus of practice theory. These short examples are raised to show that practice-theoretical concepts such as fields and practices have analytical affinities in the study of Chinese international politics. Thus this research heeds the appeal by G. Wang and Zheng to "look at domestic sources or disaggregate things that are otherwise perceived as a unified analytic unit, such as nationalism, foreign policy discourse, and even the state itself" and to critically reexamine the taken-for-granted units of analysis and processes (2008, p. 12). Indeed, lying at the heart of the practice theory project is its focus on the relational, quotidian, and lived aspects of international life.

This research draws on international practice theory to study Chinese diplomacy, its purported assertiveness, and how diplomacy evolved with Xi's assumption of the presidency, with MOFA's representational role accented. The purpose of this section is to introduce the key concepts and theoretical tools used to analyze Chinese diplomacy and to demonstrate why these concepts and tools are necessary and how they both challenge and add value to the literature on Chinese foreign policy. I proceed by furnishing a broad overview of practice theory in IR and by introducing three concepts—practices, habitus, and field—that are central to my analysis of MOFA. I end this chapter by describing my research design.

Defining Practices

The "practice turn" in IR constitutes an important development in the discipline by spelling out the multiple dimensions of world politics "in action, as part of a 'doing' in and on the world" (Adler & Pouliot, 2011b, p. 3). Nonetheless, there is no agreed-upon definition of practices. Schatzki explains that "the term practice theory designates at best a family of accounts" (1997, p. 284). Even so, they are united in taking practices as the basic social phenomenon: "It is in practices that meaning is established in social life" (1997, p. 284).

Bourdieu distills his account of practices into the formula *"(habitus x capital) + field = practices"* from his work in *Distinction* (1984, p. 101). For Bourdieu, an individual's habitus is vital in generating the most sensible practices available to him (see also Bourdieu, 1990b, p. 50). The selection of practices (or sets of action) by the individual follows a "logic of practice" in which the habitus gives meaning to objective structures (such as class) availing themselves to the actor by marking out the possibility and impossibility of certain actions at any given moment (e.g., Bourdieu, 1990b, pp. 63, 266–268). This logic also observes what he calls the "economy of practices" where it "must endeavor to grasp capital and profit in all their forms and to establish laws whereby the different types of capital (or power, which amounts to the same thing) change into one another" (Bourdieu, 1986, p. 243). In other words, human practices are dependent upon the struggle to accrue benefits. In the Chinese diplomatic landscape, actors struggle over resources such as (greater) access to the political leadership, career and political advancement, status in society, and influence over foreign policy matters.

The embodied and "commonsense" nature of practices is a recurrent theme in Bourdieu's ideas: "Practical sense, social necessity turned into nature, converted into motor schemes and body automatisms, is what causes practices, in and through what makes them obscure to the eyes of their producers, to be sensible, that is, informed by a common sense. It is because agents never know completely what they are doing that what they do has more sense than they know" (1990b, p. 69).

Thus actors' practices are generally not reflected upon by actors themselves because of this "commonsense" quality. In the words of a Chinese interlocutor, actors do what they do because it is "correct" and "commonsensical" (Interviewee 70, personal communication, November 10, 2010). Embodied practices (gestures, mannerisms, and styles) matter because they simultaneously reveal and conceal the "commonsense" rules governing social spaces. They are also indispensible in revealing organizational messages, protocols, and culture, which in turn form foreign policy perceptions in the eyes of other international actors. It is with this in mind that chapter 2 turns to an analysis of MOFA spokespersons' body gestures and mannerisms in press conferences. By contrast, bodily gestures do not feature and are dismissed in realist, liberalist, and constructivist accounts of China's international politics.

For Barnes, practices are "socially recognized forms of activity, done on the basis of what members learn from others, and capable of being done well or badly" (2001, p. 19). Bueger offers this three-part definition: "firstly, bodily movements in the form of doing and sayings, secondly, practical knowledge which might be tacit or explicit, and thirdly, objects (artifacts and things) used in a practice" (2015, p. 5). Others, like Reckwitz, focuses on the iterative, emphasizing how practices are "a routinized type of behavior which consists of several elements, interconnected to one other: forms of bodily activities, forms of mental activities, 'things' and their use, a background knowledge in the form of understanding, know-how, states of emotion and motivational knowledge" (2002, pp. 249–250). Neumann argues that practices can be both strategic and unconscious but also improvisational (2002, pp. 637–638). All in all, Schatzki is right in saying that "there is no unified practice approach" (2001, p. 11), but he also explains that despite this diversity, "practice accounts are joined in the belief that such phenomena as knowledge, meaning, human activity, science, power, language, social institutions, and historical transformation occur within and are aspects or components of the field of practices" (2001, p. 11).

Practice Theories in IR

Scholars have attempted to introduce order as a research paradigm to the practice project by conceiving it as a "theory" and a "turn" in IR. In continuation of the earlier discussion on practices, I sketch how theorists are adapting practice theory for use in IR. I therefore trace different renderings of PT and contextualize my own practice theory approach in studying Chinese diplomacy.

Bourbeau, in his review of the state of PT, notes that there are four different forms of the approach in IR, which he labels "comprehensive, complementary, discursive, and relational forms" (2017, p. 170). According to him, the comprehensive approach places practices as the foundation from which all social practices unfold and accords them ontological priority, even though it is important to note that Adler and Pouliot emphasize that their approach is not a "universal, grand theory or totalizing ontology of everything social" (2011a, p. 3). The complementary approach, on the other hand, shies away from making priority claims and instead looks at "relationship among practices, norms, and discourses in a complementary way," granting practices an important but not superior position in the social world (Bourbeau, 2017, p. 171). Perhaps the most unclear is the "relational form," where the attention is paid to how "relations are what makes the world hang together" (2017, p. 172). Bourbeau contends that this approach is concerned with the relations between actors and practices and how they recur. Bueger and Gadinger (2015, p. 22) describe five forms of PT: Bourdieu-inspired PT; the Wenger-inspired community of practice (CoP); the narrative approach; Latour's actor-network Theory (ANT); and Boltanski's pragmatic sociology. The authors determine that these forms of PT share six "core commitments" despite their differences—"Practice theory implies emphasizing process, developing an account of knowledge as action, appreciating the collectivity of knowledge, recognizing the materiality of practice, embracing the multiplicity of orders, and working with a performative understanding of the world" (2015, pp. 449–450).

Within PT, CoP scholars disentangle how practices are socially delivered and learned: "A practice is thus always a social practice, which produces meaning, provides coherence in a community and delivers learning for newcomers" (Bicchi, 2016, p. 464). Wenger (n.d., p. 1) stresses how "communities of practice are groups of people who share a concern or a passion for something they do and learn how to do it better as they interact regularly." Certainly, one can easily spot how Chinese diplomats form a "community of practice." That being said, the CoP approach does not sufficiently highlight the tensions inherent in such communities and it is also silent on the institutional effects on inhabitants (see also Glas, 2022, pp. 46–48). The tensions and synergies within the broader diplomatic community in China, as chapters 2 and 3 highlight, are important for showcasing how different actors (such as think tanks and academics) cooperate but also compete with MOFA and its diplomats.

Another strand of PT draws on Bruno Latour and Michel Callon's actor-network theory (ANT). ANT attacks traditional social theories by rejecting substantialism[12] (Latour, 2005, pp. 1–17); it does not ontologically privilege human associations and urges the incorporation of nonhuman agents or "actants" in social practices.[13] Indeed, examples such as automated computer trading in global finance (Porter, 2013), disruptive new technologies, and the daily microinteractions humans have with computers and machines (Giddens, personal communication, April 21, 2016) illustrate how *actants* interact with humans and are woven into social realities. It is important to highlight this because, as my empirical work shows, nonhumans play a substantive enabling role in Chinese diplomatic practices. For instance, chapter 5 underlines how Twitter, impelled by more assertive Chinese diplomacy in the online sphere, is having significant effects for more traditional, "face-to-face" diplomacy. In contrast, extant literature on China's international politics tends to focus on nonhumans merely as vehicles that intervene to create certain international political effects: for example, interpreting China's construction of aircraft carriers as a manifestation of its increasing naval ambition or describing how natural resources in Africa intervene in China's foreign policy decisions (Y. Sun, 2014). These approaches mask how actants can resist human agency and impel new practices. In this vein, things such as bookshelves, MOFA headquarters, architecture, seating arrangements in press conferences, diplomats' Twitter activities, and so forth are significant coproducers of diplomatic practices, as I will explain in the Conclusion to this book.

In the main, the turn toward PT was born out of a dissatisfaction with grand theory's proposition.[14] Indeed, PT approaches promise to provide the tools to allow us to rethink IR phenomena—ranging from power and warfare to international hierarchies and diplomacy—more accurately and comprehensively with its sensitivity to concrete practices taking place at the granular level.

Operationalizing Practices

Despite differences, "practices" share certain general commitments. First, practices are socially expressed and recursive. Second, they are informed by implicit and tacit knowledge, know-how, and discourse. Finally, because practice enactments are possible only in social relationships, there must be an audience to appraise these practices. For these reasons, Adler and Pouliot's definition of practices as "socially meaningful patterns of action, which, in being performed more or less competently, simultaneously embody, act out, and possibly reify background knowledge and discourse in and on the material world" (2011a, p. 4) is seen by practice theorists in IR as most persuasive. They opine that practice implies the existence "of an audience able to appraise" whether it is done correctly or incorrectly (Adler and Pouliot, 2011b, p. 7). Slightly refining Adler and Pouliot's operationalization, I take practices to be *socially meaningful, competent and incompetent performances by individuals and institutions in and on the material world*. The question of "competence" is important for my research, particularly when Chinese diplomats are evaluated by (1) key stakeholders at home and (2) an international audience. Differences in what counts as "competence" matter because what is construed as skilled diplomacy at home is sometimes interpreted as "undiplomatic" or "incompetent" by international audiences. In chapter 2, for instance, I show how the performance of China's foreign minister at a press conference in Canada was viewed negatively by Western audiences as a sign of aggression and a breach of diplomatic sensibilities. However, Wang's press conference was praised back home, signifying strength and diplomatic competence.

Thus the refinement to Adler and Pouliot's term allows me to also capture "exceptional practices" or "inappropriate/incompetent practices": That is, acts that depart from what is expected or appropriate. To borrow Duvall and Chowdhury's (2011) example, Khrushchev's shoe-banging performance in the United Nations General Assembly produced social meanings and political effects. The authors rightly highlight that "there are instances . . . where actors either reflexively or self-consciously act incompetently in order to establish their identity—or, more precisely, their identity itself is constituted by departing from what would constitute 'competent performance'" (2011, p. 341). They further note that actors can deliberately transgress and "act out" (2011, pp. 342–343). Giving practices this performative nuance would, I argue, better account for *change* and *resistance* in the field—such as whether the exceptional performances were isolated or a combination of different exceptions, and whether they altered the field or other social practices. Furthermore, this attention to performative practices by PRC diplomats allows insights into how they represent state and Party interests to international audiences. Affording this space to exceptional practice(s) also has methodological implications, as it entails paying close attention to both exceptional and mundane practices. As practices are performative, one can analyze how a set of practice is exceptional in one field but not in another, as I seek to show in evaluating Chinese diplomats' practices at home and abroad in chapter 3.

Some deliberate acts of incompetence achieve social aims and some are faux pas (accidental) but nevertheless consequential. Restricting practices to "competent practices," as Duvall and Chowdhury add, "risks precluding seemingly 'incompetent' performances that ground subjects, practices whose meaning is contested or otherwise unstable, or transgressive performances that challenge the existing order" (2011,

p. 351). Such is the case when non-Chinese diplomats either deliberately or accidentally transgress the accepted practices and "field rules" (chapter 3). What is more, Chinese diplomatic practices are often enacted for both domestic and international audiences. Owing to the complex mix of audiences, the risk of being misunderstood or construed as "incompetent" is ever present. Hence, a greater sensitivity to competency or incompetency is needed to render a more precise appraisal of the practices under study, particularly for Chinese diplomats, who are hypersensitive to appraisals on their diplomatic performances (Interviewee 25, personal communication, August 13, 2018).

Third, by highlighting organizations' role in constructing practices, I clarify how practices are not *purely* constructed from individuals but also from institutions. Without doubt, human individuals undertake acts that are competent, patterned, and meaningful, but so too do groups and institutions as collective entities. The splitting of "individual" and "groups" indicates that these are usually aligned but that sometimes contradictory practices between them can be plotted and account for "slippages" in practices (Pouliot and Adler, 2011a, p. 11; see also Voeten, 2011, pp. 275–276). As a case in point, Hansen points to "corporate practices" in international diplomacy by showing how G8 summits are performed not by singular heads of state but by large teams of representatives. These summits are acted out by communities of practice, and in that way practices can be both individual and structural (2011, p. 295).

Habitus

Bourdieu writes that habitus is "a system of durable, transposable dispositions, structured structures predisposed to function as structuring structures, that is, as principles of generation and structuring of practices and representations which can be objectively 'regulated' and 'regular' without in any way being the product of obedience to rules" (1977, p. 2). One's habitus is affected by one's personal biography, particularly one's family socialization, education, and position in the class structure (Bourdieu, 1984, pp. 23, 109). Put plainly, habitus is our embodied disposition that orients us toward certain practices. These practices are geared toward position-taking and position-preserving moves in the field. By way of illustration, a realist might explain China's assertive diplomacy as a result of China's grand strategy (Y. Wang, 2016), and a constructivist might explain China's energetic foreign policy as a result of changing notions of what it means to be a great power (Forsby, 2011). By contrast, a practice-sensitive account suggests that we direct our inquiry into the incentives in the field of diplomacy and the attendant shift in practices that enabled and promoted diplomatic assertiveness. In the Chinese case, A. D. Barnett's interviews (1985) with the third premier of China, Zhao Ziyang, precisely map out the importance of his family background, education, and class position for his foreign policy competencies and preferences. In this way, tracing collectively, the group habitus of diplomats from MOFA can uncover key historical, cultural, and organizational sensibilities to account for its current diplomatic practices. Indeed, chapter 4's investigation into the celebration and commemoration of "birth anniversaries" of deceased high-profile Chinese diplomats is instructive, as it reveals how this practice enhances group solidarity and reinforces organizational stability—fostering greater conformity and valorizing state-inflected values and practices such as self-sacrifice and loyalty to the Party and the organization.

Bourdieu (1990b, p. 55) notes that habitus, rather than having a fixed quality, is a generative scheme that inclines actors toward narrow options within the range of possibilities, while recognizing the historical and social context in each exercise of practice. This creates space for agency (see also Cornut, 2018). Bourdieu discloses that the "responses of the *habitus* may be accompanied by a strategic calculation tending to perform in a conscious mode the operation that the habitus performs quite differently, namely an estimation of chances presupposing transformation of past effect in an expected object" (1990b, p. 53). Therefore, strategizing or exercising agency is "neither intentional nor fully determined," and "strategic practices come from having a sense of the game that is generated by one's habitus" (Mérand & Forget, 2013, p. 97). Within the context of diplomatic practices, however, strict protocols exist that restrict this creative agency. For this reason, PRC diplomats often do not reveal their "backstage" and what they privately think and, as a matter of official policy, are forbidden to meet singly with visitors so as to ensure mutual surveillance and prevent deviation from official scripts.

Fields

According to Bourdieu and Wacquant,

> In analytical terms, a field can be defined as a configuration of objective relations between positions. These positions are defined objectively in their existence and in the determinations that they impose on their occupants, agents or institutions by their current and potential situations (situs) in the [wider] structure of the distribution of different currencies of power (or of capital), possession of which provides access to specific profits that are up for grabs in the field, at the same time, by their objective relations to other positions (domination, subordination, equivalents and so on). (1992, p. 20)

Put simply, a field is a relatively autonomous and hierarchical spatial-social arena where actors vie for resources and occupy positions in this configuration. It has both material dimensions (resources such as money) and ideational dimensions (norms and practices of the field and what "competence" is). Within a field, the boundaries of possible actions and the stakes of the game appear as "commonsensical" and intuitive to actors. Bourdieu and Wacquant call this "understanding" the *doxa*, which is the "immediate belief in the facticity of the world that makes us take it for granted" (1992, p. 73). This intersubjective understanding canvasses meaningful action in that field; it is an enabler and a disabler. The Chinese diplomatic field displays all the above tendencies typical of a "field," with the boundaries policed closely and tightly. One non-Chinese respondent says: "Of course, diplomatic services everywhere are tightly knit and disciplined, but the Chinese diplomats are different because of the conformity, there is immense and there is little allowance for the sort of flair you see in another place. There is no other option but to believe and act like you believe in whatever the Party decides" (Interviewee 30, personal communication, January 20, 2020).

Bigo explains how the field is not just "a collective" but "a field of individuals and of the institutions they make, as the field will not exist independently of human action and reflexivity" (2011, p. 238). Indeed, Schmidt argues that there is "no acting subject devising his or her moves in advance." Instead, the subject is a "co-player and carrier of collective complexes of knowing-how, comprehension and knowledge." Rather than conceiving individuals' reflections as subjective activities taking place in "a separate autonomous existence in some internal, unobservable mental sphere," practices treat these as collective, instantiated, and observable practices because "reflecting" and "analyzing" are "always also in things, acting bodies," and "in artefacts such as catalogues of definitions, algorithms and software programmes" (2017, p. 151). In the same way, Chinese diplomats in the game of diplomacy are not unthinking individuals who only act out political leaders' desires but are also "co-players" and carriers of "collective complexes" of institutional knowledge, capable of reflection (that may translate to changes in practice) within the limits of the field. For IR, deploying the concept of field allows us "to recognize a level of analysis that is quite distinct from the discipline's dominant currents: it is not focused on substances, such as the state and state actors, or essentialized concepts such as politics or globalization, but instead on the 'totality of relations' involving positions that are uncovered" (Pouliot & Mérand, 2013, p. 32).

Indeed, conceiving of the Chinese diplomatic landscape as a "field" gives the analysis a powerful tool to construct hierarchical relations within that domain and also a means of showing how transnational diplomatic fields are sites for contestation, resistance, and normative imposition (see Lesch & Loh, 2022). In sum, Bourdieusian and practice-theoretical concepts—practices, field, habitus—allow us to recast and rethink Chinese diplomacy in new ways—granting us a sharper focus on the concrete, everyday actions performed by diplomats and institutions. This enables the analysis to be sensitive to meaningful and productive performances, gestures, and practices that were hitherto undetected.

Research Design

To move to the methodological underpinnings of my research, I now clarify how I examine nonhuman objects, bodily comportments, and practices of Chinese diplomacy. Studying the IR questions presented here with this particular theoretical approach requires some innovation with methods. Broadly in the spirit of Patrick Jackson's *methodological pluralism*,[15] this research uses a mix of qualitative methods—field interviews, participant observation, case studies, and practice tracing.

The book's ancillary focus on "objects" is important. An exchange with a PLA interlocutor illustrates this point. A Chinese major general told me that she was part of a WeChat group consisting of other high-ranking military members and that they communicated regularly and shared news items in this chat group.[16] Chatting and sharing news is "everyday" and banal, but what was revealing was how social exclusion and inclusion were embedded in and made attainable through the techno-materiality of WeChat. The interviewee disclosed, for instance, how members had been displeased with the Foreign Ministry's handling of the SCS disputes in 2014–2016 and had shared their feelings in the chat group (and only in the chat group) in very critical terms (Interviewee 4, personal communication, June 20, 2016). This, essentially, articulated their "mastery" and "competence" over foreign policy domains at the expense of their Foreign Ministry counterparts. Orlikowski similarly comments on the techno-materiality of the Blackberry phone: its introduction, she notes, reconfigure the social realities of members in an organization in such a way that "members experience both increased flexibility (about where and when to work) and increased obligation to be continually responsive" (2007, p. 1444). Along these lines, I pay serious attention to nonhuman materials in my analysis by investigating the role of objects and their relationship with and in cocreating practices.

Moving to bodily comportments, Eagleton-Pierce regards how the "taken for granted" nature of social life in the World Trade Organization often ignores practices and embodied deeds: "The most privileged WTO member draw upon a repertoire of methods in order to control other actors. For outsiders, these forms of power are not always directly observable, because these techniques are often 'underhanded,' 'silent,' or 'gestural'" (2013, p. 2). Drawing on this insight, my approach takes silences, elisions, and gestures seriously. For instance, a longer-than-usual pause in an interview, instead of being dismissed, could be an indication that the question asked is unsettling or that the interviewee requires more time to think through an acceptable response. Such silences can be useful signposts for further probing and for constructing future interviews. Thus it is important to take as a starting point not only the "doings" of actors but also their embodied dispositions, gestures, and manners (Bourdieu, 1990b, p. 58).

For practical reasons such as cost and accessibility, it remains difficult to conduct ethnography or use interview data with those involved directly in foreign policy even as scholarship on Chinese politics has been enlivened by these microsociologically sensitive works (albeit mostly conducted in pre-Xi time periods). Weiss's contribution to Chinese nationalism, for instance, draws on "more than 170 interviews with nationalist activists, students, protesters, journalists, analysts, and diplomats" (2014, p. 11). Likewise, Iza Ding's (2022) extensive fieldwork and interviews with Chinese environmental bureaucrats was crucial in shedding light on the politics of environmental governance, revealing ubiquitous "performative governance."[17] Rühlig (2022, p. 17), for his part, conducted over 150 interviews "with party cadres, policymakers, party-state officials" to examine contradictions in Chinese foreign policy. This research adds on to these works and adopts a similar methodological approach to reconstruct the everyday world of agents' lived experiences in the diplomatic field. I also take my methodological cue from Pouliot, who emphasizes the importance of acquiring access to practices, as it forms the "raw material of social science" (2013, p. 48). "Pure" ethnographic participant observation is most ideal but, as he rightly notes, is not always possible, particularly in authoritarian regimes. The next best option is to get "proxies" of participant observation—interviews, documents, and texts that give the researcher substitutive access to agents' practices. Interviews form the cornerstone of practice scholars. Pouliot advises: "Seek to trace practices indirectly through in-depth interviewing. Focus on what they talk from—the stock of unspoken assumptions and tacit know-how that ought to be presumed in order to say what is being said. Use interviews to trace practices but also to interpret the context in which they are being performed" (2016, p. 277).

In my study of Chinese diplomatic practices, I conducted 102 in-depth semistructured interviews and conversations with eighty-four diplomatic interviewees (see Appendix B for their profiles). These were primarily conducted in person, but interviews over the phone, email, and WeChat were also conducted. Of the interviewees, forty-seven were Chinese diplomatic actors. From these, twenty-two were "primary" diplomatic actors who were directly linked or associated with diplomacy (through MOFA). Within this group, eleven were MOFA diplomats. Twenty-five of the eighty-four interviewees were "secondary" Chinese diplomatic actors—made up of players from universities, think tanks, the media, non-MOFA officials, and Party members who occupied the diplomatic field (see chapter 3 for this categorization of key and secondary actors). Out of the eighty-four interviewees, thirty-seven were non-Chinese diplomats and actors who were privy to the diplomatic practices and the diplomatic field in China. The benefits of this triangulation are multifaceted (see Appendix B). Third-party (non-Chinese diplomatic) interviews revealed practices that I would not have been able to access from Chinese diplomatic actors themselves. These interviews were conducted from 2016 to 2020. I spent time (ranging from one to three months) in China from 2016 to 2018. Most of the research was done in Beijing, but interviews were also conducted in Shanghai (2017), Shenyang (2017), Singapore (2016, 2018, 2019), Cambridge (2018), and London (2016, 2018).[18] In 2020, owing to the Covid-19 pandemic, interviews were conducted virtually or by phone. My Chinese respondents replied in Mandarin, English, or a mix of both, which I have translated to English in the text.

These contacts were made via my existing network and, subsequently, through snowball sampling. While the built-in biases and problems associated with snowball sampling are well recognized (see Biernacki & Waldorf, 1981), my goal was not to build a representative sample of MOFA. Rather, I aimed to furnish insight (via a preliminary analysis) into Chinese diplomatic practices and how such practices are perceived by others, thus teasing out the representational role of MOFA. Hence, I used a necessarily broad and open approach, where I "cast my net wide" since getting proximity to Chinese diplomats proved difficult initially. I found non-Chinese diplomats extremely useful for introducing me to other non-Chinese diplomats and Chinese nondiplomatic sources and for triangulating my data. In addition to engaging with the diplomatic community, I got in touch with reporters, scholars, and universities in Beijing—in particular the China Foreign Affairs University (CFAU), which hosted me in 2016, 2017, and 2018, and Renmin University, which hosted me in 2017.

From these interviews, I used practice tracing because it captures "observable practices without reducing to single or handful causal mechanisms. It enables making contingent causal claims and analytical generality" (Visoka, 2018, p. 9). This inductive approach, which takes the background knowledge, unspoken assumptions, and practices of practitioners as its launching pad, gave me a view into the lived experiences of practitioners and enabled me to see things that might not appear relevant or significant at first glance. As Weeden, invoking Socrates, puts it crisply, "There is never nothing going on" (2010, p. 267).

My setup was supplemented by a close reading of speeches and statements by MOFA. Specifically, this involved closely watching MOFA daily press briefings. This was done by way of the Associated Press YouTube channel (AP Archive, n.d.) (for daily press briefings), official MOFA websites (for press releases and key speeches), MOFA's WeChat account (press releases and official publications), my presence at three "live" press conferences (in 2016, 2017, and 2018) and a close watch on China's Twitter diplomats. Such sources provided extra insight into the discursive practices of MOFA actors and clearly brought to the foreground MOFA's capacity to speak for other agencies. Through this process I could observe how MOFA was discursively and symbolically representing other departments through its verbalization and defense of China's positions in domains covering economy, human rights, military security, and so forth. The scrutiny of the daily press briefing, for instance, also made apparent how controversial questions extracted similar assertive responses despite the different personalities of the three spokespersons of MOFA. Through watching diplomatic press conferences, I could see the variations and similarities in gestures, tones, and body language from diplomats in different settings on different issues. As Vennesson observes, "*Intensive, open-ended interviewing, participant observation and document analysis* help to understand the meaning and role of established regularities, and can help to suggest ways to uncover previously unknown relations between factors" (2008, p. 234).[19]

Illustrative case studies (particularly in chapter 2 but also chapter 3) formed an integral part of my methodological approach. In themselves, illustrative cases are particularly apt ways to examine manifestations of social, structural, and agential conditions in the field and to excavate underlying mechanisms of phenomena under study: "Empirical phenomena may be selected for comparison for explicitly political or 'interested' reasons or because we suspect them of having similar determinants. But they also should be selected because they are believed to be relevant to uncovering or illuminating the causal mechanisms and structures of interest" (Steinmetz, 2004, p. 393).

Indeed, an extra analytic dimension was added when I confronted interviewees with these cases, such that I was able to obtain different articulations and perceptions for the same case. In addition to interviews, I leveraged my time working as an analyst in a think tank in Singapore from 2013 to 2015. There I participated in and organized track-2 and track-1.5 events where Chinese interlocutors were sometimes present. These served as unique sites where I was able to participate and observe my Chinese counterparts. Additionally, I had the opportunity of working under a diplomat in the think tank to interact with Chinese interlocutors.[20] Beyond that, during my fieldwork I was able to insert myself into closed-door conferences where diplomatic actors were present. The broad goal during these observations was to capture as much information as possible on the practices of diplomats. This was therefore a necessarily liberal approach. This yearly affair (2016–2018) culminated with a visit to MOFA headquarters to attend their daily press briefings. In these meetings, I was able to pose questions and observe diplomatic actors at work. With that in mind and going back to my earlier point on the "representativeness" of my MOFA interviewees, the plurality of methods that I used to support my interviews strengthens my account of MOFA's contemporary diplomatic practices. This research design was also meant to mitigate against potential biases inherent in interviews where interlocutors might not give an accurate representation of diplomatic practices. First, I tried to triangulate oral testimonies by interviewing both non-Chinese diplomats (see Appendix B) and secondary diplomatic actors (think tank members, former Chinese diplomats, media personnel, PLA officials) so that they could corroborate and help me more robustly reconstruct Chinese diplomatic practices. For some interviewees, I tried to establish second rounds of interviews, both to probe deeper and to check for accuracy on previous statements made. Second, I sought to inject greater data diversity by buttressing interviews with textual analysis of official PRC documents, speeches by key officials, and PRC diplomat tweets. This was further complemented by the case studies as well as the field observations outlined above.

In the following chapters, I study the *practices, sites, institutions,* and *materials* of diplomacy in China in a bid to understand MOFA's representational role in Chinese assertiveness. First, I look at the *practices* of diplomatic actors and how these have incrementally shifted toward acquiring a more assertive character and have come to assume an increasingly representational position. Through that, I also show how, far from being a weak player, MOFA is in fact being empowered to do more by the political leadership. Next, I assess the *sites* of diplomacy and give an account of *where and how* diplomacy is executed. In doing so, I gesture toward the importance of fields as fertile sites to analyze Chinese political assertiveness and international resistance to such efforts. Subsequently, I investigate the *institution* of MOFA itself and contend that the organization produces significant identity effects for China. Finally, focusing on Twitter as a nonhuman diplomatic *material,* I point to the ways in which it has impelled new diplomatic practices through the generation of "discursive power" for Chinese diplomats.

TWO

Diplomacy's Ascendancy

In the past no one cared about what a Chinese vice foreign minister said. Now, what a vice foreign minister says will move financial markets around the world.

(INTERVIEWEE 77, personal communication, November 16, 2018)

There has been a curious neglect of China's MOFA, its diplomats, and the role it plays in international politics. Even though the organization and its actors assume a limited role in domestic politics, Chinese diplomats have occupied key and often leading roles in China's foreign policy across a range of issues big and small—from weakening and hampering the issuance of ASEAN statements on the South China Sea (SCS) to managing the release of detained Singaporean armored vehicles. The elevation of Yang Jiechi—China's former foreign minister—to the twenty-five-member Party Politburo in 2017 at China's Nineteenth Party Congress and Xi's call in 2013 for Chinese diplomats to "tell China's story well" (A. Huang and Wang, 2019) join a long list of examples demonstrating the growing profile of MOFA in China's foreign policy and its representational role (Song & Gao, 2017). Indeed, in recent years much more international media attention has focused on China's assertive behavior stemming from its diplomats.[1] We are also witnessing greater coordinating and facilitating powers of MOFA over other domestic actors: for instance, when it led and coordinated economic recovery efforts in Wuhan in the wake of the pandemic in 2020 or when it served as the main conduit for managing the Doklam standoff with India in 2017. MOFA has also taken on a more prominent role in the Special Administrative Region of Hong Kong, where the Office of the Commissioner of the Ministry of Foreign Affairs has been more conspicuous in articulating Hong Kong's political future, electoral reform, and the role of Hong Kong's "mini constitution" (Cheung et al., 2021).

Focusing on the diplomatic practices of MOFA actors, I make three interrelated arguments in this chapter. First, I complicate claims of MOFA's weakness in diplomacy by illustrating how diplomatic institutions and diplomats have grown more assertive and influential since 2009. Through an investigation of diplomatic practices and three case studies, I show how MOFA regularly exercises influence through its *capacity to implement, counsel,* and *coordinate.*[2] Second, and closely related to the first, I add to current understandings of Chinese "assertiveness" to show how diplomatic assertiveness contributes to the overall assertiveness leitmotif. PT helps us visualize and trace this assertiveness in practice. Thereby, I bring attention to various communicative practices of MOFA as a vital component of the expression of diplomatic assertiveness, and to the ways material objects interweave to coproduce such practices.

Finally, I make a distinction between *corporate practices* and *individual practices* to underscore how competing practices and styles generate tension and conflict in the diplomatic arena. The analysis of the three cases here—the Special ASEAN-China Foreign Ministers' Meeting; the Chinese foreign minister's meeting with the Canadian prime minister; and the detention of nine Singapore Armed Forces armored vehicles in Hong Kong—were also instances where China applied its diplomatic leverage in a demonstrably robust manner.[3] They are also apt analytic points to begin my investigations into Chinese diplomatic practices. It is germane to recall that PT invites adherents to take seriously the bodily comportment, gestures, speeches, statements, and activities of actors as units of analysis. These are materials and data that would have been discarded by predominant theories analyzing China's international politics. With that in mind, the attention to the quotidian and "unseen" allows us to assess if indeed and in what ways MOFA and its diplomats are "assertive" in concretized, corporeal forms.

The chapter proceeds as follows. First, I briefly describe existing accounts of MOFA's role in China's international politics and map out the changes in the PLA-MOFA dynamic to highlight how PLA is ceding some control over foreign policy issues to MOFA. From my empirical investigation of Chinese diplomatic practices, I work my way "up" and show how Chinese diplomats play a leading role in foreign policy and how an incremental instantiation of assertiveness follows from an enlargement of MOFA's diplomatic influence. Finally, I turn to the three specific cases mentioned and work my way down toward the practices of actors. Thus I get diplomatic actors themselves to articulate what their positions are in connection to cases of purported assertive diplomacy. Through this movement between practices and cases, I also show how MOFA exercises influence in implementing, coordinating, and counseling. Finally, I tease out differences in corporate and individual practices and the translation of these effects to China's international politics.

China's Foreign Policy and Diplomacy

Some observers of Chinese politics—scholars and practitioners alike—have a low regard for the Chinese Foreign Ministry. An Asian diplomat bluntly observes: "They have always been quite low [ranked]. Definitely nothing like the State Department [of the United States] or the Foreign Office in the UK" (Interviewee 5, personal communication, July 27, 2017). To be clear, I am not claiming that MOFA is a domestic powerhouse. My claim is modest (but important): regarding diplomacy, it has seen its influence and its function as the key representation of Party and country grow. This gain parallels the uptick in assertiveness starting in 2009 in Chinese foreign policy. This is an important distinction to make because scholars have alleged, until only very recently, that MOFA is weak *internally and externally*. While its lack of influence domestically is not disputed, claims of its weakness in foreign policy are problematic because little evidence has been offered to support this belief. Furthermore, while it may be self-evident to say that MOFA, as the organization responsible for diplomacy, has influence in diplomacy, the claim that it has exhibited increased diplomatic assertiveness and a heightened profile is certainly worthy of closer scrutiny.

Scholars who call MOFA weak contend that its top diplomats are toothless (Breslin, 2013, pp. 1280–81) or assert that it is overburdened and conclude that MOFA has been marginalized by the leadership (J. Sun 2016). They point to the ministry being just one of the many "groups influencing [China's] international agenda, including its ever-expanding military and large state-owned companies that have significant investments overseas" (Hatton, 2013, para. 5). For Stenslie and Gang, MOFA has had to occupy a "middle position" in foreign affairs, implying that it is sandwiched between other, more powerful foreign policy actors (2016, p. 129; see also Brown, 2017, pp. 42–44; H. Wang, 2000, p. 489; Hale & Urpelainen, 2020, pp. 32–34). Relatedly, Jakobson asserts that China's foreign policy fragmentation has resulted in a situation where "MFA [MOFA] faces competition for influence from among other bodies: the Ministry of Commerce (MOFCOM), the National Development and Reform Commission (NDRC), the Ministry of Finance, the Ministry of State Security, the Ministry of Public Security." Consequently, there is "intense rivalry both with the MFA and with other official foreign policy actors" (2016, p. 138). MOFA "lacks the power to effectively enforce its mandate to coordinate among various foreign policy actors" and "MFA's weak standing within the Chinese foreign policy decision-making apparatus" means that "MFA is often not informed by other agencies about incidents or decisions pertaining to China's international relations" (2016, p. 141).

In contrast, my interviews with military personnel show an increased deference to Xi Jinping and, notably, to MOFA (albeit begrudgingly),[4] with specific regard to the SCS issue, where we see MOFA increasingly playing the role of the overall coordinator. My findings also dispute the claim that MOFA's role has diminished because of the proliferation of foreign policy actors. On the contrary, precisely because of this proliferation, greater powers to coordinate have been given to MOFA by top leadership. As a senior colonel told me: "In terms of the South China Sea issue, we listen to MOFA. Now they are the ones with power to coordinate" (Interviewee 4, personal communication, June 20, 2016). Another senior colonel concurred: "We cannot do things on our own [in the South China Sea]. We must all listen to top leaders' decisions. In overall [mandate] terms, it is MOFA facilitating the SCS issue" (Interviewee 6, personal communication, July 29, 2017). This is an important point, as he explained: "In the past, from 2009 to around 2014, the South China Sea issue was very messy. Why? Because there were too many people involved! It was decided that MOFA would coordinate, so what you see after that is less messy" (Interviewee 7, personal communication, June 29, 2017). More directly, one MOFA source told me, "MOFA can tell private companies when to stop [oil] drilling in the SCS. Not all the time and not without reason. But [MOFA] does have the power to do so" (Interviewee 8, personal communication, June 2, 2018). My sources further described certain tensions between the PLA and MOFA. As one PLA interviewee contrasted "diplomats versus soldiers," "We belong to different worlds. We are trained to fight, but they are trained to prevent fights" (Interviewee 14, personal communication, July 1, 2016). A former PLA officer echoed this: "We have different perspectives, and MOFA will want to solve things differently. The military will have its own perspective" (Interviewee 15, personal communication, August 28, 2017).

Earlier, I described how a major general and her fellow counterparts partook in collective castigation of diplomats, in a WeChat group, for not taking a strong enough position on territorial disputes.[5] Yet as I looked more deeply into the differences between the two actors, it became increasingly apparent that military actors were yielding to MOFA, with regard to the SCS, in spite of their misgivings. "It is not true that we do not have a say. We don't report to or tell them what military exercises we are conducting. But it is correct to say that MOFA has the say now. They are the ones coordinating it." This was a reply I received from a senior military member when I sought an update on the SCS (Interviewee 18, personal communication, August 2, 2018). This affirmation of MOFA is increasingly recited by PLA actors and other secondary diplomatic players. Similarly, when quizzed publicly in an interview in 2017 on the stalled progress of a Code of Conduct (CoC) between China and ASEAN, Senior Colonel Zhou Bo demurred, saying that the Chinese foreign minister had made it clear that the matter was open to further negotiations (Lin, 2017). One high-ranking officer told me: "Yes, we have influence on MOFA, but this is exaggerated. There is a misconception of our actual role. Certainly, in terms of security matters, we come down hard, but *they are the experts on foreign policy*"[6] (Interviewee 16, personal communication, August 1, 2018).[7]

We can also see MOFA's ability to coordinate in a very tangible way in the 2017 Doklam-China standoff. A senior military interviewee expressed impatience at the impasse but said in no uncertain terms that it had to be solved by diplomatic talks and that MOFA was working hard to resolve this security issue (Interviewee 23, personal communication, July 31, 2018). Indeed, it was MOFA that was publicly taking the lead on the deadlock—releasing pictures of alleged trespassing by Indian troops and showing a map with Doklam as part of Chinese territory during its daily press conferences. Subsequently, they produced and published a fifteen-page report entitled *The Facts and China's Position Concerning the Indian Border Troop's Crossing of the China-India Boundary in the Sikkim Sector into the Chinese Territory* (Ministry of Foreign Affairs, 2017). This depicts, quite clearly, their capacity to coordinate and produce expert, authoritative knowledge. When I questioned another PLA officer on the criticism that MOFA received from the military, he revealed: "Maybe we do not make good comments on each other, but this doesn't mean we dislike each other. Also, looking at how one defines diplomacy, there is military diplomacy, and this is diplomacy conducted by the PLA *under the ambit and framework of MOFA* but not at its direction. This is part our overall diplomacy [*zheng ti waijiao* 整体外交]" (Interviewee 17, personal communication, August 2, 2018).[8]

Significantly, this PLA-MOFA cooperation corresponds with disciplined and disciplining communicative practices on MOFA's part. Thus MOFA's competence and mastery over valued communicative practices cannot be ignored. When China's MND started conducting regular monthly press conferences in April 2011 (Ma & Zhou, 2011), it sought MOFA's help and advice (Interviewee 13, personal communication, August 27, 2017).

Failing to recognize the above-mentioned changing MOFA dynamics, some scholars have argued that MOFA has lost so much leverage that it has been "reduced to . . . a mere spokesperson and translator for other ministerial agencies" (Sun, 2016, p. 419). Yet on March 21, 2013, one week after assuming the premiership, Li Keqiang announced the structure of the new State Council (the government of China) and ranked MOFA as the top ministry of the twenty-five under its jurisdiction, followed by the Ministry of National Defense (MND) and the NDRC. This restructuring made Wang Yi, the foreign minister until 2022, the top minister in the Li cabinet.

Remarkably, Sun interprets this development as meaning that "under Xi, the MOFA's secondary position in China's decision-making hierarchy has been formalized" (2016, p. 427). In contrast, my own case studies and investigation of diplomatic practices make clear that Wang's influence (and that of his ministry) is palpable. In addition, Wang Yi was promoted to state councillor in 2018 (Goh, 2018). The implication of this move cannot be overstated. It demonstrated Xi's approval of MOFA and recognition of its importance. Though Sun states that according to official data from 1998 to 2002, "164 people quit their jobs at the MOFA" (2016, p. 431), I found from the same data source that during that time period 158 people left their jobs at the Ministry of Foreign Trade and Economic Cooperation and 107 quit their jobs at the People's Bank of China—both comparable numbers to the number of job leavers for MOFA. That same report notes: "In some of the government departments where there are more stringent professional demands on its employees, such as the Ministry of Education, Ministry of Information Industry, Ministry of Finance, Intellectual Property Office, Ministry of Construction, Ministry of Science—the losses of people are *even more serious*" (H. Wang, 2003).

On top of this, my interviews with students and faculty in Beijing at CFAU (which supplies many of MOFA's employees) show that jobs at MOFA are viewed positively and competitively applied for. One CFAU student and aspirant says: "The pay is not so good, but many of us want to apply to MOFA because it is a government job that is very prestigious" (Interviewee 9, personal communication, June 25, 2016). A professor at the university adds: "In my observation, even as the [Foreign] Ministry's work gets harder, people still apply. It is still very competitive and attractive as a career for young people" (Interviewee 10, personal communication, June 27, 2017).[9]

Data pointing to the strengthening of China's diplomatic institutions is commonly omitted in the literature. For instance, over the past decades, MOFA has quickened its pace in retiring older diplomats and replacing them with fresh talent who can speak better English and local languages. A 2005 Xinhua report estimated that half of the country's four thousand diplomats are below the age of thirty-five (Kurlantzick, 2007, p. 227). The reorganization of China's Leading Small Group on Foreign Affairs to become the renamed and institutionally more important Central Foreign Affairs Commission in 2018 (Xinhua, 2018) is also indicative of the increased attention paid to diplomatic work.

Furthermore, MOFA's increased presence and activity on Twitter from 2019 onwards, which I investigate in chapter 5, point to its heightened profile generally. Only recently (in 2020) have analysts begun paying attention to China's diplomats and their assertiveness with the description of a "wolf warrior diplomacy." And even so, they do not systematically explore if and how China's diplomats and foreign ministry have increased their status, or point to the representational role that MOFA has progressively adopted across domains. As one Chinese diplomat revealed to me, one important recent development has been the increase in job rotation opportunities available to envoys: "They join state-owned enterprises and local governments to be vice-mayor (*fu shi zhang* 副市长), mayor (*shi zhang* 市长), deputy governor (*fu shen zhang* 副省长), and so on so that they can gain more experience and exposure. This was different in my time! They can even work before they enter MOFA now" (Interviewee 77, personal communication, November 16, 2018). While MOFA's workload has grown, so too have the professionalism and resources it has at its disposal, as evinced above through its guidance and assistance to other Chinese institutions with its external-facing elements. Its expansion is manifested through its increasingly assertive diplomatic practices and through its implementing, coordinating, and counseling practices.

Diplomacy and practice theory present ample opportunities for cross-fertilization: "Diplomatic studies have a lot to learn from practice theory; so does practice theory from the study of diplomacy" (Pouliot & Cornut, 2015, p. 298). Thus it is fitting that research focus both on the practices of individual diplomatic agents and on MOFA's corporate practices. In this chapter I additionally (1) provide an account of MOFA's communicative practices in its conducting of diplomacy and demonstrate the importance of the institutional body in these practices; (2) highlight the importance of corporate practices in diplomacy and how these are performed in and through agents; and (3) shed light on the understudied processes of MOFA's implementing, counseling, and coordinating functions. Bourdieu himself was closely concerned with the body, and his idea of habitus was formulated to capture the "permanent internationalisation of social order in the human body" (Eriksen & Nielsen 2001, p. 130). The expression of practices cannot have meaning without attention to the human body and observations of bodily movements.[10] This addition to the literature on Chinese security studies is important because it redefines the ways in which "assertiveness" and "diplomacy" are hitherto understood by expanding them beyond the military domain or state-level actors while providing an embodied account of state representation through diplomacy.

Embodied and Communicative Chinese Diplomatic Practices

In this chapter, I present three diplomatic cases—Wang Yi's 2016 Canada visit, China's blocking of ASEAN's statements on the SCS, and China's detention of Singapore's Terrex vehicles—to illustrate the significance of MOFA to China's international affairs. Through an analysis of those cases and my own field data, I introduce embodied and communicative instances of Chinese diplomatic practices that personify "assertiveness." To be clear, I am aware that an increase in assertiveness does not imply an increase in influence. But as I will show, this assertiveness can be explained not only by diplomats' heightened sensitivity to signals from top leadership but also by an increase in MOFA's symbolic and material resources.

Wang Yi Visits Canada

In June 2016, China's foreign minister, Wang Yi, traveled to Canada for a scheduled visit. While there, he broke diplomatic protocol and demanded to meet with Canada's prime minister, Justin Trudeau. Observers immediately highlighted how odd this was (Vanderklippe & Fife, 2016). When notified that Trudeau might not be free for the requested meeting, MOFA doubled down and intimated that the entire trip might be canceled. The Canadians thus acceded to Wang's request. In the same trip, Wang also took issue with a reporter's question on China's human rights record. He scolded the reporter, wagging a finger at him while insisting that he had "no right to speak on this" and telling him not to "ask questions in such an irresponsible manner." He further questioned the reporter: "Have you been to China? Do you understand China?" (Buckley, 2016, para. 8).

According to one analyst, Wang Yi had shown "the kind of aggressive and unpleasant behaviour by senior Chinese officials that makes Canadians less and less enamoured with China" (Bruk, 2016, para. 1). But China's ambassador to Canada, Luo Zhaohui, later penned an editorial to defend Wang. He painted his visit in glowing terms, insisting that Wang had achieved "positive results" (Luo, 2016, para. 1).[11] It is useful to recall Bourdieu's attention to detail on bodily gestures as actions that convey and produce social meaning. Such a reading views the finger-jabbing, the staring, and the condescending "look" as components of meaningful corporeal-diplomatic activity. They tell a story of a confident China that will brook no criticism. This is not simply a matter of Wang Yi being "rude" (that is not to deny he can be perceived as such) but of a comportment that Wang and other agents bring to bear in diplomacy. When questioned on this particular instance of assertiveness, a Chinese diplomat told me that there was "nothing wrong" with Wang Yi's behavior and that "this, more accurately, shows confidence. It is a natural response to others in the Western world who harm our interests" (Interviewee 11, personal communication, July 1, 2017). Indeed, the daily press conferences of MOFA show embodied diplomatic behavior reminiscent of Wang Yi, although on a much smaller scale.[12]

Of course, one must be careful not to overinterpret what one sees from MOFA diplomats' gestures and bodily comportment. They do not frown all the time. Sometimes they smile, and they can, in rare instances, joke with reporters. It is also expected that diplomatic spokespersons of any country adopt a disciplined style and keep relatively close to diplomatic scripts. Yet I found from my interactions with different MOFA spokespersons[13] that these individuals had different personalities offstage even as they maintained a consistent demeanor in press briefings. Thus, in public forums,[14] their diplomatic habitus cohered in such a way that individual diplomats' gestures and tones become similar.

It is important to remember that these diplomatic styles and gestures (in press conferences) are performed to domestic and international audiences. Pouliot (2011, p. 555) reminds us that such arenas give diplomats "an immediate opportunity to gesture, frown, or grimace live. . . . As a result, the multilateral diplomat must be skilful so as to signal ambiguously enough to please different publics." Questions about who can legitimately frown, raise their voice, or speak "over" another tell us where their "sense of place" is and their rank within that arena (2011, p. 556). In other words, diplomatic gestures, tones, and "look" are not apolitical or trivial but are always politically meaningful. In one participant observation in London,[15] I noticed an example of this divergence between "front stage" and "less front stage" demeanor.[16] The Chinese diplomat in question was frequently interrupting the Philippine diplomats when they referred to disputes in the SCS. He interjected incessantly to push his point across, while reserving particularly unkind words for the Philippine diplomats and their president. However, once the meeting was over, he turned collegial in his interactions with his Philippine colleagues (although never crossing into being "friendly").

One Southeast Asian diplomat I spoke with recalled how "Chinese [diplomats] have always acted properly in their interactions with me. Generally, they are professional. But if we go to a private dinner at the Chinese embassy, you will see this most clearly in how they behave. They act like they are a big power. You *see it in their demeanor*, how they talk to you and words they use" (Interviewee 2, personal communication, July 11, 2018).[17] MOFA and its diplomats' communicative practices are thus an important generator of perceptions of assertive diplomacy.

One aspect of communicative practices raised by several interviewees was diplomats' choices of various communicative media. Techno-material objects such as WeChat, emails, and fax machines intervened to coproduce diplomatic practices. The fax machine, an arguably outdated object, remains central to getting access to MOFA. Thus some see China as remaining "stuck in the past" through its insistence on this mode of communication—leading to some mockery and frustration among international diplomats. One diplomat mockingly told me, "They have a fear of emails as a modern form of communication, it seems" (Interviewee 29, personal communication, August 17, 2017). Another diplomat complained, "It is undiplomatic and unprofessional for Chinese diplomats to not even reply to emails. If they are not free, they just ignore. This is ridiculous and frustrating and gives the impression of aloofness and snobbishness" (Interviewee 12, personal communication, June 27, 2018). That being said, MOFA does not always ignore emails: these can be a main means of communication, particularly for diplomats stationed in embassies overseas.[18] And one journalist who enjoys close links to MOFA told me he could communicate with Chinese diplomats on WeChat—though he noted that this usually happened only in the context of urgent and fast-developing events. Even then, he added with some incredulity, "They have to first type their response on their letterhead, print out their response, and snap a picture to me! Guess what? Their response to me was 'We have no comments'!" (Interviewee 13, personal communication, August 27, 2017) (figure 1).

Yet the avoidance of email and instant messaging and the reliance on faxing are practices that are not unique to the Chinese and do not depart widely from what is required in the field.[19] And from the Chinese perspective, there is a logic to relying on slower and more formal means of written communication and using them sparingly. Some diplomats lack confidence in using the English language.[20] Others may wish to restrict themselves as much as possible to "directly quoting from government reports and official speeches" so as to "reduce the chance they will make a career-damaging mistake" (Qiu, 2018, para. 8).

While the actions of Wang Yi and his foreign ministry in Canada were viewed negatively in many quarters, they "went down well in Beijing where all agencies from the Party Propaganda Bureau to CCTV [China Central Television] are being urged

FIGURE 1. Picture of my respondent's phone with MOFA's message that translates to "We have no comments," August 27, 2017.

to promote party ideology" (Stephens, 2016, para. 10). The dismissiveness and forceful bodily gestures of Wang were not expected of typical diplomatic practice (Buckley, 2016). To the international diplomatic community and certainly to the Canadians, they constituted "exceptional practice" and indeed "incompetent practice." Note, however, that this "incompetence" and transgression in the bilateral field translated to plaudits back home. Many of the non-Chinese diplomats I spoke with expressed (initial) surprise at the assertive language and behavior of Chinese diplomats. Nonetheless, this is increasingly normalized. One non-Chinese interlocutor told me: "Honestly, we are used to it. To me, it is not right but it is no longer abnormal." When pressed on when this assertiveness was first noticed, he added: "It is difficult to say exactly when, as it is a gradual process seen in the past four to five years" (Interviewee 21, personal communication, July 1, 2017). Another told me: "They are more demanding now: they always say, You cannot do it this way! (*Bu ke yi zhe yang!* 不可以这样), and they are quite stubborn. The reasons are complex, but the short answer is that they have much more in the way of resources" (Interviewee 3, personal communication, July 10, 2018).

A Chinese diplomat described this purported assertiveness pithily: "In the past no one cared about what a Chinese vice foreign minister said. Now, what a vice foreign minister says will move financial markets around the world" (Interviewee 76, personal communication, November 16, 2018). What is more, MOFA's coordinating capacities—particularly in diplomatic protocol arrangements—are used to signal hierarchy and power. When US deputy secretary of state Wendy Sherman visited China in July 2021, there was contention over whom she would meet. Sherman wanted to meet directly with Xi's inner circle and China's foreign minister, but MOFA offered only a meeting with Vice Foreign Minister Xie Feng, as they felt she was not ranked high enough in the US leadership hierarchy (Sevastopulo, 2021). In the end, a compromise was reached when MOFA offered "talks" (*huitan* 会谈) with Xie and a "meeting" (*huijian* 会见) with Wang (Xinhua, 2021), with the latter being a downgraded diplomatic event, as a diplomatic "meeting" does not have the same importance or significance as full diplomatic talks. This was commensurate with what China's diplomats felt was a mismatch of rank between Wang and Sherman, thus elucidating the politically productive nature of seemingly apolitical diplomatic protocols. Indeed, shortly before the meeting in Tianjin, Wang promised Sherman a "tutorial" in treating countries fairly (Zhou & Jun, 2021).

Without a doubt, these assertive diplomatic practices would not have been possible if not for the material and immaterial capital that MOFA could apply in its diplomatic activities, the awareness of these resources, and the requisite skills and "competence" that actors such as Wang Yi could invoke.[21] Significantly, in the case outlined above, the foreign minister was successful in his demands to meet with Trudeau. One could certainly argue that in doing what he did, Wang Yi overreached, doing more than what most other foreign ministers would have attempted to do, and did so successfully.[22] The interviews above also underline how embodied diplomatic practices are, with a tightly knit communicative logic disciplining utterances, sayings, silences, bodily comportments, and material objects.[23] What is more, an updated appraisal of the PLA-MOFA dynamic reflects a situation where the military, in some cases, accedes to MOFA's coordination functions and even (as in the case of its own press briefings) solicits MOFA's expertise.

This section also reveals the importance of bodily gestures, comportments, and demeanors. Practices, as Bourdieu points out (see also Mattern, 2011; Schatzki, 1996), are not only instantiated in actors' activities but also actualized in bodies in a way that is not fully articulable by agents. Thus my interviews with Chinese diplomats and my interviews with non-Chinese diplomats differed in the "sense" and "feeling" that I took away from them, with non-Chinese diplomats being more open, friendly, and relaxed. Chinese interlocutors are curt and more uptight. This bodily reserve is important because it has consequential diplomatic effects, as the Wang Yi example shows. A former consultant to United Nations writes how Chinese diplomats "go directly to their seats, only talking to each other, with no interaction or greetings with delegates from other countries. They are usually silent, except on those occasions when they read China's position aloud from prepared scripts. When meetings are over, they usually make straight for the exits; rarely are they seen at networking events and receptions inside the UN compound" (Qiu, 2017, para. 2). We glean from the bodies and gestures of Chinese diplomats the embodiment of assertiveness in "a kind of strong language, especially when they want to press home a point" (Interviewee 19, personal communication, August 3, 2017).

Second, the embodiment and bodily gestures in these contexts potentially become more sharply defined, the more "public" or "official" the setting is. Practices are iterative performances. The larger the audience, the more vivid the performance needs to be, as Wang's forceful performance demonstrates. Yet it would be a mistake to assume that diplomats cast off this embodiment completely in the private sphere.[24] On the contrary, one diplomatic interviewee observes how "they can tone it down. But sometimes they tone it up. Ultimately, they never depart from the main message even in private settings. That's how they are" (Interviewee 20, personal communication, August 1, 2017).

Third, we see MOFA's *capacity to coordinate* clearly. If MOFA is as toothless as some say, would it have the wherewithal to (threaten to) cancel an important scheduled trip to Canada? A comment by the former Mexican ambassador to China, "Usually, China does not give foreigners the same courtesies it asks or demands for itself," encapsulates how China's diplomacy has undergone an assertive turn (Vanderklippe & Fife, 2016, para. 29).

ASEAN's South China Sea Statements

The SCS territorial disputes have long been a source of tension between Beijing and rival claimant countries in Southeast Asia, namely Vietnam, the Philippines, Brunei, Malaysia, and Indonesia (C. Huang, 2016). Ten countries in Southeast Asia are part of ASEAN, and they have inadvertently been caught in the crossfire. MOFA has delayed the process to conclude a legally binding CoC regarding the SCS since this was first proposed in 1992 (Thayer, 2013). An examination of China's wrangling with ASEAN members, collectively and individually, highlights the indispensable role of the Chinese Foreign Ministry and its diplomats in exerting influence in the organization and show how Chinese diplomatic practices have progressively been institutionalized.

When a joint communiqué from the Forty-Ninth ASEAN Foreign Ministers' Meeting in Ventiane was issued in July 2016, it omitted references to the ruling against China in a case brought by the Philippines to the Permanent Court of Arbitration (PCA) regarding China's claims in the SCS, including the legality of the so-called nine-dashed line.[25] It later emerged from media reports that ASEAN could not refer to the ruling in its communiqué because Cambodia prevented it (D. Loh, 2016). Chinese leaders saw the adulterated statement as a diplomatic triumph and expressed their gratitude toward Cambodia. China's foreign minister stated, "History will prove that the Cambodian side's maintained position is correct" (Baliga, 2016, para. 3).[26]

The above incident is not a one-off. In July 2012, during the ASEAN Foreign Ministers' Meeting, the bloc failed to issue a joint communiqué for the very first time in their history. The prominent role that Cambodia played in frustrating the issuance of the statement—allegedly instigated by China—was shown to be critical to that result (Bower, 2012). Furthermore, shortly before the July 2016 Foreign Ministers' Meeting, a comparable incident took place during the Special ASEAN-China Foreign Ministers' Meeting in Kunming, China, in June. At first, a robust ASEAN statement was issued by Malaysia concerning the SCS matter. Just three hours later, the document was retracted as Cambodia and Laos stopped its final release. Singapore's foreign minister left the meeting before it ended, despite being the meeting's cochair. Nonetheless, Wang Yi downplayed his absence, emphasizing that the meeting had gone well (Zulfakar, 2016). In the aftermath, Liu Zhenmin—China's vice foreign minister—said that Singapore, as a nonparty to the disputes, should "butt out" of the SCS issue and urged Singapore to do better in coordinating dialogue between China and ASEAN (Siow, 2016).

Here China's assertiveness not only was perceived and expressed through MOFA but also was the main conduit through which the PRC's influence was brought to bear—underlining the representational role that MOFA assumes. During the June 2016 Kunming meeting, Chinese diplomats were going around warning representatives from the other countries not to mention the SCS issue—giving rise to ASEAN diplomats' frustration at their "tone." Comparing his experience with the Chinese military and MOFA personnel, one diplomat's words are particularly illuminating: "When I meet with their military guys, even they can be more friendly and less assertive than the MOFA people I deal with!" (Interviewee 29, personal communication, August 17, 2017).

It is not surprising that China, by virtue of its national capacity and resources in relation to its ASEAN counterparts, has significant influence over the bloc: the same could be said for other active major powers, such as Japan or the United States. Still, it is notable that perceptions of assertiveness come across most strongly with regard to the PRC. For instance, a 2020 survey of ASEAN elites revealed that a majority of respondents (53.6 percent) would choose to align with Washington over Beijing, and a 2021 survey showed that 61.5 percent of respondents would do so, with worries of China's assertiveness in the region being a key motivator (ISEAS-Yusof Ishak Institute, 2021, p. 4). So a turn to China's diplomats can provide insights into the means and practices that construct perceptions of China's more resolute foreign policy.

At the 2016 Kunming meeting, China was insisting that ASEAN sign onto China's own statement or issue nothing at all (Parameswaran, 2016). Beyond embodied (assertive) practices, non-Chinese diplomats have noted that MOFA diplomats threaten or try to coerce others by enlisting nondiplomatic actors, such as businesses, to further their diplomatic cause. An ASEAN official told me that MOFA was "now more organized as a whole in *bullying other sectors to serve foreign affairs interests.* They use local businesspeople in China to pressure us. Telling these big businesses that our government is causing damage and will harm their interests. So, what happened? These companies come and pressure us!" (Interviewee 2, personal communication, July 11, 2018).[27]

This is another example of how MOFA can use its capacity to coordinate and to mobilize other diplomatic actors and nondiplomatic actors to support certain MOFA practices. While MOFA's strategy of inducement and pressure is a state-backed effort, the ministry holds considerable influence in selecting targets and sites to exercise that influence. MOFA officials thus hold some authority and have some flexibility in implementing state coercion. A diplomat discloses that "after the announcement of the PCA award, the very next day, MOFA put up a press conference and called foreign and local media. It gave copies of a slickly produced publication that clearly was done long ago and was able to mobilize media, academics, and retired officials to great propaganda effect in the following days. Very impressive" (Interviewee 29, personal communication, August 17, 2017).

"Exceptional practices" are practices that diverge from normal or expected practices, while "incompetent practices" are ones that are judged to be incorrect or inappropriate by audiences in the field. Undeniably, interfering in other countries' domestic politics and in ASEAN departs from "typical" diplomatic practice, particularly in ASEAN, where this is highly sensitive. ASEAN countries, by and large, saw the maneuvering as evidence of China's assertiveness, while the Chinese celebrated the tepid ASEAN statements as a victory (Farrow, 2016; D. Loh, 2018). A Southeast Asian diplomat explained to me: "They [MOFA] are skillful and will definitely make you feel the pressure. Once they invited all the other ambassadors but none from our country because of a perceived slight" (Interviewee 24, personal communication, August 15, 2017). Southeast Asian officials detected a palpable increase in lobbying and strong-arm practices. To be sure, diplomats of all stripes, particularly from major powers, can engage in coercive tactics in the service of national interest. Nonetheless, no other external power has come close to Chinese diplomats in disrupting ASEAN norms and practices and in provoking internal reflection on solidarity and centrality (D. Loh, 2018b). What is more, Chinese diplomats are increasingly assertive over a wide range of issues in ASEAN and outside ASEAN, including cyber security, trade, human rights issues, and China's own domestic politics—realms that MOFA has increasingly come to represent and speak for (see *Global Times*, 2021).

Such diplomatic and discursive practices, far from being exceptional for MOFA, are its *modus operandi* as it assumes and represents Chinese assertiveness internationally. But as the 2020 and 2021 ASEAN surveys noted above indicate, these practices can be self-injurious as others grow wary of Beijing. Of MOFA's actions, a Southeast Asian official says: "We know they have money and we need money. But China is greedy and, for us, is not 100 percent reliable. Their diplomats always play us against our domestic adversaries. But because we need money and they have a few strings they can pull, we have to smile. Our diplomats made it a point to tell the Chinese that we are 'everybody's friends'" (Interviewee 30, personal communication, May 10, 2018). Another Southeast Asian diplomat adds,

> It is not true that they are suddenly assertive now or that in the past they were very meek or quiet. They have always been ideological, [even] decades ago. But now they become very easily agitated, unduly sensitive, and believe that they can do no wrong. I don't know if this is their real personal belief. I suspect it is. I also think maybe it's a requirement to get into MOFA that becomes worse after they get in. (Interviewee 25, personal communication, August 13, 2018)

In the same vein, another relates: "They believe in their own hype, that China is a rightful major power and all that. They exude confidence, for example, in their repeated view that the US 'can't do us in' and how China has the resources to deal with all these challenges. This is not bluff; they genuinely believe this to be true. They assert their point of view and have plenty of self-confidence [*zi xin* 自信]" (Interviewee 31, personal communication, July 19, 2018).

MOFA's assertive diplomatic practices have been successful (from the Chinese perspective) in protecting China's interests. In particular, ASEAN's failure to come up with strong statements on the SCS issue has largely been a result of MOFA and its diplomats. Their Department of Asian Affairs and their various embassies in Southeast Asia authorize what constitutes "legitimate knowledge" on Southeast Asia and in diplomacy and thus have a monopoly over it. As Yun writes: "Within the bureaucratic system of the MFA, its field offices [Chinese embassies] are the primary sources of information on issues of bilateral relations" (2014, p. 20). So while it might be true that theoretically "the upper echelons of the Communist Party can overrule the desires of the foreign ministry" (Hatton, 2013, para. 6), in practice this rarely ever happens, particularly in its day-to-day operations. A Chinese source reveals that "top leadership are too busy, and they cannot possibly know everything. MOFA is the main source for information because of their embassies and people. Of course, they [leadership] decide, but [the] Foreign Ministry's information is crucial. This actually also means they can proceed in their way" (Interviewee 32, personal communication, July 11, 2017). Even Chinese academics, seen as purveyors of "objective knowledge," assent to MOFA. For example, policy recommendations from academics normally go through MOFA. "Whether this actually makes any changes or goes to top leadership I don't know. They [MOFA] do not tell us what they do to it and if it becomes policy. Although I think so" (Interviewee 26, personal communication, July 25, 2018). Another academic adds, "Yes, in recent years, they do want more ASEAN research. They do meet us. MOFA sometimes invite us to HQ for this and sometimes they come to ASEAN-related academic conferences. We submit our research and hope they use it!" (Interviewee 34, personal communication, June 27, 2016).

Here we see MOFA increasingly acting as a gatekeeper of knowledge. They exercise discretion in selecting producers of expert knowledge who could lay claim to legitimate knowledge and determine how to operationalize it. Through its *capacity to counsel*, as the official, natural bearer of IR- and country-specific knowledge, MOFA acts through its expertise. Diplomatic practices, then, are also informed through the politics of knowledge production over which MOFA holds sway.

MOFA's activities have created a sense of unease in ASEAN and in the leaders of member countries by disturbing ASEAN's norms and practices (see D. Loh, 2018b). One Southeast Asian official says: "The Chinese are increasing the pressure, particularly over SCS matters in recent years. This is understandable, but some tactics are very blunt. This has definitely made us [ASEAN] concerned" (Interviewee 35, personal communication, June 25, 2016). What we see, beyond embodied practices, are practices that persuade, threaten, and coerce. These practices are increasingly sedimented and institutionalized, as every staging of the practice reinforces them even further, particularly when one considers how little goes into counteracting them.[28]

Detention of Singapore's Terrex Armored Vehicles and the "Power" of Diplomatic Protocol

On November 23, 2016, nine Singapore Terrex armored vehicles traveling back to Singapore from a military exercise in Taiwan were seized in Hong Kong's Kwai Chung Container Terminal in a suspected breach of Hong Kong's laws. Two days later, Singapore's defense minister hosted the Chinese ambassador to Singapore to a game of golf, adding that "China and Singapore have enjoyed good bilateral relations built up over the years through close cooperation across many areas such as economy, trade, defence and people-to-people relations" (E. Ng, 2016). Several days later, in its first official response to the incident, MOFA warned Singapore about its activities with Taiwan—with Foreign Ministry spokesman Geng Shuang demanding that "Singapore strictly abide by the One-China principle" (Gan & Liu, 2016, para. 2).

On January 9, during Singapore's parliamentary debate, it was revealed that Singapore's prime minister had communicated Singapore's request for the return of the vehicles to Hong Kong's chief executive (Today, 2017). Further, Singapore's defense minister announced in parliament that the vehicles were "protected by sovereign immunity" and "cannot legally be detained or confiscated by other countries." The reply from China was swift, with MOFA spokesman Lu Kang saying, "I hope the relevant parties can be cautious in their remarks and actions" (Clover & Cheung, 2017, para. 5). On January 24, 2017, Hong Kong announced that the detained vehicles would be returned to Singapore, and the vehicles eventually reached Singapore on January 30, 2017 (Chua, 2017).

While it is customary practice for MOFA to issue statements in response to other countries' activities, it is pertinent to underscore the effects of this diplomatic practice. Although it is debatable how much influence MOFA has in formulating policy, MOFA clearly played a leading role in verbalizing Chinese positions and eventually resolving the issue—accenting its representational responsibilities. It was through MOFA that China's displeasure with Singapore's military cooperation with Taiwan—widely seen as the crux of the issue—was clarified and expressed. Tellingly, despite reports saying that Singapore would have to deal with Hong Kong to resolve the issue, it was announced that the Singaporean authorities "will have to contact the Chinese Ministry of Foreign Affairs to secure the return of the armored vehicles," essentially bypassing the Hong Kong government (Chong et al., 2016, para. 15). Though Singapore's long-established security exercises with Taiwan since 1975 have been an open secret that China has long tolerated, Beijing had hoped that the seizure of the vehicles would teach Singapore a lesson for its perceived recent diplomatic snubs—ranging from its refusal to side with China over the SCS to its military ties with Taiwan. When I told a Chinese interlocutor that the seizure of military assets by China had been interpreted by some in the region as an unreasonable act, he chided me: "Your [Singapore's] Ministry of Foreign Affairs has failed. Your government has failed. It is your [country's] failure. If Singapore wants to fight [with China], it is like a five-kilogram [object] going up against fifty kilograms! It cannot win! China and MOFA did what it had always done and what the international community agrees on, which is insisting on the One-China principle" (Interviewee 36, personal communication, July 4, 2017).

While I claim no special knowledge of any backchannel diplomacy concerning this incident, some instances of "behind the scenes" courting of Chinese diplomats can be teased out. For instance, on January 17, 2017, it was announced that the Joint Council for Bilateral Cooperation—"the highest-level forum between China and Singapore"—would be held in February of that year. On the same day, China's vice foreign minister met with Singapore's permanent secretary of foreign affairs to discuss impending exchange and bilateral matters (*Straits Times*, 2017). Of Liu's appearance and meeting in Singapore, it was noted that he was "certainly senior enough to re-inject momentum into the China-Singapore relationship" and that there was an expectation for resolution of "the [armored vehicles] issue . . . around the same time as the meeting is taking place" (Jaipragas, 2017, para. 11).

Exactly as predicted, several days later (January 24) it was reported that the military assets would be returned to Singapore. Clearly, the vice-minister and MOFA played a significant role in securing the release of the vehicles. It is interesting to see the ways in which foreign affairs are implemented and how this implementation is politicized. In this regard, Bode and Kalsrud observe how an analysis of "implementation through practices" recasts the "process of implementation as a site where normative content emerges through practices rather than considering it as technical or apolitical" (2019, p. 461). While implementation seems like a sterile activity, for MOFA, the *capacity to implement* is a capacity that was fought for. On this matter, a senior ASEAN official tells me how (and it is worth quoting at length here):

If they allow things to proceed without them being in charge, then they certainly cede power. In the past, the State Council, PLA, etc., could bypass MOFA and do something but not inform them. One time, I had to deal with the NDRC,[29] and the guy was Chen Deming. We were fine-tuning agreements to the Mekong Basin development project. I said, I will need to bring in our MOFA and can log it with ASEAN secretariats so that we can have proper representation to the Chinese MOFA. He was so adamant that he did not have to get the Chinese MOFA involved as "the budget, money, everything is from NDRC!" He was irritated by my insistence to involve China's Foreign Ministry. Now things are different. They [MOFA] know they cannot cede control and must be the people who implement, if not at least coordinate. Yang Jiechi was firm about insisting that MOFA would do this and that and in advancing MOFA's role. He is very sound and assertive in meetings—very assured in saying, "We are in charge." There was a project involving the Commerce Ministry, and Bo Xilai was then commerce minister.[30] He kept saying, "This is a matter of foreign commerce, not foreign affairs" [*Bushi waijiao shi waimao* 不是外交是外贸] to keep out MOFA. But Yang insisted on bringing MOFA back and did so successfully. (Interviewee 3, personal communication, July 10, 2018)

While it now appears natural to consider MOFA's role as foreign policy implementers, this had to be competed for. The upshot has been that MOFA increasingly finds itself leveraging its competencies to coordinate, counsel, and implement—playing a crucial role in grand initiatives that were previously not under its radar such as the Belt and Road Initiative (J. Yu, 2018, p. 228; S. Chen, 2018). To an important degree, MOFA is able to strategically play off its "capacity to implement" to generate significant political effects. One diplomat confesses how, "after the incident [PCA court case], MOFA was able to use its scheduling powers to disinvite the Philippine diplomats. So all the ASEAN member countries were at that event but not them" (Interviewee 25, personal communication, August 13, 2018). This example brings into sharp relief how the functional capacity of "scheduling" is a consequential diplomatic practice, with important ramifications for expressions of power and assertiveness. One interviewee told me: "My frequency of meeting with the Taiwanese representative here is important. I do meet him, but I cannot meet him too often. Which events, small ones versus big ones, that I appear together with the Taiwanese rep is also important. Otherwise, if I don't judiciously select, the Chinese will make noise" (Interviewee 75, personal communication, November 16, 2018).

Another interviewee mentioned how MOFA can leverage its functional and implementing abilities in multilateral settings: "You can feel it. Since President Xi, they [MOFA] have been more forceful in their diplomacy. For instance, in our experience [in the ASEAN context], they will draft a document and demand that you respond within a couple of hours. This of course puts us under pressure, and they clearly know that we do not have the resources to respond in time. They seize the initiative this way. They play with these" (Interviewee 29, personal communication, August 17, 2017).

One Southeast Asian diplomat adds: "They can prioritize whom they schedule your leaders to meet, and which Chinese leader they send to meet, to put a message across. Depending on your country's importance or on the current relationship, MOFA can do all these things. Planning for your visits, who will receive you when you land, whom they attach to you, the attention that they pay to you, where you stay, the time they give to meet important people, etc." (Interviewee 37, personal communication, August 3, 2018).

MOFA's ability to control protocol and who visiting delegations can meet with is not unique to China, nor did it emerge only recently. Nevertheless, existing literature on China disregards such protocol-controlling activities and does not conceive of these practices as an exercise of power and influence. In another example, a Commonwealth envoy described how "the Chinese embassy boycotted a South Korean film fest because of the THAAD [Terminal High Altitude Area Defense][31] deployment issue. The sponsors of the film festival were Korean companies, not the [Korean] government, and I don't think Beijing told them to boycott this, but they decided to do that. Of course, it sends a signal, and they [South Korea] feel it" (Interviewee 75, personal communication, November 16, 2018).

In this way, as implementers, far from being powerless, MOFA staff have compelling competencies across a range of functional competencies available to them—particularly in how they implement, when they implement, and what is implemented. A Chinese military source close to MOFA surmises: "They are not decision makers, but they can use the process and, in the process, use their influence to influence decision makers" (Interviewee 38, personal communication, July 11, 2017).

It is also important to consider how these different capacities are mutually entangled. Implementation, for instance, is often instructed by MOFA's own capacity to counsel. The ASEAN example brings out this point plainly. MOFA coordinates and organizes multiple events tapping into the Ministry of Commerce, the Ministry of Culture, and provincial governments to host visiting ASEAN delegations for various trade shows and exhibitions. Through this, they are able to dictate the concrete forms (dates, location, content) and the styles (how "important" and how big of a delegation) that such exhibitions will take (Interviewee 20, personal communication, August 1, 2017).[32] This, in turn, is informed by their assessment of ASEAN and issues that they believe are important and productive to China. Pouliot and Therien's (2017, pp. 166–167) observation that the practices of global conferencing are highly productive and political in generating inclusion and exclusion for participants is worth bearing in mind. From this perspective, MOFA's dictation of the forms and styles of international summits, meetings, and conferences reinforces its institutional and political importance as an implementer. It also generates expectations of preferential treatment in the international arena, particularly when MOFA's demands for control of events are frequently met (Interviewee 75, personal communication, November 16, 2018).

Against this backdrop, counseling, implementing, and coordinating are not separate sets of practices—they interlock and support each other. When I asked a Chinese diplomat to reflect on the ways MOFA was important (or not), he mentioned both coordinating and implementing capacities: "MOFA cannot care about everything, but we care about the most important things to China! Look at all the most important things involving China and Xi Jinping. These are the G20, BRICS, APEC, ASEAN Summits. In of all these, it is MOFA that is coordinating and implementing. Of course, for the matters that are most important for China, we are there" (Interviewee 77, personal communication, November 16, 2018).

Turning back to the case study, the recursive practice of chastising and criticizing countries/actors that keep relations with Taiwan has come to be an established, *institutionalized, and corporate practice* that is collectively enacted. In the Terrex example, it achieved the effect of reiterating China's Taiwan stance, registering its annoyance toward Singapore, and attempting to nudge Singapore into ceasing military cooperation with Taiwan. Precisely this practice and the manner in which it was performed led to perceptions of Chinese assertiveness, corroborated by earlier interactions with Singaporean and Southeast Asians diplomats. When pressed on how they saw evidence of this, they pointed to MOFA's way of "treating others" (Interviewee 31, personal communication, August 31, 2017) and "the way they acted" (Interviewee 21, personal communication, August 2, 2016). In answering the empirical question of MOFA's weakness or strength, the Terrex case goes to show how MOFA is significant to China's foreign policy. This case study also differs from the Canadian example in showing different "levels" of diplomacy at work. Here we see a "state-to-state" issue being resolved through interpersonal work, whereas the Canada example concerns a "person-to-person" issue scaling to generate broader diplomatic results (see also Bouris & Fernández-Molina, 2018).

Corporate Practices and Individual Practices

In the examples above, I have featured a range of individual and corporate practices. Echoing Emanuel Adler (personal communication, November 8, 2018; see also Adler, 2019), I suggest that a greater sensitivity to the distinction between the two is useful. Corporate practices can be understood as "practices that are performed by collectives in unison. In world politics, most practices belong to this type: war, for example, is a socially meaningful pattern of action which, in being performed more or less competently, simultaneously embodies, reifies and acts out background knowledge and discourse in and on the material world" (Adler & Pouliot, 2011b, p. 9).

The authors further explain that corporate practices "are not the action of one corporate agent (a state) but that of a community of representatives whose members enter in patterned relations, within an organized social context, thanks to similar background dispositions" (Adler & Pouliot, 2011b, p. 10). Using diplomatic summits as examples, they emphasize that "it is more appropriate to conceive of G8 summits as one aggregate practice; a study into intergovernmental rites, however, may want to zoom in at a lower level" (Adler & Pouliot, 2011b, p. 9). Beyond differences in levels, corporate and individual practices can be qualitatively different. Consider the example of warfare presented by Adler and Pouliot. While it is a collective practice that acquires meaning and force in the community of soldiers, it is also nonetheless an embodied practice—the camouflage paint that one puts on the face, the decision of how and when to fire a gun, the muscle-molding that goes into being "fit for combat," and so forth. Most of these social practices fit hand-in-glove with corporate practices. However, consider the frequent cases of insubordination or desertion where soldiers' own moral and safety practices override the corporate practice of fighting a war (Albrecht & Koehler, 2018). That is to say, social practices and corporate practices are usually aligned but the possibility of contradiction is always present.

From this distinction, I lay out two observations and discuss their implications in the Chinese case. First, individual practices and corporate practices are co-implicative and constantly shape each other. For example, the corporate practice of "criticizing Taiwan" sets the tone for how agents conduct their own performances and fix the contours of what is acceptable or not. In the case of China, there is almost no conflict between the performance of embodied and social practice and enactments of corporate practices. A diplomatic source from Southeast Asia divulges: "MOFA personnel actually do believe in what they are doing. They buy into the propaganda. They believe that many countries are trying to do them in, and they also think that the way to practice major power diplomacy is to assert themselves more in the world" (Interviewee 37, personal communication, June 24, 2016).[33]

Another instantiation of this co-imbrication can also be seen in relations between ASEAN and China with regard to MOFA's recent history of hindering the goals set forth by ASEAN's chair and by foreign ministers in the time period under study here (D. Loh, 2018b). These diplomatic practices have become the norm for Chinese diplomats as they get "rewarded" for their diplomatic behavior. These rewards manifest in material forms (performance appraisals and promotions) and symbolic forms (praise from the media, the public, or one's superiors) (Interviewee 37, personal communication, June 24, 2016). While corporate and individual practices affect each other, they do not do so equally: corporate "standard operating procedures" and practices still serve as the lodestar of individual diplomatic practices. Indeed, the structure of the diplomatic field is such that President Xi holds overwhelming power over state and society, and the space for innovation or change from within is limited (though never absent). Even so, one North America diplomat cautions against interpreting too much from one person: "We should not overstate Xi because even if some other person was in charge, Bo Xilai or Li Keqiang, we might see some style changes, but the general thrust is going to be more and less the same. But I do concede that Xi has certainly accelerated this diplomatic drive and the assertiveness observed" (Interviewee 39, personal communication, July 19, 2018).

Agents are not automatons, but their space for virtuosity is finite. Consequently, the corporate practices of MOFA tend to take precedence over individual practices, and deviations from expected individual practices or corporate practices are swiftly sanctioned. One example can be seen from MOFA spokesman Lu Kang's comments on June 30, 2017, that the Sino-British Joint Declaration had "no realistic meaning" and that it had value only as a historical artifact (Ng, 2017, para. 3). This caused consternation in the United Kingdom. MOFA, after several days, was compelled to clarify the remarks, saying that the Declaration was still legally binding and that Lu Kang was misinterpreted (J. Ng, 2017). One interviewee told me, "He [Lu Kang] needs to be more careful. Sometimes, some [diplomats] can try to do too much" (Interviewee 40, personal communication, July 16, 2018). Another example would be spokesperson Zhao Lijian's promotion of a debunked conspiracy theory that Covid-19 was released by the US military in China. He was criticized for his remarks not only internationally but by some diplomats within China, and he later backpedaled on his initial claims (Hadano, 2020).

While individual practices and corporate practices can be at odds and perhaps even a source of change, diplomacy in China shows no visible tension because discipline and loyalty are pervasive. As my discussion in chapter 4 will reveal, a similar dynamic is at play regarding MOFA's institutional habitus, which guides, orients, and disciplines individuals' habitus in a multitude of ways, ranging from mutual surveillance, to legislating rules that forbid diplomats' resignation, to a stronger emphasis of political loyalty than in pre-2009 periods. One European diplomat opines: "China's MOFA has always been tight. Even more so after Xi took over. You see very few gaps [public disagreements in foreign policy orientation], and their messaging is really watertight" (Interviewee 28, personal communication, August 29, 2017).

Conclusion

What appear as "normal" diplomatic practices to the Chinese are not similarly viewed by their Southeast Asian or Canadian counterparts and can be considered "odd" (see Glas, 2022) or a breach of diplomatic decorum. If decorum can be understood as "conduct that is judged to be appropriate within a particular social and spatial setting"

(McConnell, 2018, p. 364), paying attention to diplomatic breaches and how MOFA tactically "plays" with diplomatic protocol, brings "into sharp relief . . . the assumptions underpinning diplomacy" (2018, p. 373). Helpfully, McConnell adds that diplomatic decorum-breakers throw light on "the hierarchies and social boundaries that are inherent to the diplomatic profession" (2018, p. 373). Regular decorum transgressions or "incompetent practices" thus reflect a diplomatic hierarchy commensurate with China's emerging status. Nevertheless, it can be contended that the belligerent behavior of diplomats has been approved and encouraged by Party leaders.[34] Even so, this chapter tells us that Beijing is increasingly relying on MOFA and its diplomats to express their desires and send their messages across various audiences. This reliance on MOFA by top leaders is reflected in the increased prominence of its diplomats and material increments to expand its capacities.

To be sure, this chapter has not stated that MOFA and its diplomats have grown more influential independent of Xi and the central government. Rather, *MOFA's influence and assertiveness are made possible only by the president's and the top leadership's enabling.* Chinese assertiveness also did not "suddenly" appear because of leaders' wishes. Indeed, claims of Chinese assertive behavior on the international stage go as far back as the 1990s (Jerdén, 2014, p. 70). What has changed, however, is the intensity of such performances and the increased tendency among the broader diplomatic community to notice and remark upon that intensity. We can draw several observations from the analysis in this chapter. First, international perceptions of Chinese "assertiveness" now extend beyond the military domain, where assertiveness has traditionally been recognized. The tendency in the literature, when invoking Chinese assertiveness, has been to couch it in security terms. The evidence suggests a more complex construction of how these perceptions are emerging—not least through Chinese diplomatic practices, which analysts are only now starting to come to grips with, such as China's Twitter diplomacy (see chapter 5). Certainly, the encroachment of MOFA activities into nonofficial and nonmilitary domains of other countries demonstrates the influence these functional competencies have. One non-Chinese academic told me: "MOFA keeps a detailed list of people—a list of academics who write what they think are 'anti-Chinese' articles on the South China Sea and other issues. They also know who the non-Chinese academics are that write positive things about China, and they can go cultivate or strong-arm people" (Interviewee 22, personal communication, February 11, 2015).

Similarly, a 2018 Wilson Center report on PRC interference and influence in US academic communities underscores how the PRC, "unlike most foreign governments," "employs its diplomats to assess and influence potentially sensitive academic activity on American campuses" (Lloyd-Damnjanovic, 2018, p. 50). Some of the cited examples show the PRC diplomats' coordinating capacities. On one occasion, "the

Embassy sent an email chiding members of GW's [George Washington University's] chapter of the Global China Connection in late 2016 for holding an event about infrastructure development in Xinjiang, according to a student member from the PRC who viewed the email. The email emphasized that the event was inappropriate and that students should refrain some holding similar events in the future" (Lloyd-Damnjanovic, 2018, p. 54).

Consider, also, instances where Chinese envoys attempt to induce academics to publish pro-Chinese products:

> University of Wisconsin-Madison faculty member Edward Friedman said that Ministry of Foreign Affairs officials approached him while he was visiting the PRC for a conference in the early 2000s and offered him $25,000 to write a book touting the PRC's growing global profile. . . . The senior official told him that they were aware Friedman held views critical of the CCP, but that they also knew he believed "China was winning in international relations." The Ministry was interested in producing a short introduction to China and wanted Friedman to write it. (Lloyd-Damnjanovic, 2018, p. 58)

A caveat must be added here. From this chapter, it is easy to get the idea that Chinese diplomats and diplomacy are unreasonable and assertive in a complete and totalizing way. That is untrue. Certainly Chinese diplomats do cooperate, can be reasoned with, and can switch on the diplomatic charm. That said, the theme of assertive diplomatic behavior finds resonance within the (non-Chinese) diplomatic community. While it was always, historically present in manifold forms and to different degrees, this leitmotif became more pronounced in 2009, intensified from 2013 onwards, and saw online manifestations from 2019.

Second, and relatedly, this assertiveness is indicative of MOFA's enlarged role. Through the interrogation of assertive practices, I identify how MOFA is able to exercise its *capacity to counsel, implement,* and *coordinate* to cogent ends. A Chinese diplomat showed self-awareness of these capabilities when he said to me: "What we can do *comes out from our own capabilities*: how to arrange relationships with others and how to conduct negotiations. Definitely for diplomacy and MOFA, because we have that knowledge and those capabilities. Even in economics, we will have state-to-state relationships, and these naturally involve MOFA. We execute our original mission, and in this execution we influence things" (Interviewee 77, personal communication, November 16, 2018).

Above all, it is evident that MOFA and its diplomats play a critical representational role in foreign policy and possess an influence in foreign policy matters that is not commonly acknowledged. One could even make a tentative case that its power has also grown in the domestic sphere. For that purpose, I gave examples of MOFA's

national coordinating role and how the ministry can leverage this coordination ability strategically to gain further resources. In a press conference amid the "two sessions" in 2020, China's foreign minister answered a question on MOFA's assistance
to Hubei Province during the Covid-19 global health crisis—the hardest-hit province,
as it was the epicenter of the pandemic. Wang Yi recounted how MOFA had helped
Hubei and Wuhan get through the initial crisis but, more strikingly, said MOFA
would play a key role in supporting Hubei's economic recovery efforts and would coordinate with other national agencies to bring more international opportunities to
the region (CGTN, 2020). Claims that "MFA is less important than MOFCOM or
NDRC" (Hale et al., 2020, p.32) thus need to be rethought: MOFA is able to coordinate issues in the SCS, intervene in grand initiatives such as the BRI, and, most
recently, coordinate and promote China's Covid-19 efforts. Crucially, it can guide
and coordinate nondiplomatic and domestic actors according to its purposes and be
said to speak legitimately on domains that are not traditionally considered within the
ambit of MOFA. Such prominence is an offshoot of China's rise as its foreign policy
demands have grown, but it was certainly not automatic: it had to be struggled over.
Organizationally, MOFA has undergone a series of changes that make it a more professional outfit since 2008. For example, it was only in 2011 that MOFA began holding
press conferences five times a week, reflecting the greater demands of foreign affairs
and the increased importance of MOFA's duties.[35]

A word about strategy and agency is in order here since I gesture toward how
MOFA "plays" its role and "strategically leverages" its power to implement. A PT approach does not obviate considerations of strategy and game playing—a point that
was made in the previous chapter. Actors do not "think" or calculate how assertive
they need to be or what to do to express that—they often act because it is *practical and sensible* to them in the field. Similarly, when an agent such as Yang Jiechi insisted on placing MOFA front and center on multiple external issues, his agency was
not about "'defying' structures by making choices independently of them" (Pouliot,
2008, p. 264). The basis for practice obtains from one's *habitus*, which is constituted
"by conscious and unconscious learned experience on the one hand and by cumulative
impact of practices on the other" (Jackson, 2008, p. 164). In other words, the exercise
of strategy and of game playing is enabled and bounded by the conditions of the field;
agency cannot be thought of independently of practices within particular social fields.

Finally, I have emphasized the role of embodied practices by showing how "ri-
gidity," "discipline," and "assertiveness" are personified through speeches, gestures,
and demeanor. I have also pointed to the functional necessity of material objects—
WeChat accounts, documents, and fax machines—in making and enabling the de-
livery of practices, particularly in facilitating MOFA's communicative practices and
embodying its representational role. Carrying out Adler and Pouliot's suggestion to

distinguish between corporate practices and agent practices, I have argued that these co-implicate and hold the potential to challenge and transform each other. Yet in the Chinese case, because of multiple disciplining variables, corporate practices and individuals' practices align very well. The issuing of statements to denounce Taiwan and parties that maintain ties to them is an example of a MOFA corporate practice. This practice works its way into an agent's habitus and practices, which get acted out in the agent's diplomatic work and even in private spheres.[36] Even as it is acknowledged that actors are unique individuals with different personalities, such is the impact of the institutional habitus (chapter 4) that, short of leaving MOFA, actors display these diplomatic practices consistently in multiple public arenas. And far from being in retreat, China's diplomats and diplomatic influence are, in fact, ascendant. From this observation the next chapter takes as its assignment mapping out the field of diplomacy in China.

THREE

The Field of Diplomacy in China

It becomes natural to be suspicious and view everyone else as an enemy, especially foreigners. This feeling is very common when you are inside.

(INTERVIEWEE 54, personal communication, April 27, 2018)

This chapter investigates the diplomatic field of China and constructs the relationships between diplomatic actors there.[1] In the previous chapter, I underscored how the diplomatic practices of MOFA have increasingly been marked by an assertive turn. This is instantiated in MOFA's embodied and communicative practices, and through MOFA's implementing, counseling, and coordinating capacities. From these observations, a natural question emerges: What are the (field) conditions that allowed for the emergence of diplomatic assertiveness in the first place? To answer the question, this chapter "zooms out" to consider MOFA in the broader structure of diplomacy in China. In that way, and in dialogue with my previous chapter on practices, I show the dynamic interplay between structure and practices, empirically fleshing out the link between diplomatic actors and the local diplomatic field.

As Pouliot has noted, "In the normal, everyday practice of diplomacy, practitioners operate in a relatively self-contained social environment, with its own ways of doing things" (2016, pp. 36–37). In deploying Bourdieu's concept of field, I have sought to comprehend what this "self-contained social environment" contains in China's diplomatic context. To do so, I sketch out the hierarchical relations of actors in the diplomatic field to give a sense of how actors struggle for stakes and *how actors cooperate*. This is imperative because while struggles and competition lie at the core of Bourdieu's sociology (e.g., Bourdieu, 1990a, pp. 143–144; see also Martin-Mazé, 2017,

p. 212), cooperative practices are largely unseen in field analysis despite their ubiquity. Analyzing both struggles over and cooperation toward goals gives us more complete assessments of the diplomatic field. More significantly, few studies examine cooperation and competition between domestic Chinese diplomatic actors and the subsequent effects on China's foreign policy. This chapter advances our understanding of this cooperative/competitive dynamic through a field analysis. With that purpose in mind, I zoom out even further, to the transnational diplomatic field, to stake out the effects on practices and "local" fields, at the spaces where fields "meet" and overlap. In this oscillating movement between macro and micro,[2] I begin my chapter and turn my gaze toward an individual: President Xi Jinping.

Much has been said about Xi's centralization and expansion of personal power and authority and its effects on domestic politics (e.g., G. Wang & Zeng, 2016). However, comparatively little attention has been paid to the modality through which such efforts to expand power are conducted and its implications for China's diplomacy. Indeed, Xi has strengthened his power comprehensively (Economy, 2014) and assumed top posts in state and Party apparatuses, including those on foreign affairs (C. Li, 2016). This represents a significant change from the previous two administrations. Brown notes that "Xi's predecessor, Hu Jintao, maintained a low profile, barely figuring in international affairs. His silence . . . was infamous." In contrast, he adds that Xi's leadership is "more willing to speak openly about external issues" (2017, p. 64). Lampton concludes that Xi's decision to create a National Security Commission in 2013 helped him better coordinate domestic and foreign policy, resulting in "control over internal security, foreign, and military policy that his predecessor Hu Jintao did not possess" (2015, p. 775). Foot, meanwhile, argues that under Xi, China has largely embraced a more activist foreign policy and that this represents a departure from Deng's mantra of "biding one's time" as China under Xi seeks to be more "globalist" (2014, p. 1087; see also Yan, 2014). Mao aside, Xi's power grab is unprecedented in modern China, and the effects of his control over diplomacy have yet to be fully understood. Unlike his predecessors, the president has considerable autonomy to implement and achieve his foreign policy objectives. How and in what ways has Xi contributed to diplomatic assertiveness? How has Xi enhanced MOFA's representational role? While many analyses have focused on Xi and on military assertiveness (e.g., Yahuda, 2013; I. Chan & Li, 2015; You, 2017), there has been little attention to the effects of Xi's drive for power on MOFA.

This chapter proceeds as follows. First, I leverage the concept of "field" to study MOFA's position and role within the broader structure of the diplomatic landscape in China. I show how Xi has (re)gained control of diplomatic actors through socialization, restriction, and displays of fealty. This, in effect, incentivizes diplomatic assertiveness. Second, I explain what this accumulation of power means for the field of diplomacy in China. I suggest that MOFA and other diplomatic actors are socialized into a more politically disciplined outfit, one that predisposes itself toward robust diplomatic displays. While doing that, I furnish a way to analyze fields through the identification of primary and secondary actors and a mapping of the relationships between them, thus providing a novel relational charting of China's diplomatic field. Finally, in investigating the transnational diplomatic field, I introduce the notion of "transversal disruption"—the potential of a field to disrupt and introduce change when fields overlap. This chapter contends that we can profit from field-sensitive accounts of China's IR that recognize the productive and generative effects of fields. This is illustrated with field interviews, while specifically drawing on a series of participant observations in track-2 settings.

A Shift in the Field(s)

Glas (2017), in his study of ASEAN, shows how habits, dispositions, and practices of peace serve to limit violent conflict. Focusing on the distinction between tactical and strategic practices and the reflective nature of practices, Bode (2018) argues that UN officials, member states, and NGOs' practices influenced the United Nations Security Council's decision-making process. Other such examples of practice-focused diplomatic studies are already furnished in chapter 1, so I will not revisit them. Suffice it to say that studies of diplomacy take practices as their analytical starting point. On the other hand, it is well noted that "social fields are the macro concept that structure Bourdieu's thoughts and that represent the entry point for Bourdieu's further concepts" (Walther, 2014, p. 8).

Despite its significance, the concept of "field" has not received commensurate attention in IR. Of course, there are exceptions (e.g., Pop, 2009; Adler-Nissen, 2014; Pouliot, 2016, pp. 193–253), but these exceptions prove the rule.[3] How can we understand "change" in Chinese diplomacy—particularly when PRC envoys seek to impose their vision of diplomatic propriety, hierarchy, and power in multilateral arenas? Such changes in Chinese diplomacy, I submit, can be captured through a field analysis that takes both the practices of diplomats and the structure of the diplomatic landscape seriously. For far too long, interpretations of Chinese behavior in multilateral settings have tended to ignore the role of diplomats themselves (e.g., H. Wang, 2000; M. Li, 2011) while regularly overlooking the position that quasi-diplomats play in track-2 multilateral arenas. This chapter thus illustrates how the concept of fields can be useful in understanding (the attempt to spur) diplomatic change and the representational aspects of PRC diplomats.

Studying Fields

According to Bourdieu,

> In analytical terms, a field can be defined as a configuration of objective rela-
> tions between positions. These positions are defined objectively in their exis-
> tence and in the determinations that they impose on their occupants, agents
> or institutions by their current and potential situations (situs) in the [wider]
> structure of the distribution of different currencies of power (or of capital),
> possession of which provides access to specific profits that are up for grabs in
> the field, at the same time, by their objective relations to other positions (dom-
> ination, subordination, equivalents and so on). (Bourdieu & Wacquant, 1992,
> p. 20)

In brief, a field can be understood as a relatively autonomous and hierarchical
social arena where agents vie for resources and benefits and occupy positions. This autonomy, however, is never absolute. To Bourdieu, fields are arenas where actors compete over what are legitimate rewards in an exercise of "symbolic violence." His work
in *Distinction* sets out one example of this process. First, what are considered desirable
or legitimate cultural practices and products are captured by the dominant class by
virtue of their ownership of economic and cultural capital. Then these products and
practices of consumption eventually diffuse "downwards" and become popularized
as the middle classes mimic the dominant classes in their consumption patterns in a
bid to be "legitimate" consumers. Yet that very practice undermines their challenge
to the dominant class because as these products/practices gain wider currency, the
dominant groups start abandoning them in favor of more unique, haute items and
practices (1984, pp. 247–255).

For Bourdieu, competition is central to social life. He says colorfully, "Within a
field, people fight to the death over things that are imperceptible to those who find
themselves in the next room" (2014, p. 318). However, it is important to bear in mind,
contra Bourdieu, that actors in a field frequently cooperate as well. This is certainly
true of the international diplomatic field, for diplomats cooperate and negotiate to
reach agreements even as they seek to defend their national interests. Similarly, diplomatic actors within a country collaborate as they work toward achieving national
foreign policy goals. Indeed, as I shall highlight later, cooperation among actors is frequently observed in the local Chinese diplomatic field. Jackson describes how the field
is "structured by the positions of various actors within them, by the written and un-
written rules and conventions that condition (but do not determine) the strategies of
actors and, finally, by the various forms of capital—primarily power and influence—
for which actors compete" (2008, p. 167). Within this space, boundaries are policed to

exclude others from entering. In the diplomatic field, knowledge of IR/politics (both theoretical and practical) is normally a key requirement. To formally participate as a central player, say in China, strict conditions need to be met—educational accreditation, political fidelity, and so forth.

Importantly, while autonomous, fields overlap and map (sometimes resistantly and always imprecisely) onto each other and are not completely self-contained. As mentioned above, some important works in the PT program put the concept of fields to good use. Pop (2009) investigates the "EU field"[4] in analyzing EU enlargement and the dynamics between central and eastern European countries. Through the case of the Roman Empire, Nexon and Neumann (2018) provide a field-theoretic account of hegemony by showing how hegemons leverage their dominant positions in economic and military fields to exercise *metacapital*[5] across multiple social fields and fashion their vision of international order. Even so, the authors, like many others, take struggles as their central concern (2018, p. 674). At any rate, Nexon and Neumann take the conversion of capital[6] almost as a seamless operation without acknowledging the dynamics (and frictions) of field interactions. It must be added that while these works engage with and scrutinize what happens within fields, they do not look at relations *between fields.*[7] On that subject, a handful of scholars have acknowledged the interactive elements of fields (e.g., Swartz, 1997, pp. 136–140; Abrahamsen & Williams, 2011, p. 316). For instance, Jackson writes that "the field was also structured by elements from outside its parameters. The most important of such elements were the dynamics of both French domestic politics on the one hand and the conditions of international politics on the other. Important changes in either of these larger fields forced the Foreign Ministry to adapt its strategies to new conditions" (Jackson, 2008, p. 170).

In the main, however, little has actually gone in the way of studying these dynamics and their concrete effects at points of overlap. This is not simply a matter of agents from one field entering another and experiencing hysteresis there.[8] It is possible also to focus on the productive, generative, and restrictive effects of the field itself and that which comes to the fore when fields encounter and meet. Certainly, one important benefit of looking at the transnational is that it dissolves the "divide between the 'inside' (the nation state) and the 'outside' (the global) by focusing on the interplay between several national contexts" (Kauppi, 2018, p. 186).

Accordingly, the questions this chapter seeks to answer are: What happens when diplomatic fields are misaligned? What happens when there are competing or outright contradictory stakes at points of field overlap in China's diplomacy? As I will demonstrate in this chapter, there are potentially disruptive effects with significant practical implications for Chinese diplomacy and multilateralism. To clarify at this point, transnational fields are fields that cross national boundaries, whereas transversal disruptions are resultant effects of overlapping, cross-cutting fields, regardless of national boundaries. For example, while the field of multilateral diplomacy is trans-national in nature, it retains a transversal quality, as it is "inherently intertwined and imbricated with national fields . . . as well as with transnational fields" (Pouliot, 2016, p. 212). The complex, cross-cutting qualities and the effects/disruptions that spring from them are best captured by the vocabulary of "transversal disruption." However, the presence of transnational or overlapping fields should not be taken to automatically imply disruption—even as that possibility is always present. In the next section, I examine the Chinese diplomatic field and describe some of the ways that actors compete and cooperate before going into the cases of transversal disruptions in multilateral, international diplomatic fields.

The Chinese Diplomatic Field

Bigo provides a guide on how to quantify a field:

> To speak about a field supposes that empirical research has been carried out, which shows what is specifically at stake in the game played by the agents. From this specificity of the stakes involved, it is crucial to understand how agents position or distinguish themselves in that game, along what lines, what kinds of positions are taken in relation to others, and what kind of resources in terms of power they can mobilize in order to play. A field also supposes a certain period of time for the rules of the game to have an effect and to have a certain degree of autonomy. (2011, p. 240)

On that score, it is important to stress that fields are not conceptual substitutes for "context" or "space." A field has its own regulative logic and history and the concept is particularly useful for exploring the struggles over stakes in an arena (Bourdieu & Wacquant, 1992, pp. 97–88). As Swartz has noted, "Conceptions of social location, such as 'milieu,' 'context,' or even 'social background,' fail to highlight sufficiently the conflictual character of social life," which can be captured by the concept of field (1997, p. 119). Field analysis can therefore link the struggles, hierarchies, cultures, and structures that are present in social life in a systematic and methodical way (Swartz, 1997, p. 293). Bernhard adds that "field analysis is less confined than constructivism to some facets of social reality (such as ideas, culture, and discourse) at the cost of neglecting others. Epistemologically, relationalism implies that a single element of the social (for example, an idea or an actor) can never be fully understood in isolation. There is no inner quality, substance, or 'essence' that defines these elements as such" (2011, p. 428).

My construction of the diplomatic field in China involves three interrelated steps. First, building on Bigo (2011) and following Bourdieu and Wacquant's emphasis on the relational nature of fields (1992, p. 96), I first identify the *primary and secondary players* involved in the diplomatic space. Then I map out, hierarchically, the agents and institutions that constitute the Chinese diplomatic field. This allows me to study cooperative and competitive practices in the field in relation to MOFA. Finally, I outline the material/immaterial and normative/institutionalized boundaries of the field.

Hence, the Chinese diplomatic field is demarcated by MOFA as the central institution but also by the CFAC, the PSC, and the Central Military Commission (CMC) owing to its defense diplomacy work. Notably, several secondary actors within the diplomatic field exercise some influence on the foreign policy process and the execution of diplomacy. These include think tanks and (mainly Beijing- and Shanghai-based) universities,[9] prominent academics, retired politicians/officials, and media outlets, with varying degrees of prominence and influence.[10] My criteria for assessing who these secondary and primary actors are both subjective and objective: they come from subjective self-referentiality (the actors noting their own contributions, limitations, and influence) and objective assessment (measurements of direct influence/impact on the field, such as adopted policy recommendations and "face time" with MOFA and PSC leaders).[11] These assessments are triangulated with those from third parties in the field from whom I have received information on specific actors' influence and practices.

To locate actors in the field, I first determine what the most important stake in the field is. In the Chinese diplomatic field, I suggest this is social capital (translatable to economic capital) and in very specific terms: *access to and impact on diplomacy and, externally, the maximum number of international friends* (see Bjola & Kornprobst, 2018, p. 4). To be sure, despite this scoping, the definition of fields remains ambiguous—a point I concede. However, it is important to remember that a field cannot be reduced to purely objective standards because fields are, by nature, approximations. Therefore, this imprecision is acceptable to derive the "benefits that can be gained by thinking about social relations in general, and foreign policymaking in particular, in terms of relatively distinct 'fields'" (Jackson, 2008, p. 167). After determining the stake, I establish the current possession of this "stake" by actors, which maps unto its direct or indirect impact on diplomacy. So whether or not actors are direct organs of the state and Party for the purposes of external affairs orients their rank. For actors that I do not have direct access to, such as state-owned enterprises (SOEs), I rely on secondary literature to categorize them. Moves to increase access to foreign policy can be seen as a stake-accumulating activity. Activities that set an individual apart from others in the field in having a direct line to top policymakers are also seen as hallmarks of distinction. For example, an academic from CFAU regularly mentions the lectures he has delivered to the PSC of China. This serves as a distinguishing feature of him, the person, separate from the institution. Other secondary players in the field, particularly think tanks and academics, reference this scholar—"Advising the top leadership and giving them a lecture, that is the highest achievement!" (Interviewee 34, personal communication, June 27, 2016)—not only reinforcing the distinction but also reifying it as a valuable stake in the field.

For further clarity, let me outline the steps I took to locate CFAU as a secondary actor. First, I assessed their "direct effect" on diplomacy. Are their views sought by MOFA and PSC? How aligned are they with these diplomatic players? I supplemented this through field interviews with actors where they signaled their alignment and closeness to MOFA. Objectively, I established whether personnel who occupied leadership positions in the school were directly linked to MOFA (its leadership team is staffed with current and former MOFA officials)[12] and how some scholars also took up positions within MOFA (an uncommon occurrence). Finally, this account was corroborated by my interviews.[13]

All in all, I categorize primary and secondary actors as shown in table 1.

This categorization is, in turn, reflected in figure 2 to portray the hierarchical relations, where the actor closest to the core has the largest effect and impact on diplomacy.

This charting is an ideal type and should not be taken to map unerringly onto the "reality" of the field. While I do identify specific actors and institutions, listed actors do not exhaust the categories. The table and figure are presented simply to illustrate who the typical, main actors are in each class and how they relate to each other. Indeed, within Bourdieusian theory, positions are relational, and the concentric graphic in figure 2 is meant simply as a shortcut for readers to visualize the uneven power dynamics (closest to the core having the most influence) and how each actor correlates to the others. Furthermore, fields are always shifting, and players move about in their games. For instance, while academics and think tanks have different influences on diplomacy, they are nevertheless grouped together in the diagram to locate them within the field in a general way for the sake of clarity. Therefore, this composition of the field automatically results in a static snapshot because of temporal-spatial limits of the research. Nevertheless, when I showed the mapping to four different sources,[14] they broadly agreed with this evaluation. Obviously, agreement with the model by practitioners themselves is not tantamount to the accuracy of the model. Be that as it may, the concordance it finds with field actors is, at least, indicative of the mapping's fitness.

In his magisterial exposition of class distinction through consumption and lifestyle patterns, Bourdieu used, in addition to qualitative methods, questionnaires with multiple correspondence analysis (MCA) in his construction of field and practices.[15] Elsewhere, Pouliot (2016) also employs MCA[16] in his mapping of the diplomatic field

TABLE 1. Primary and secondary actors of Chinese diplomacy.

Primary Actors	Secondary Actors
Politburo Standing Committee	State-owned enterprises[1]
Ministry of Foreign Affairs	Retired officials[2]
Central Foreign Affairs Commission[3]	Think tanks[4]
Central Military Commission and PLA	Key universities[5]
International Liaison Department of the CCP[6]	Academics[7]

1. SOEs primarily extend Beijing's economic policies, but their involvement in foreign policy and diplomacy should not be understated. While they are not the focus of my research here, SOEs nevertheless "are directed by Beijing's geopolitical and mercantilist priorities," and their overseas expansion is crucial to China's rise (Jones & Zou, 2017, p. 743). SOEs are also heavily involved in key geopolitical projects such as the BRI. Some of the largest SOEs are Sinopec Group, China National Petroleum, State Grid Corporation, Industrial and Commercial Bank of China, China Mobile, China Railway Construction, Sinochem Group, Bank of China, China National Offshore Oil, and Ping An Insurance (see also Jakobson and Knox, 2010).

2. These "retired" officials are influential because they tend to remain active in an unofficial "semiretired" role embedded in former or new units. These include Zhu Chenghu (former PLA), Yao Yunzhu (former PLA), Yang Yi (former PLAN), Sha Zhukang (former Chinese ambassador to the United Nations), Wu Sike (former special envoy on Middle East Affairs), Fu Ying (former MOFA official), and Yu Hongjun (former ambassador), among others.

3. Formerly known as the Central Foreign Affairs Leading (Small) Group.

4. The most influential of these are the China Institute for International Strategic Studies (CIISS), the Chinese Academy of Military Sciences of the People's Liberation Army, Shanghai Institutes for International Studies (SIIS), China Institutes of Contemporary International Relations (CICIR), the Chinese Academy of Social Sciences, the China Institute of International Studies (CIIS), and the China Foundation for International Studies. See also Zhao (2012, pp. 128–129), Glaser (2012, pp. 92–93), and Brown (2017, pp. 57–58).

5. The ones identified here are CFAU, Renmin University, Tsinghua University, Peking University, BFSU, Fudan University, Shanghai International Studies University, and Shanghai Jiaotong University.

6. By virtue of it being the CCP's foreign policy "arm," whose broad goal is to build ties with foreign political parties.

7. These academics include respected scholars domestically and internationally. They are usually affiliated with the influential secondary diplomatic think tanks and universities. They include scholars like Yan Xuetong (Tsinghua), Sun Xuefeng (Tsinghua), Gao Fei (CFAU), Ruan Zhongze (CIIS), Yang Jiemian (SIIS), Chen Dongxiao (SIIS), Qin Yaqing (CFAU), Shi Yinghong (Renmin), and Wang Jisi (Peking University), among others. Obviously, this is not an exhaustive list, nor is the goal here to provide one.

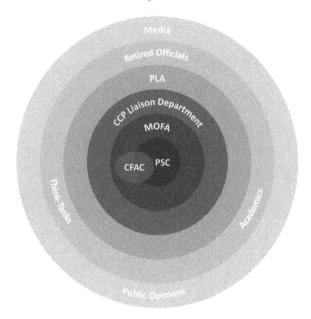

FIGURE 2. Visual representation of the diplomatic field in China, 2019.

of logics in UN and NATO pecking orders. Yet without the advantages of a large enough sample size, technical expertise, clean access to data, and questionnaires for my subjects, I turned to a wholly interpretive, qualitative construction of the diplomatic field. In that regard, we can see from Neumann (2002), Adler-Nissen (2011), A. Cohen (2011), and Autesserre (2014) how a field can be mapped through qualitative means.[17] Suffice it to say, getting at the "objective positions" of the field need not employ only statistical methods—there are ways of understanding objective positions without resorting to quantification.

One way to map the field is to look at where the borders end. While it is well established that borders are dynamic and porous (Bigo, 2011, p. 240), there needs to be some level of temporal fixity for a field to be properly studied and accessed. Adler-Nissen suggests that the field ends where the effects of the capital in that field end (personal communication, April 5, 2018).[18] Bourdieu himself stresses how the task of determining the "limits of the field is a very difficult one." He also adds that "the boundaries of the field can only be determined by empirical investigation." He suggests that the limits of the field are located "at the point where the effects of the field cease" and that "various means" must be used to measure the point at which "these statistically detectable effects decline" (Bourdieu & Wacquant, 1992, p. 100). My approach here is to identify (1) the current participants and (2) the limits of their diplomatic and foreign policy influence. Another strategy is to focus on the "core" of the field and not the edges. In this chapter, this involves listing out all the diplomatic actors who are at the heart of the field—MOFA, the PSC, the CFAC, the president, the CMC, and so on—and placing them in concentric circles where actors who have the most immediate relationship with diplomacy are sited nearest to the center. This way, one can acknowledge but avoid falling into the trap of "resolving" the unresolvable border issue in the establishment of a field while still being able to parse out the state of play in the space under study.

Having mapped out the Chinese diplomatic field, I turn my attention toward empirical analysis. How has President Xi changed the structure of that field? And how do these changes affect primary and secondary players? I argue that three interconnected processes of *selection and socialization*, *restriction*, and *fealty displays* are at work in affecting primary and secondary actors in the field of diplomacy.

President Xi Takes Control

When Xi took power as president in 2013, there were hopes that he would be a liberal reformist (Branigan, 2012). Those hopes were dashed as he undertook sweeping reforms, including his much-publicized anticorruption drive, to consolidate and strengthen his power (Economy, 2014). Xi's disquiet over his predecessor's foreign policy was obvious. Lampton mentions how Xi did not "sound like someone fully satisfied with the foreign policy and domestic security policy-making processes that he inherited" (2015, p. 762). Xi's drive to impose his vision of foreign policy meant exerting control over MOFA and the attendant players in the Chinese diplomatic field. In that regard, his reorganization of the Central Foreign Affairs Leading (Small) Group to become the renamed and institutionally more important Central Foreign Affairs Commission in March 2018 is reflective of his ongoing campaign to "upgrade" China's diplomatic apparatus. Looking at his speeches, we can observe how Xi's personality and thinking shape his worldview. Lam's (2016) analysis of Xi's speeches (contrasted to those of Hu Jintao and Jiang Zemin) points clearly to a discernible shift in Xi's approach to foreign policy from that of previous administrations in that Xi has given MOFA greater importance and responsibility. Lam (2016) and He and Feng (2013) reach similar conclusions in their analysis of Xi's speeches. They observe that Xi's worldview inclines China toward an international strategy that is more assertive. At any rate, in the diplomatic field, Xi's power accretion efforts have resulted in a subsequent shift of the field (structure) itself. In that connection, I tease out these structural effects—which, subsequently, filtered downstream to diplomatic actors. The following sections will detail some of these effects.

Selection and Socialization

MOFA personnel are drawn mainly from the top universities in Beijing and Shanghai—primarily Peking University, Tsinghua University, CFAU, and Beijing Foreign Studies University (BFSU) owing to its language training. First, students from these universities (and across the country) are drawn into the foreign service through the annual civil service examination. Then CFAU, and to a limited extent Peking and Tsinghua, supply a significant portion of their top students to the ministry. This is done through two ways. Faculty members identify suitable candidates and submit a list of around thirty names a year to MOFA, which then proceeds to place them through the necessary tests and training (Interviewee 42, personal communication, August 13, 2017). Second, MOFA, from time to time, gives CFAU a quota to fill. Finally, in a process unique to CFAU and some individuals from influential think tanks, senior scholars who are deemed capable have the opportunity to "transfer" to MOFA while retaining the option of heading back to academia after working for three to five years (Glaser, 2012, p. 133; Bondiguel & Kellner, 2010, p. 9). Those regarded as unsuitable are weeded out through the process of selection.

One academic who was seconded to Japan told me, "The embassy thought I had something to contribute through my participation in conferences and writing reports. I could give some knowledge in that process" (Interviewee 7, personal communication, June 29, 2017). The same academic noted: "We do have disagreements but on nothing fundamental or anything too critical," further adding that "once a decision is made, we must support it and we most definitely cannot write or go public disagreeing." This also shows how actors cooperate—through the circulation of talent, documents, and ideas in the field. The release of academics to MOFA helps the organization develop ideas and "new ways of thinking," as a diplomat puts it (Interviewee 8, personal communication, June 2, 2018). This practice also helps academics and the university by adding the luster of practical real-world experience to their scholarly endeavors. Put differently, such moves help both MOFA and the academics and universities in the field. For MOFA, they allow oversight of knowledge production. Academics and universities obtain a distinguishing mark of their ability to "impact" policy. That said, there is no equivalence in cooperation between secondary and primary players, as these arrangements tend to be initiated only at the behest and coordination of MOFA. An academic with close ties with MOFA states, "We cooperate closely with MOFA. Of course, some think tanks and academics enjoy closer relationships, but I would say that they [MOFA] wish to get some research thinking and views from us" (Interviewee 43, personal communication, August 22, 2017). This is echoed in Glaser's study of think tanks, where one academic says, "The first problem is getting [an official] to read it and pass it up to the senior officials in the MFA [for their approval]. Then, the second problem is whether the MFA leadership likes it and is willing to support it" (2012, p. 118).

"The first quality that MOFA looks for is loyalty—political loyalty" (Interviewee 9, personal communication, June 25, 2016), notes one MOFA aspirant who failed to get through to the latter stages. He adds that while grades are important, these are of secondary importance to one's political leanings and discipline in obeying orders. While this was always the case, he emphasizes that it has been ramped up as a criterion under Xi. This account is corroborated by a MOFA source who notes that "surely, political loyalty and discipline is one of the most important considerations" (Interviewee 44, personal communication, September 1, 2017). Another MOFA diplomat says that there is no shortage of talent to promote, so a crucial factor is "loyalty to country and also Party and to our politics" (Interviewee 40, personal communication, July 16, 2018).

Nonetheless, one must be careful in drawing a direct link from Xi to these hiring practices because the criterion of political loyalty has always been important. "It is not just what the General Secretary [*zong shuji* (总书记, Xi Jinping] says. We are increasing our professionalism; we are increasing discipline, and we need more talented people. All these are the reasons [for hiring candidates]" (Interviewee 40, personal communication, July 16, 2018). In other words, a general shift in the diplomatic field created conditions for the kind of scrupulous selection processes we see today. This is a shift that accelerated and was made more discernible under Xi. There is a growing awareness that MOFA needs to admit more people from non-MOFA affiliated schools to diversify the organization (Qiu, 2017; Interviewee 46, personal communication, July 30, 2017), but this recognition does not always translate to concrete practice, as CFAU and the language universities continue to supply the bulk of MOFA talent owing to their preponderant position. An academic from Peking University says, "I agree that we should have more diversity [in MOFA], but how can we replace CFAU and BFSU?" (Interviewee 45, personal communication, July 31, 2017).[19] A 2017 survey of four hundred MOFA officials' educational backgrounds is enlightening as it reveals the top-supplying universities for PRC diplomats, ranked as follows: (1) BFSU, (2) CFAU, (3) Peking University, (4) University of International Business and Economics, (5) Shanghai International Studies University, (6) Renmin University, (7) Beijing International Studies University, (8) Communication University of China, (9) China University of Political Science and Law, and (10) Wuhan University. Apart from Wuhan University, which is based in Wuhan, Hubei Province, and Shanghai International Studies University, the universities are all in Beijing (Fengling, 2017). While an exact breakdown of the numbers was not provided, BFSU (first) and CFAU (second) remain the main sources of MOFA officials, with almost half of the four hundred diplomats polled hailing from these two institutions (Fengling, 2017). Peking University follows in a distant third place.

When an agent enters the institution, the socialization process quickens. The learning of what is "right and wrong" and "dos and don'ts" is well documented in socialization theory (Clausen, 1968). Bourdieu (1984) himself wrote extensively on the reproduction of social structures in schools and remarked how agents learn through "institutional inculcation" and training. In short, the socialization process that agents are put through in MOFA and in the entire diplomatic apparatus under Xi enjoins agents, as a Southeast Asian diplomat puts it, to "be firm and to be able to get their message across very forcefully and skillfully. That is their training" (Interviewee 47, personal communication, August 31, 2017).

Restrictions

Meeting diplomats, researchers, and reporters is part of normal diplomatic activity. In China, however, Foreign Ministry personnel are not allowed to meet singly with visitors; they must meet at least in pairs (Interviewee 14, July 1, 2016, personal communication; Interviewee 53, personal communication, July 28, 2018).[20] This practice departs from that of most countries, where diplomats are generally free to have meetings individually. Speaking from experience, it is only with the Chinese diplomats that I have encountered situations where there is at least one other person present.[21] There are several reasons for this, chief among them to prevent wayward messaging, keep up surveillance, and restrict the movements and utterances of agents. A North American envoy says, "We simply cannot be friends with them, not for want of trying, but it is just not possible" (Interviewee 48, personal communication, June 24, 2017). This is substantiated by other diplomatic actors who see a "friendship problem" as particularly acute with the Chinese. A European diplomat recalls that he once invited his Chinese counterpart for dinner at home and, to his surprise, the Chinese diplomat turned up with a couple of other colleagues dressed and behaving in a very "officious manner," turning what was intended as a friendly, personal interaction into one that was semiofficial, if not entirely official (Interviewee 41, personal communication, June 27, 2016). By way of comparison to the past, one Commonwealth diplomat recalls:

> When I was in the UN in New York in 1998, the Chinese diplomats were very friendly to me. I was particularly close to this current high-ranking diplomat. We were close on a very personal level, where he would ask their friends and family to host me in China. In fact, I would even bring stuff from their family to him and vice versa when I went to Beijing. He and his wife came to my house very often too! Back then, the junior ministers from China very happily

accepted our beer and food in our homes. Maybe they were very deprived, so with some food and drinks, they became very grateful! (*laughs*) (Interviewee 75, personal communication, November 16, 2018)

On the state-to-state level, such micropractices in the field effectively undermine China's attempts to "introduce friendship" and project a "friendlier kind of great power" (Nordin & Smith, 2018, p. 390). Secondary actors can play off this accessibility issue to carve a bigger space for themselves by receiving guests wanting to know more about Chinese foreign politics. For instance, several think tankers encouraged me to turn to them for information if I faced obstacles with MOFA. "They definitely will not be so accessible. We are different, we don't have so many problems with meeting up" (Interviewee 49, personal communication, August 7, 2017). MOFA, in a few instances, introduced me to their sources in think tanks too, highlighting how actors cooperate even as they compete.

Be that as it may, secondary actors are also not free from mutual surveillance and often require the presence of another colleague. While secondary diplomatic players such as think tankers, university academics, and retired officials have slightly more latitude than primary actors, they do not have unalloyed freedom. They too face increased restrictions in their movements under Xi. One told me: "If my official travel documents say two days, I must travel within two days' time and get back to China before then. I cannot extend or visit friends outside this travel period" (Interviewee 50, personal communication, September 27, 2016). Another retired official told me how he had had to turn down several requests to attend overseas conferences because "they only allow me to apply a few times and they approve a fixed number. I can definitely say [restrictions] have been greater in the past few years" (Interviewee 73, personal communication, August 1, 2018).[22]

Beyond restrictions on their movements, speeches, and friends, MOFA personnel are advised not to participate in alumni meetings and not to meet with foreigners unless on official work (Interviewee 11, personal communication, July 1, 2016). Like other civil servants in China, they are not allowed to travel abroad for personal reasons without official consent, and their nondiplomatic passport is kept by the state. And when the field is tamed, objects are also disciplined. Take the example of gifts and diplomatic courtesies. A Chinese diplomat told me: "I like Moutai.[23] In the past, embassies had Moutai, and in Russia we served it. I collected them too. But now we just serve water (*laughs*). It is a good thing because of Xi's anticorruption drive! All these things are now seen as wasteful and discouraged. No one brings them out now, not even to display at home" (Interviewee 51, personal communication, August 1, 2018).

Such restrictions on speech, body, and relationships have been most pronounced since 2016—particularly in 2017 in the lead-up to the Nineteenth National Congress of the Communist Party of China—and they persist to the present day. Many of my primary and secondary diplomatic Chinese interviewees told me that the atmosphere is "more restrictive" and that "we have not seen anything like that for a long, long time" (Interviewee 50, personal communication, June 23, 2017; Interviewee 42, personal communication, August 13, 2017). It would be wrong, however, to assume that they are resenting Xi: many of my Chinese interviewees believe that he is making the right moves in foreign policy even as this comes with some personal costs.

Diplomatic actors' primary asset is social capital (Bicchi, 2014). In the diplomatic field, such access would be easily translatable to other capitals. For some secondary actors, such as academics and retired officials, this means having a packed schedule of meetings with leaders and top officials of foreign countries. It also means that the locally administered social capital can extend into social capital at the level of the transnational diplomatic field. In a closed-door working group, a retired Chinese admiral announced that he wished to join us for lunch but had to leave because he was meeting with an ambassador of a major power. During our meeting, he masterfully wove his work experiences into his responses to our questions. He underlined his involvement in setting up the China-owned Djibouti base and provided valuable, private information on it. This left the six other participants—who were (non-Chinese) diplomats and international academics—keenly impressed.

This social capital can also translate into economic capital. A vice president of an academic institution, well known for his connections to the PSC and in particular for having delivered a lecture on foreign policy to them (a distinguishing mark), noted candidly that this allowed him to get more funding for his research (Interviewee 52, personal communication, July 29, 2017). Additionally, it made him a highly sought-after scholar in prestigious Western institutions—institutional affiliations that would increase his social, economic, and cultural capital even further. One former diplomat-turned-academic revealed: "My inside knowledge on China's diplomacy helps me in my academic career, definitely. How many Chinese academics can say they have worked in a regional desk for MOFA?" (Interviewee 53, personal communication, July 28, 2018). Indeed, he is the holder of prestigious "academic chairs" in Europe and appears on local media frequently to comment on China's international affairs.

Retired Chinese diplomatic officers thus frequently leverage social capital for further cultural and economic gains. These usually take the form of sales of autobiographical books and lucrative postdiplomatic career positions. Some examples include former ambassador Fu Ying, who then served as the chairperson of the National People's Congress Foreign Affairs Committee; former ambassador Wu Jianming, who then served as the president of CFAU; and former ambassador Dai Bingguo, who then served as the chairman of Jinan University. Such plum postgovernment career positions are not exceptional. The point in highlighting this movement is to illustrate the fungibility of capitals and to show the importance of preserving and fighting for these capitals. Another instantiation of the hierarchical relationship between primary and secondary players can be seen in the reports that academics, think tanks, and university departments make. In the previous chapter I alluded to how MOFA can monopolize and guide the means and the ends of knowledge production. Journal articles, policy briefs, and commissioned reports are some ways these secondary players influence policymaking. This process is, nevertheless, mediated by MOFA. A MOFA contact told me: "We can tap into all these researchers' knowledge to help us. For sure, we use them. But we must also choose and select. There are too many of them. Even after I submit, there are other levels. At each level, there will be modifications made in reports" (Interviewee 11, personal communication, July 1, 2017).

Displays of Fealty

During a meeting with Geng Shuang (one of MOFA's then spokespersons), he was asked how the outside world should understand the sometimes-opaque Foreign Ministry. He replied: "Study the Communist Party and you will understand China and you will understand the Foreign Ministry."[24] Yang Jiechi, one of China's most important foreign policy figures, penned a long op-ed praising Xi Jinping's thoughts on diplomacy, giving him a chance to display his personal loyalty. Yang was fulsome in his praise, emphasizing how Xi had "great foresight and a comprehensive perspective" and how "General Secretary Xi Jinping's thought on diplomacy is a comprehensive and profound system of theories with rich connotations" (D. Zhang, 2017, para. 5). Wang Yi, MOFA's minister, was equally effusive in his applause, writing that Xi's diplomatic thought "innovates upon and transcends the past 300 years of traditional Western international relations theory" while dubbing him a "reformer and a pioneer" (Martina et al., 2017, para. 7). Such ritualized tribute paying, particularly to the Party and the president, is field pervasive. A member of an influential think tank told me that aligning with the Party and, most importantly, espousing and promoting Xi's foreign policy vision made papers "safe" politically (Interviewee 44, personal communication, September 1, 2017).

Such displays of fealty do two things. First and most important, they make visible the practice of pledging loyalty or *biao tai* (表态) to Xi. The president has already installed key allies in important posts and removed people with links to either Jiang Zemin or Hu Jintao through either retirement or corruption purges.[25] Ostensibly and publicly (re)asserting loyalty prevents one and one's organization from being seen as an alternative power center. Second, under Xi, the field has shifted so that tribute paying has become established practice (M. Lau, 2015). Beyond written words and speeches, actors are expected to embody this new spirit. Diplomats frequently invoke their subordination to Xi and the Party. Whenever questions of decision-making on foreign policy come up, discussion invariably ends with "The president is the decision maker." This does not, however, mean that there are no contending voices or that MOFA has little influence. If anything, because of Xi, MOFA has grown bolder, more assertive, and activist in its diplomatic activities (D. Loh, 2020b).

The recent increase in praise is quite clear. In 2013, references to Xi were not so apparent. Around 2014 to 2015, attributions and praise to Xi started appearing during my work meetings (when I was in a Singapore think tank) with Chinese interlocutors. Subsequently, in 2016 (when Xi was named the "core" of the Party), 2017, and beyond, Xi's name has never been absent from discussions on China's foreign policy, and this is also reflected in MOFA-sponsored publications.[26]

Since MOFA is a central player in the field, increased control over it results in more disciplined MOFA corporate and individual practices—ones that incentivize activism and assertiveness and discourage "weakness." This has some related knock-on effects for secondary players. First, the scope of what they can say and do has been curtailed. Whether self-disciplining or otherwise, secondary actors have exhibited a rising tendency to restrict information, but this is always delicately balanced with a desire to fill the void (and meet) where official MOFA players cannot. Second, and following from the earlier contention, despite the restrictions, secondary diplomatic actors still have greater freedom of movement and speech compared to primary actors. This has not departed greatly from the past. What has shifted, however, is the amount of ostensible deference to President Xi *and to primary actors such as MOFA* as its representational role gets emphasized even more.

As Australia's former prime minister Kevin Rudd observed of diplomacy under Xi—"In short, the system was given the mandate to contest, assert, and where possible to lead in the various councils of the world. And this was new" (2018, p. 2). Xi Jinping himself was unequivocal, saying that "diplomacy represents the will of the state, and the diplomatic power must stay with the CPC Central Committee, while the external work is a systematic project" (Xinhua, 2018). Moreover, secondary actors' access to social capital is the most important stake in the diplomatic field, but inside information, access to policymakers/leaders, and having their opinion heard have all been curtailed, and their subjection to the primary actors in the local field is entrenched. Paradoxically, however, as access to official players such as MOFA diminishes, secondary players can positively position themselves to carve a niche.

In sum, the field, as a structure, has important constraining and enabling effects on inhabitants' practices. Perhaps the people who are best at teasing out the effects of the field on one's practices and habitus are those who have left the field and are able to assess their "previous selves" at arm's length. A former diplomat put it this way:

I felt very restricted, that is why I left. I felt stifled when I spoke and met others. I had this natural distrust of people [*dixing* 敵性]. It becomes natural to be suspicious and view everyone else like an enemy, especially foreigners. This feeling is very common when you are inside. I have to be extra careful with my words and behavior even when I am with my friends. I can never let my guard down and try to be very careful even to local Chinese. Because they watch you too! It is impossible to speak with you like this (*laughs*). As with other ministries in other countries, there is also a so-called one-year quiet period before you can travel or study after leaving. Some of my former colleagues also want to leave, but [they stay] because of the Beijing residence permit (*Beijing hukou* 北京户口), it is still valuable. (Interviewee 54, personal communication, April 27, 2018)

Transnational Fields

It has already been observed that fields can overlap and imbricate each other (Lesch & Loh, 2022; Adler-Nissen, 2011; Bigo, 2011; Mérand, 2010). A sociological view of institutions generally suggests a dynamic approach to understanding transnational fields; it highlights how transnational fields, from time to time, function as catalysts for significant changes that would often be politically unachievable on the national level, where such strategies are much more constrained by formalized politics and institutional frameworks (Madsen, 2016, p. 18). Let us also not forget that while the transnational diplomatic field is "structuring" (fields, practices, agents, and objects), it is concurrently being structured as well. While most scholars have focused on it being a structuring force, I show that it is analytically productive to look at it dynamically, *as an object and a subject of structure*. I now turn my attention toward exploring cases where fields "meet."

Many scholars look at field movements from a perspective of actors "leaving" and "entering" a field. This dissonance, they argue, creates an impact on the actor and on his actions. My contention is that actors never completely leave or enter a field: they are more or less situated in relatively stable fields and do not make a clean break as the lexicon of "leaving" and "entering" suggests. Rather, actors are enfolded in layers of fields, with some always being stronger than most and providing the girth for structural stability. That said, this constancy can be disturbed when fields come up against each other (Lesch & Loh, 2022). This is not normally a problem when fields are aligned, but what happens when fields that are not so aligned are embedded or overlap? Häkli puts it this way: "Arguably, it is precisely this aspect of field theory in the study of transnational processes that should be developed further. Instead of

looking at how the national and international fields 'overlap' or 'interact,' it is important to employ field theory to account for what dynamisms are at play in the emerging
transnational realm of social thought and action, and how these processes relate to the
nation-state as (one significant) context of action" (2013, p. 347).

How can we understand the transnational diplomatic field? Bourdieu emphasizes
how fields can be used "at different levels of aggregation" or scales, from as small as one
construction firm to as big as the "housing economy" (Bourdieu & Wacquant, 1992,
p. 102). Vauchez argues that "transnational fields have a perennially hybrid structure.
As a matter of fact, they entail elements of both 'settled' fields and 'emerging' ones."
He further emphasizes how these are "weak fields" in the sense that they are "interstitial" since they are additive to other more firmly established fields (2011, p. 342).
It is natural, then, that the transnational field represents an upward aggregation of
the state-bound field. Like local fields, it has its own structural logics, boundaries
(although fuzzier), and key and secondary actors (although less anchored), and it
produces generative effects (on and in practice). I will spotlight these effects in the
transnational diplomatic space where the key players are the institutional and human
participants of the representing countries while the secondary players are policymakers, academics, and think tanks.

Key to the power relations, as I will demonstrate in my cases, is that Chinese actors
are hierarchically better placed than others in the transnational diplomatic field.[27]
Furthermore, in the transnational field, where there is no arbiter in the sense that
the state (and Party) can metadefine various capitals, the stakes are more fluid and
contested. In that respect, the transnational (multilateral) diplomatic field is different
from the local diplomatic field in two ways. First, the stakes are different. Rather than
competing for diplomatic influence locally, competing performances of diplomacy are
enacted for, and competence is assessed by, the outcomes of "national interests" or
"regional interests." Second, in the local field, the boundaries are much tighter and
less contestable, since the activities that constitute the field (bilateral/trilateral negotiations, issuance of a joint communiqué, and so forth) are more specific, although they
are never completely closed.[28]

The tying of the "transnational" to the local is important because, "more often
than not, the literature on transnational fields indeed tends to overlook both the national structuration of social fields, and thereof the specificities of emergent global
fields" (A. Cohen, 2018, p. 205). Additionally, transnational fields are more fluid.
Sometimes they may consist of just two actors in the bilateral diplomatic field embodied in the two foreign ministries; at other moments, multiple players can be identified,
as is the case of regional forums. Most importantly, owing to this "transversality,"
disruption and change are always possible.

Rules of the Game

Bourdieu sees fields as universes where institutions and individuals "integrate" with the rules (*règles*) of the field. While fields are relatively autonomous, Walther writes that Bourdieu "also qualifies that the autonomy is only relative as fields are embedded in a social space. For instance, the intellectual field may also be influenced by the politic, the economy or religion" (2014, p. 8). This is an important observation because fields affect each other—closely related, embedded fields such as the diplomatic fields even more so. How should we understand *règles* or "field rules"? It is enlightening to hear Bourdieu's elucidation:

> We have *stakes* (*enjeux*) which are for the most part the product of the competition between players. We have an *investment in the game, illusio* (from *ludus,* the game): players are taken in by the game, they oppose one another, sometimes with ferocity, only to the extent that they concur in their belief (*doxa*) in the game and its stakes; they grant these a recognition that escapes questioning. Players agree, by the mere fact of playing, and not by way of a "contract," that the game is worth playing, that it is "worth the candle," and this *collusion* is the very basis of their competition. (Bourdieu & Wacquant, 1992, p. 98)[29]

In the forthcoming examples, I show how the field has had its rules altered. This modification does not necessarily (and often does not) result in abandonment or lessen actors' participation in the field. Likewise, the institutionalized internal/external structures, informal and formal practices, artifacts, and immaterial and material resources that are carried literally and figuratively in their conduct and practices only make sense within the context of the field.

Transversal Disruption

Disruptions always have an element of surprise that departs from or does not comport with the taken-for-granted assumptions and field rules. These disruptions, I argue, do not necessarily need to come in the form of crises (as the "hysteresis argument" rests on), nor are they simply slow, accumulative changes inherent in practices themselves. They are instead grounded in "moments" and "spaces" where rules are disrupted and subsequently altered perceptibly to engender a shift in the field. However, this movement is not extensive enough to bring about a rupture. I argue that when disruption happens, the field typically realigns or resists. I now turn to empirical cases of transversal disruption through three international diplomatic fields: (1) a track-2 international diplomacy field; (2) multilateral fields, particularly that of ASEAN; and (3) a bilateral field (China-Malaysia).

A TRACK-2 DIPLOMATIC FIELD

In a track-2 meeting in 2013, during a lunch break, a Chinese delegate—a secondary diplomatic player—tore a page off all member countries' conference booklets containing "Taiwan" as a participant.[30] Members returned to some shock but stopped short of punishing the Chinese delegate. In fact, the Chinese delegates intimated strongly that they would not tolerate any "formal" reference to Taiwan ever again.[31] China's unhappiness and anger over the officialization of Taiwan is well known—this anger, however, became more pronounced when primary and secondary actors became more emboldened after Xi took over.

When I brought up this incident to a Chinese diplomatic contact, he opined that the way the delegate had done this was "not right" but that there was "nothing fundamentally wrong with their actions" (Interviewee 1, personal communication, November 20, 2016). It is also important to observe that while the delegate's unorthodox practice was aimed toward changing a practice in the field, he and the other Chinese delegates nonetheless tried to respect the logic of that space in how they wished to see such changes made. The same contact told me, "We were not going to say that we were going to withdraw if changes were not made. Of course, we valued our participation and the organization. *We still need to play by the rules of that organization*" (Interviewee 1, personal communication, November 20, 2016).[32] In this example, secondary actors, through a highly visible act of disruption, which can also be seen as a breach of decorum or a "deliberately incompetent practice" (see chapter 1), caused a shift in the field that resulted in a change of field rules. This shift made the transnational track-2 diplomatic field more aligned with the Chinese local field. The consequence of that episode was that regulations were tweaked so that "Taiwan" could now be referred to only as "Chinese Taipei." The Taiwanese were not given a seat at the table (literally) and could participate only as observers. The diplomat's action left a lasting impact through the changing of formal rules (procedures and regulations regarding Taiwan as a participant) and informal rules (microaggression/shaming of Taiwanese participants).

Scant resistance was met in the field as actors found themselves aligning quickly to the field's altered *modus vivendi*. Beyond this change in formal rules, the later field effects were even wider ranging. Following the Chinese action, participants were careful not to talk about Taiwan or Taiwan-related issues. A party present when this took place told me that a Western delegate had said to him: "This is a track-2 arena, so we can let it slide. Anyway, in this field, the matter [Taiwanese delegate] is not so important to us," while also adding that he saw the PRC participants as underlining China's diplomacy role in representing the Party and the state much more than before (Interviewee 55, personal communication, February 26, 2015). The action also resulted in others shunning the Taiwanese representative. Such microshaming and neglect have significant social and political consequences that "spill over." Mealtimes are an example of this. The same person also recollected that, "quite clearly, the Taiwanese representative, if she even attends, has lunch by herself" (Interviewee 55, personal communication, February 26, 2015). This confirms my own observations, in 2014, of little to no interaction between the Taiwanese delegates and everyone else.

The change of the field rules in this transnational track-2 space, engendered by Chinese actors, can have a chilling effect for Taiwan's future participation in such events. In this context, countries are also compelled to make clear their "One-China position." Simultaneously, this also reinforces and legitimizes microaggressions by Chinese officials and semiofficials against Taiwanese representatives. We see this dynamic played out in official diplomatic fields too. When the US Speaker of the House Nancy Pelosi visited Taiwan in 2022, China got ASEAN and individual member states to respectively reiterate and voice their support on the "One-China policy" at the Fifty-Fifth ASEAN Foreign Ministers' Meetings in August that year (H. Yang, 2022). In this way, we can observe how a change in the field rules led to a consequent change in practices. Yet the structure of the field itself was first changed through the practices of the Chinese actors who relied on their own field operative logic. This example illuminates both the "structuring" and "structured" nature of fields acutely. A secondary Chinese diplomatic player told me, "We have to push for our interests. We have so many interests in the world. This is nothing special or shocking. It is very normal." In any event, he also admitted that "we have our own way of doing things and we bring that into the international arena. Sometimes, others disagree. But we are also aware in these places, we cannot just follow our own way all the time" (Interviewee 49, personal communication, August 7, 2017).[33]

The track-2 meeting incident also highlights something Vauchez speaks of, the emergent and "weak" structure that is symptomatic of transnational fields and makes them ripe for disruption. From the Chinese perspective, there is a tension in such spaces between a natural inclination (informed by its own field logic and practices) to bring the location into one's own fold and some awareness that the transnational location is "different" from the local diplomatic field and cannot be treated entirely as such. An important point to stress here, is that in this track-2 space, China regularly pulls diplomatic levers in a way that has resulting effects on "official diplomacy." While many countries have multiple tracks of diplomacy, China is unique, in the eyes of Singapore's former top diplomat, in that it does this "more insistently, much more systematically, and with a greater institutional apparatus devoted to the different tracks than any other country I know" (Kausikan, 2018, para. 14).

MULTILATERAL FIELDS

Another important type of transnational site is the multilateral field, most promi-
nently the (multiple) ASEAN-China field(s) where most ASEAN-China diplomatic
activity happens.[34] One sees intensified attempts to change the formal and informal
field rules, but at several sites this is met with resistance. Take the ASEAN Foreign
Ministers' Meeting in Phnom Penh, Cambodia, in July 2012. At the conclusion of this
meeting, a regular joint communiqué failed to be issued. Commentators attributed
this to the "spoiler role" that Cambodia had played in disrupting the joint communiqué—an outcome actively sought by China. Four years later, a similar incident took
place during the Special ASEAN-China Foreign Ministers' Meeting in Kunming,
China. A strongly worded statement on the SCS was first released by Malaysia near
the conclusion of the meeting. Less than three hours later, it was cancelled, purportedly because of Chinese pressure. In this way, China's visible and invisible interference disrupted vaunted ASEAN norms and rules.

Some Southeast Asian diplomats whom I interviewed noted that Chinese officials' behavior was "undiplomatic." "Within ASEAN, disagreements were plenty,"
noted one envoy, "and these were fiercely contested, but there would still be mutual
respect, give-and-take" (Interviewee 29, August 17, 2017, personal communication).
Crucially, however, they noted that members had come to expect disruptive behavior
from China. Yet this does not mean there is no resistance. In fact, resistance from
countries such as Singapore and Indonesia, and from ASEAN itself, has been crucial
in preventing alignment with the Chinese diplomatic field. Singapore, for example,
highlighted ASEAN's important role in the SCS and published its most public and
forceful message about China's assertive activities in the SCS in 2016 (Prime Minister's Office, 2016).[35] Indonesia too, has resisted—firing live arms at encroaching
Chinese vessels (Areddy, 2016), renaming part of the SCS as the "North Natuna
Sea" (Allard & Munthe, 2017), and, more significantly, insisting that ASEAN take a
common stand on the SCS issue (Gutierrez, 2017). One diplomat from the countries
putting up resistance tells me: "We want to have a good relationship with China. Everyone does. But we must make it clear to them that we have our national interests.
We must also ensure that ASEAN stays free from interference" (Interviewee 2, personal communication, July 11, 2018). When probed on instances of such interference
in the China-ASEAN field, he stated: "They [China] don't want to break up ASEAN.
It is not in their interest. But when they want to apply some pressure, they are most
willing to do so. They will do it by applying individual pressure on each delegate,
that is very clear. To an extent, they have succeeded with their cultivation of certain
countries in ASEAN. This is a challenge to the norms of neutrality and ASEAN centrality" (Interviewee 2, personal communication, July 11, 2018).

Prior to 2012, ASEAN and foreign ministerial statements were banal affairs. Post

2012, these statements have become politicized as objects that are fought for. Thus there are ongoing struggles over ASEAN statements' wording when reference to the SCS is made. For instance, in 2016 and 2017, the usual language in the statements of ASEAN chairs and foreign ministers were watered down through the removal of all references to the South China Sea; yet in 2018, these made a reappearance with reference to "concerns on the land reclamations and activities in the area, which have eroded trust and confidence, increased tensions and may undermine peace, security, and stability in the region" (ASEAN Secretariat, 2018).

What used to be exclusively an internal ASEAN matter has now increasingly found itself under pressure from extramural forces (see D. Loh, 2018b). According to one official, China "want[s] to change the rules of the game in ASEAN. They know they can make use of the principle of consensus and play us, and they did" (Interviewee 56, personal communication, August 28, 2017). A senior ASEAN diplomat similarly asserts:

China's ASEAN diplomacy, since around 2010, has generally insisted on China defining everything from the trivial—which hotel delegations stay at, the timing of meetings, and so forth—to the consequential, like the pace, timing, and substance of the CoC negotiations in a kind of conditioning that is made more effective with some added coercion. They want to slowly change the way things are done in ASEAN, bring about changes to the whole edifice and not even let you notice things changed. (Interviewee 3, personal communication, July 10, 2018)

Another ASEAN diplomat says of his experience in this transnational field:

Within ASEAN, it is very predictable and straightforward. We have disagreements, of course, but [we] disagree within ASEAN. In ASEAN-China meetings, there is something different. They bring something different, and for us [ASEAN], it is not just merely an ASEAN meeting. Also, we have so many China-ASEAN initiatives compared to the past. Much, much more face time with them. Think about it, if they are indeed changing how we do things in the China-ASEAN, it will eventually change ASEAN itself for good or for bad. (Interviewee 20, August 1, 2017, personal communication)

Are there any lasting changes in the ASEAN field? There have been some shifts—not tectonic but not insignificant either. First, the "rules of the game," both the formal and informal,[36] in this field are increasingly being contested, challenged, and weakened. But there is resistance. The act of resisting clarifies what the field rules are: what exactly the "ASEAN way" connotes, how to practice it, and how important it is.[37] Shanmugam, Singapore's former foreign minister, maintained that ASEAN must keep speaking out on the SCS issue and not be silenced: "If ASEAN keeps quiet and loses credibility, it would not be in China's interest" (Chang, 2014, para. 2). It is this ongoing self-reflective resistance that is preventing the widening of cracks into fissures, even as this resistance is by no means guaranteed to succeed. All the examples presented above have had the effect of reinforcing the local Chinese field—clarifying the stakes, reaping the rewards, increasing the confidence of actors within the Chinese diplomatic field. Bringing up ASEAN examples where norms or field rules have changed, a European diplomat says, "They can get away with plenty and they know it. If they can get away with it, of course they would do it repeatedly" (Interviewee 41, personal communication, June 27, 2016). Indeed, Chinese diplomatic actors have met little successful resistance that seriously challenges their field rules so that they would reconsider their actions. In that respect, a Commonwealth diplomat says: "If they [Chinese diplomats] have a field day pushing, they will, of course, push all the way! Nothing to resist or stop them from doing so, they will naturally keep pushing and pushing" (Interviewee 75, personal communication, November 16, 2018).

Beyond the ASEAN-China transnational space, we can see such practices emerging in other multilateral fields too. For example, it was reported that a Chinese diplomat—Du Qiwen—walked out of the Pacific Forum Islands Meeting in 2018 after his demands "to be heard when [Tuvalu's] Prime Minister was about to speak" were not met. He reportedly strode around the room to show his unhappiness before leaving. Nauru's president, Baron Waqa, expressed anger at the envoy's behavior: "He insisted and was very insolent about it, and created a big fuss and held up the meeting of leaders for a good number of minutes when he was only an official. So maybe because he was from a big country, he wanted to bully us" (Doherty & Davidson, 2018, para. 4).[38] In a remarkable sign of resistance, Nauru's president subsequently called on China to apologize for its diplomats' "crazy behaviour" (*South China Morning Post*, 2018b, para. 1). Here, once again, we observe the characterization of such practices as exceptional (or "crazy"); yet seen from a Chinese diplomatic perspective, they are part of an established and valued diplomatic style—so-called wolf warrior diplomacy.[39] When queried on Chinese attempts to change field rules in the transnational space, a secondary Chinese interviewee said: "We do not think this view of others seeing us as assertive as accurate. This view comes especially from the West. For us, to use assertiveness is to be more active (*jiji* 积极). It has positive connotations, more like confidence, rather than negative connotations. These activities that you see from our diplomats reflect that confidence. It comes with China's rise. It is natural you see this on the world stage" (Interviewee 57, personal communication, June 28, 2017).

THE CHINA-MALAYSIA BILATERAL FIELD

Beyond the multilateral arena, we see instances where Chinese diplomatic practices are creeping into the bilateral-transnational field. The China-Malaysia bilateral relation is illustrative. Two cases spring to mind. The first is the apparent interference by former Chinese ambassador Huang Huikang in Malaysia's domestic politics in 2015. That year, he appeared in an ethnically Chinese street in Malaysia when pro- and antigovernment protests were raging owing to the "1MDB [1 Malaysia Development Berhad] scandal."[40] In his visit, before a planned progovernment rally, he "warned that Beijing would not fear voicing out against incidents which threaten the interests of the country, infringe upon the rights of its citizens in doing business, or disrupt the relationship between Malaysia and China." This was widely seen as meddling in the domestic affairs of Malaysia and as stoking pro-Chinese sentiments at a racially sensitive moment (Tariq & Chan, 2015, para. 3). After being summoned by the Malaysian Foreign Ministry for clarification, Huang's aides told them he was very busy and demanded instead that the Foreign Ministry officers go to the embassy to see him. Huang then went on to lobby Ong Ka Ting, Malaysia's special envoy for China, and several other ministers, who reportedly let him off the hook (Parameswaran, 2015, para. 5).

Next, in the 2018 general elections in Malaysia, it was observed that the Chinese ambassador, Bai Tian, campaigned for the incumbent candidate, Liow Tiong Lai, from the Malaysian Chinese Association, which was a major component of the then ruling coalition Barisan Nasional. The Chinese ambassador was a constant presence at the campaign rallies held by Liow (Xi's image even appeared on the Association's campaign posters) and the ruling administration, leading to murmurs that Beijing was openly supporting the pro-China Najib administration (Ho, 2018; *Borneo Post*, 2018). Nevertheless, their gambit backfired. Mahathir Mohamad's "Pakatan Harapan" coalition emerged as the new government after the elections, and he moved swiftly to suspend the China-backed USD $20 billion East Coast Rail Link project and a natural gas pipeline project in Sabah, citing the unfair nature of the deal (Reuters, 2018). Mahathir also sounded a warning against "a new version of colonialism" in a thinly veiled reference to China during a state visit to Beijing (Hornby, 2018, para. 1). China's assertive diplomatic practices here reveal a greater willingness generally to engage in and with the domestic politics of other countries, even though China has consistently articulated a strict "non-interference policy" (Li, 2019).

When I suggested to a Chinese diplomatic source that China's moves in Malaysia could be seen as interference, he was self-exculpatory: "This is being misunderstood. We always insist on noninterference. It is normal that as China grows we have more resources; we expand and protect these." He also brushed off Malaysia's moves, saying,

"No, this is not a reaction to the so-called 'interference' or 'debt trap.' First, there is no such thing. Next, it is their negotiating tactic for the East Coast Rail line" (Interviewee 51, personal communication, August 1, 2018). What was left unsaid, of course, was that China had materially grown for decades but that the recent assertive turn had become most apparent over the last ten years.[41]

Whether in multilateral fields, such as ASEAN, in the bilateral China-Malaysia space, or in the track-2 diplomatic field, this *diplomatic assertive turn* has been a recent development coinciding with Xi's efforts to exert control and the heightened representational role of MOFA over various domains in state and society. As a Southeast Asian diplomat describes it: "They are importing their brand of diplomacy into Southeast Asia bilaterally and multilaterally through ASEAN. Publicly of course they have to say otherwise [that there is no domestic interference]. If you study what they actually do, you see how they apply their own ideas and try to apply them elsewhere" (Interviewee 58, personal communication, September 3, 2017). Thus we see how Chinese interlocutors are prepared to bring their local operative logic to bear on transnational fields and also how these transversal disruptions are, on occasion, resisted.

As stated at the start of this chapter, the account of change in diplomacy provided here is a *via media* between incremental change and sudden exogenous shocks, even as it has elements of both. Change potentially occurs when fields meet: a process understood here as the dynamics observed in transnational diplomatic fields when seemingly separate "local/national" fields come together. In this case, change is brought about by practices informed by the local Chinese diplomatic field entering an unfamiliar (but not completely novel) transnational field. Resistance can spring up, but even so, this transnational space is never fully defended against forces external to it. Indeed, change and resistance in international fields are affected by and always shifting in tandem with broader, more systemic forces in a mutually reinforcing and constitutive way.

Thus in interviews Chinese respondents describe their interactions in multilateral and bilateral fields by pointing to the "changing currents of the world" and a "changing international order" that is increasingly "favorable" to China (Interviewee 51, personal communication, August 1, 2018). What is important to note is that Chinese practitioners treat this as a fact and that their practices are informed accordingly. Indeed, various external, internal, and in-between field forces act together to "tip" changes one way or another. Though discussions of China's more assertive behavior in the period after 2008, Xi's rapid assumption of a grip on state and society after 2013, and the emergence of "wolf warrior diplomacy" in 2020 often speak of these changes as "sudden," they actually were not abrupt but were simply seen as more intense after reaching tipping points. As McConnell and Dittmer explains: "Outliers are actualisations that resemble the ideal form less and less, until they become closer to another attractor in this multidimensional space and tip into a different basin of attraction. For this reason, increasing intensities will seem to have little effect on an assemblage until suddenly it reaches a 'tipping point' and the elements re-territorialise in a new form, unleashing energies that can ripple through neighbouring assemblages sharing common elements" (2017, p. 143).

Conclusion

In this chapter, I suggest that field analysis can provide nuanced understandings of change in Chinese diplomacy, particularly in multilateral and international arenas. To demonstrate this, I charted the diplomatic landscape within China and gave a novel relational account of how fields can be identified, marked out, and analyzed. This involved mapping the "primary" and "secondary" actors and the hierarchical relations between them. Next, I catalogued shifts taking place within and how these have resulted in a correspondent and (constant) realignment of actors in the arena. Following that, I introduced the idea of "transversal disruption" and what this entailed. Using the transnational fields of track-2 diplomacy, the multilateral ASEAN-China field, and the bilateral Malaysia-China space, I exhibited some effects of field overlaps. Specifically, I displayed the ways in which transnational fields can be sites of change, particularly because of their "transversality"—more than established "local fields," where boundaries, actors, and field rules are less contestable. Hence, such fields hold potential for disruption in which field inhabitants, informed by their own operative logic, introduce change to the structure of the transnational field itself.

Empirically, I demonstrated how Xi's quest for control in foreign policy further tweaked the local diplomatic field's structure and incentives. His sizable political power, compared to his predecessors, Hu and Jiang (Brown, 2017), gave him the necessary space and capital to impose his vision on the state, even though it is important to recognize the limits of one man. This imposition, for its part, gave rise to bolder, more proactive actors and consequently a more activist diplomacy that also demonstrated how MOFA is increasingly representing both the state's and the Party's interests on the world stage. The result is somewhat mixed for China. In some arenas, their assertive performances have been met with success, and in others they have faced strong resistance. Nevertheless, up until the intensification of US-China rivalry in 2019, there was no clear case where Chinese diplomats were successfully challenged or resisted enough for them to reflect on and rethink their own rules and practices. Importantly, these assertive performances were widely praised back home by domestic audiences, including political elites, intellectuals, and large segments of Chinese society (D. Loh

& Loke, 2023, p. 14). In fact, even if resistance or challenge did occur, no diplomat would want to be the "bearer of bad news" to his Chinese superiors (Interviewee 59, personal communication, June 19, 2017; Interviewee 43, personal communication, August 22, 2017). Thus far, I have scaled down to look at diplomatic practices and panned out to study the field. Closing that loop, the next chapter moves to scrutinize the institution of MOFA through the conception of "institutional habitus."

FOUR

Institutional Habitus and MOFA's Identity Effects

The Chinese [MOFA] have a remarkable memory. They will be able to look through their files and cite precisely what you said in the 1950s. They keep detailed records of everything you say, and this can be easily referred to. I have personally experienced this. They pull out things I have said before many years ago!

(INTERVIEWEE 63, personal communication, July 19, 2017)

Foreign ministries play a critical role in international relations—they are key actors of international political life.[1] Yet as chapter 2 highlighted, they are relatively neglected as targets of scholarly analysis and scarcely feature in discussions of state identity.[2] I extend the discussion on practices and fields from the previous two chapters to study the habitus of PRC's MOFA as both the "*tool* of investigation" and the "*topic* of investigation" (Wacquant, 2011).[3] I argue that foreign ministries develop dispositions, perceive the social world around them, and react to the world from these orientations. I do so by introducing the concept of *institutional habitus*, a concept with long-standing roots in sociology, to understand MOFA with regard to the paths by which this habitus is sustained and the diplomatic practices it engenders. I thus empirically illustrate how China's foreign ministry contributes to its state's identity and "actorness." I suggest that MOFA's institutional habitus manifests and preserves itself in three ways: iterative reinscription of institutional memory and invocation of history; displays of fealty; and organizational and personal self-regulation. MOFA is a paradigmatic case, where "strong instances of particular patterns of meaning" are present (Leonard 1989, p. 54; see also Flyvbjerg 2006, pp. 230–33), owing to the prominence of history, discipline, and control across bureaucracies in China (e.g., Harding, 1981).

This chapter makes two primary contributions. First, I make a case for the importance of China's foreign ministry to its state "actorness" and identity. When scholars speak of "state X doing Y" or "state X condemning state Z"—what is acting is often not the state but a state's foreign ministry (or a state institution) that is acting on behalf of the state. How is this "actorness" reconciled with the fact that states cannot be said to possess any inherent agency shorn of their agents?[4] My argument here is that MOFA "gives content" to perceptions of the state—derived through the everyday practices of China's diplomats and representatives—so that it is possible to speak of China "doing things" in and acting on the world. In other words, perceptions of China's identity by other officials, diplomats, and representatives *are commonly derived* from MOFA and its diplomats. Two facets of this identity stand out. First, the assertiveness of MOFA's agents and institutions comes to characterize China from the perspectives of other non-Chinese diplomats. Second, the requirements of the MOFA habitus for personal discipline often translate into an impression of Chinese "coldness" and inaccessibility.

Next, I contribute to the literature by using the concept of *institutional habitus*—an institution's relatively durable worldview and disposition—to study Chinese diplomacy. This maneuver heeds Joseph and Kurki's call for practice theorists to pay greater attention to the "relation between structures and practices" (2018, p. 87), which as they point out has been ignored. Furthermore, habitus, particularly the notion of group habitus, has received less attention than Bourdieu's other concepts. Pouliot's (2010a) scholarship on the security practices of Russian and NATO interlocutors is one important exception in theorizing group habitus, and this chapter builds on and also contributes to that endeavor. Indeed, habitus is a powerful tool for explaining social reproduction and cultural perseverance and is key to understanding how practices unfold. Accordingly, observing how institutions develop and sustain a habitus gives us an analytical perspective to understand, imagine, and study institutions and political communities in new ways, especially in highlighting the role that norms, history, and nonhuman materials play in and through institutions. A puzzle that animates this discussion on MOFA's habitus and state identity is this: *In what ways are diplomatic interactions between Chinese diplomats and non-Chinese diplomats significant?*

As will be clear in the rest of this chapter, an important upshot of this interaction is that other diplomats procure significant meaning and, consequently, impute China's identity from these interactions. The modest claim that foreign ministries are consequential in identity construction and have significant identity effects is an important one to make, as the literature on state identity often leaves out this institution in their analysis or assumes a link but does not empirically document it. Studying the identity effects of MOFA also brings to the foreground the ministry's increased profile and representational role since 2009.

There are three sections in this chapter. In the first, I briefly discuss Bourdieu's concept of habitus and show how the study of China's international politics can benefit from it. The concept of habitus, I suggest, allows one to empirically unlock important international-political effects and practices springing from the institution itself. In the second section, drawing on field interviews, I present MOFA as a case to concretize institutional habitus. Following that, I map out the effects of institutional habitus on inhabitants' diplomatic practices. In the third section, I engage with the scholarship on state identity to underline the critical role that China's foreign ministry adopts in identity construction and show why this recognition is important.

Institutional Habitus

Bourdieu writes that habitus are "systems of durable, transposable dispositions, structured structures predisposed to function as structuring structures, that is, as principles which generate and organize practices and representations that can be objectively adapted to their outcomes without presupposing a conscious aiming at ends or an express mastery of the operations necessary in order to attain them" (1990b, p. 53). Habitus allows for the range of possible strategies—conscious and unconscious—in a particular social field to unfold when actors compete to acquire more resources or gain more capital. By that same token, institutions are participatory actors in their respective social fields. They thus possess, accumulate, and deploy capital to fight for resources. In sociology (particularly the sociology of education), the concept of institutional habitus is fairly mature (see Lahire, 2010, p. 16; Atkinson, 2011, pp. 333–335). Burke et al (2013, p. 173) explain how "social institutions are constituted by individuals and it is the members of institutions and their collective practices that are the analytic focus of the collective habitus." For McDonough (1997, p. 107), an "organizational habitus" underlines "the impact of a cultural group or social class on an individual's behaviour." Similarly, Lahire (2010) suggests that an individual may have various "habituses" intersecting across domains and institutions. Critically, Burke et al. (2013, p. 166) argue that the concept of institutional habitus is important "to theorise the collective practices of groups of individuals rather than individuals per se." While Bourdieu himself did not conceptualize habitus as institutional or collective, he gestured at this possibility by noting how practices are "collectively orchestrated without being the product of the orchestrating action of the conductor" (1990a, 53). Moreover, he argues that institutional inhabitants can partake in "history" personified and manifested in institutions—an important theoretical point that is empirically fleshed out in this chapter (Bourdieu, 1977, 1990b, pp. 56–59).

The notion of an "institutional habitus" can also help explain the connection between collective agency and habitus. Callaghan points out that "although more difficult to discern, collective agency exists in the daily routines of life at least as much as in overt social movements" (2005, p. 4). Hence, the exercise of collective agency or, in other words, practices born from groups (or an institution) is more than simply the practices of individuals arrayed together.[5] That said, Emirbayer and Johnson caution that "one might speak here of an organizational habitus, were it not for the dangers of reification inherent in such a usage, dangers to which Bourdieu himself points whenever he invokes such generalizing notions as the class or group habitus" (2008, p. 19). Crucially, however, they add that this does not mean disavowing it:

> What remains truly useful, at any rate, about the notion of an organizational habitus is its highlighting of the fact . . . that organizations, even business firms, are never driven solely by considerations of self-interest in the narrowest sense; they are also driven by interests specific to the game in which they are taking part, interests, to be sure, perceived and acted upon in different ways depending on the different positions these organizations occupy within the field at hand. (2008, p. 19)

Tying the concept of habitus with workplaces, Vaughan observes how, in modern societies, work organizations are now the key sites of socialization and, as a result, the place where one's habitus is molded (2002, p. 33). While this observation is not new (see Wanous, 1992, pp. 187–234), recognizing, as this chapter does, that organizations develop dispositions and orientations that have effects beyond their inhabitants adds a novel dimension to existing accounts of institutions in international politics.

In IR, the analytical potential of institutional habitus is not fully unlocked, even as some scholars hint at this. For instance, through a study of the United Nations and the Rwanda genocide, M. Barnett notes how organizations contain "discourse and formal and informal rules that shape what individuals care about and the practices they view as appropriate, desirable, and ethical in their own right" (2002, p. 5). He notes how bureaucracies and organizations "produce social optics that policymakers and bureaucrats use to see the world" (2002, p. 60). In other words, organizations mediate how agents navigate the social world. What is more, as much as the organization molds an individual's habitus, the reverse is also true: individuals' habitus shapes the institution's habitus (see Lahire, 2010). The individual-organization habitus nexus thus opens up intriguing ways to study institutions and political communities. It complicates state-centric epistemologies by adding an interstitial layer or "image" between the individual and the state.[6] The payoff from this is that far from seeing local, global, and transnational institutions as epiphenomenon or peripheral, we can better understand how and when institutions drive global politics.

I suggest three conditions that allow for the development of the institutional habitus.[7] First, the habitus of an individual and that of the organization need to be more or less synergistic. That is to say, the habitus of an individual and that of the organization do not contradict each other in any major ways. This is best seen in the employment process of organizations. Beyond instrumental benchmarks (qualifications, work experience, salary, etc.), "fit" is an increasingly important criterion in hiring decisions (Wanous, 1992, pp. 44–46). In previous chapters, I pointed to this "fit" between the individual and MOFA such that "political correctness" is viewed as a key trait. There is no denying that one's habitus can conflict with an institutional habitus, as when coercion is used to bring an individual into an institution[8] or when individuals (or the organization) discover that their habitus—worldview, dispositions, skills, and so forth—are at odds. In such instances, a split is likely to eventually occur where the individual exits the organization or undertakes mitigating strategies.[9] With each exit, the institution "sharpens" its habitus. Interviewees with former PRC envoys show this disjuncture quite clearly. Describing recently departed Chinese diplomats, a Southeast Asian envoy told me, "People left because of higher pay elsewhere and because the work hours are long at MOFA. Those who don't 'buy into' MOFA cannot stay long" (Interviewee 37, personal communication, August 3, 2018). Simply put, there must be some level of mutual socialization and *conformity* between individuals and the institution. Institutions with too many innovative agents would find it difficult for the sedimentation of culture, practices, and memory to take hold as the institution would get pulled in different directions. A Chinese envoy, discussing the turnover rate at MOFA with me, stated, "It is natural for big organizations to have people leave. We can afford to choose because core people stay and they have the right values and motivation" (Interviewee 40, personal communication, July 16, 2018). This indicates how MOFA can retain a "core" set of values, norms, and inhabitants that sustain its institutional habitus.

There must be persistence of institutional work culture, habits, and dispositions for a habitus to be identified. That said, institutions do not unceasingly reproduce themselves, and agents do not inexorably tend toward compliance and conformity (cf. Oberfield, 2010). In a study on institutional "practice breakdowns," Lok and de Rond (2013, p. 205) explain how "institutional scripts can be stretched to temporarily fit practice performances that appear to diverge from them without necessarily causing permanent structural change." This "institutional plasticity" allows change to take place and accounts for the emergence of practices that contest the organizing principles and institutional habitus without fundamentally altering its core character.

Second, the institution in question must have some "historical stability." This allows institutional memory to develop, which is crucial to sustaining and reinscribing an institution's habitus. Phrased differently, the institution should have a durable historical continuity to allow the habitus to take hold. Commonly evinced from conversations with Chinese diplomats is the importance they place on history—the institution's, the Party's, and that of certain heroic diplomats. One source discloses, "There are no formal IR history courses, but there is certainly training on modern Chinese history that begins from Mao. That is most important" (Interviewee 60, personal communication, July 9, 2018). It is revealing that, compared to other foreign ministries, where a background of IR knowledge is typically requisite, Chinese diplomats and diplomats-to-be do not strictly demand it: most of MOFA's talent pool instead comes from foreign-language schools (see chapter 3), MOFA is professionalizing and diversifying its hiring pool (see C. Wang, 2022), but a 2017 survey of four hundred Chinese diplomats indicated that 46 percent of them still had "languages" as their majors and 38 percent had "English and/or international relations" as their majors (Fengling, 2017, para. 6).

Finally, there must be a meaningful field for the development and deployment of a habitus. In other words, it must not be a transient institution that does not support a critical mass of agents.[10] If we believe that the organizational sum is larger than its human parts, then the "institution" as the key configurative principle in one's life course is not merely the aggregation of individuals' habitus. The institution—owing to its collective institutional memory and registry of practices—lasts longer than its agents. Consider how the individual's embodied habitus "consists of a set of historical relations 'deposited' within individual bodies in the form of mental and corporal schematic perception, appreciation and action" (Bourdieu & Wacquant, 1992, p. 16).

I am quick to add that this account of institutions does not deny the presence or influence of entrepreneurial agents or exceptional individuals who possess an almost monopolistic hold on capital (such as Xi Jinping).[11] These individuals can bring about an inordinate amount of influence and change. Nevertheless, such power is not unfettered: the individuals are constrained by larger commitments, rules, and norms of the diplomatic field within which MOFA is situated. Stated another way, as powerful as Xi is, this power is nevertheless circumscribed by institutional design, whether through the Party (Brown, 2016, pp. 609–610) or the broader diplomatic field. When I asked a Chinese diplomat whether Xi's administration, relative to previous ones, "cared more" about MOFA, he was circumspect:

> All leaders care about diplomacy. It is the same everywhere, and in our case our leaders have always cared about it. Yes, our standing has improved, but it is not simply that he cares more but that diplomacy takes up more of his time and attention compared to previous leaders! Of course, MOFA is important to him, but it might not be that he places more emphasis *but that he has no choice but to devote more time and resources to it!* (Interviewee 77, personal communication, November 16, 2018)[12]

At this juncture, it is germane to make clear how the concept of institutional habitus differs from BP, "organizational culture," and "community of practices" (CoP) approaches. The difference from the first is clear—BP is concerned with intraorganiza-tion politics and conflicts and the effects that these engender. Such an approach takes politics—particularly an agent-centric one—as the driver of change/stability (Allison & Zelikow, 1999, pp. 255–294), whereas the concept of institutional habitus sees the organization collectively as an actor, in its own right, acting on the world beyond merely being a function of politics. The distinction between institutional habitus and organizational culture, at first glance, seems blurrier. Indeed, there are compatibilities between them, particularly in organizational culture's emphasis on collective values, beliefs, and habits (Needle, 2004). However, they differ in at least three important ways. First, "Conceptualizing organizational culture as habitus may give the organiza-tional researcher the opportunity to avoid static and one dimensional accounts of or-ganization and to infuse the dynamic nature of the organizational culture" (Özbilgin & Tatli 2005, p. 864). Thus, while the habitus of MOFA may be entirely fitted to the diplomatic field, it may be maladapted to the domestic political field and its associated struggles for stakes there.

    Second, it is unclear how organizational culture, as an amorphous force guiding the organization and its agents, works in practice. Bourdieu warns us against moving from a descriptive observation that fits the regularity to a rule that "directs, governs and orients behaviour," as if practices ineluctably followed some conscious law, such as cultural codes. And a view of the culture as doing "unconscious regulating" makes the motivator of social action a kind of "Deus ex machina, which is also a God in the Machine" (Bourdieu, 1990b, p. 40). Third, and most crucially, an institutional habi-tus (unlike "culture") does not in itself arouse social action. What it does, instead, is generate the possible conditions for practices to emerge, reiterate, and sustain it. Insti-tutional habitus, then, is not an untethered guiding law; it is "a system of internalized, embodied schemes which, having been constituted in the course of collective history, is acquired in the course of individual history and function in their *practical* state, for *practice*" (Bourdieu, 1984, p. 467).[13] The introduction of institutional habitus thus also allows for a heuristic concretization of what organizational culture frequently references: norms, values, beliefs, and history.

    Institutional habitus also differs from the CoP (Wenger, 1998) approach in at least two significant ways. First, the location and importance of objects are not cen-tral concerns of CoP. In contrast, I take seriously the role of objects in coproducing practices. Second, because of this emphasis on materiality, the conception of insti-tutional habitus is wedded to an "actual" physical organization. While a CoP can include physical organizations, it is much more amorphous since it conceives of com-munities nebulously—from people meeting for lunch regularly to overseas diasporas (Wenger & Snyder, 2000). Additionally, because of its emphasis on social learning, co-participation, and spontaneity, CoP is "resistant to supervision and interference"

(Wenger & Snyder, 2000, p. 140). By contrast, in foreign ministries in general, supervision and interference are established practices. Having profiled these differences, I turn to describing MOFA and its institutional habitus.

Establishment and Growth of MOFA

MOFA was founded in September 1954 (Ministry of Foreign Affairs, 2013)[14] after the establishment of the PRC in 1949. MOFA had over three thousand employees in the 1990s and is currently estimated to have over five thousand diplomats and support personnel under its organization (Zhongguo Xinwen, 2009c).[15] It has come a long way since 1954; it has enhanced its professionalism (Glaser & Saunders, 2002) and seen its diplomatic corps grow.[16] At the risk of repetition, I point to five concrete manifestations of MOFA's growth. First, Yang Jiechi (China's top foreign policy official) was elevated into China's elite policymaking Party body—the twenty-five-member Politburo—at the Nineteenth Party Congress (Chong, 2017). Second, the institution is getting greater material support, with its diplomatic spending in 2017 rising to USD $7.8 billion, almost doubling the spending in 2013 (Bloomberg News, 2017). Third, MOFA's reforms under Xi meant that in 2019 "most agencies stop[ped] replacing staff in Chinese embassies . . . , giving ambassadors direct control over their portfolios," in contrast to the past, when different embassies were influenced by different ministries. Substantially, MOFA now "wield[s] a veto over financial and personnel decisions at embassies," with a report stating that the "Foreign Ministry could weaken the very agencies such as the Commerce Ministry that have helped China establish interests around the globe, but the government has decided it is worth the risk" (Bloomberg News, 2018, para. 12). Fourth, the Central Foreign Affairs Leading Small Group—the highest strategic decision-making body for foreign policy—has been restructured and renamed the Central Foreign Affairs Commission, elevating its status and importance, with Xi as chair and Vice President Wang Qishan as deputy chair (Z. Yu, 2018). Finally, Xi has pushed for the increased importance of diplomats as the vanguard in defending China's interests and in telling "China's story" well (A. Huang and Wang, 2019).

Mapping MOFA's Habitus

Plotting the institutional habitus of MOFA requires some methodological innovation. In more precise terms, I rely on MOFA statements and agents' diplomatic practices that inform MOFA's habitus—specifically, how the habitus is sustained and instantiated—and explore how the habitus affects diplomatic practices and state identity. I triangulate the data through third-party interviews with non-Chinese diplomats who have experience working with their Chinese counterparts. In other words, I am taking a synchronic snapshot of a diachronically constructed habitus. The following sections will draw out particular features of MOFA's institutional habitus. Within the discussion of each "strand" of the habitus underlined, a discussion on the effects of that feature will follow.

Institutional Memory and History

One's biography and historical experiences are critical for one's habitus to develop. In the same vein, institutional memory is crucial for the institutional habitus to emerge since it furnishes the institution "some measure of consistency and continuity to function" (Autesserre 2014, p. 44) and since "institutional memory develops through the sharing of knowledge across time and space" by inhabitants (Hardt 2017, 123). Significantly, institutional knowledge "flattens and shoehorns history into already established boxes and cubicles" (M. Barnett, 2002, p. 59). This self-reinforcement permits the stability from which a durable "we-ness" emerges and reveals itself in "institutional myths, legends, and stories . . . *behavioural routines*, procedures and scripts" and "in *physical artifacts*, which embody, to varying degrees, the results of prior learning" (Moorman & Miner, 1997, pp. 92–93).[17]

Building on these interpretations, I define institutional memory as the "*stored material and immaterial knowledge, beliefs, norms, and behavioral routines that may be used in the present.*" One instantiation of material artifacts embodying institutional history is texts—particularly texts that diplomats rely on for meetings and briefings. Cornut notices how newly arrived diplomats "usually rely on briefing notes written by their predecessor. This helps to preserve a form of institutional memory, but it also reinforces existing frameworks of analysis" (2015, p. 393). Evidence from the Chinese case affirms Cornut's conclusions. MOFA spokespersons, in their daily press briefing, rely extensively on a thick book of preprepared notes. Remarkably, in the three press briefings I sat through, and in the many others I watched online, almost all questions had a "ready-made" response drawn from the book.[18] Furthermore, despite the vastly different personalities of MOFA diplomats off- and onstage, the responses to questions were similar. Indeed, a former Chinese diplomat writes how "over ten diplomats" work on crafting every conceivable question and answer to prepare the spokesperson. What is more, some potential responses require the approval of higher leadership or other state agencies (J. Li, 2019, para. 17). In essence, the book, as a physical artifact (beyond the substantive content), "holds" organizational institutional norms and beliefs. MOFA itself has described the press briefings, which only became a daily affair in 2011, as an extremely important duty; there are "more than a dozen assistants behind the team and this team has the backing of the entire MOFA and even other ministries and commissions" (Li, 2019a, para. 18).[19] Thus the notes serve a symbolic function: as a material thing reminding the diplomat of the correct utterances and demeanor by functioning as a repository of institutional norms and beliefs.

Pouliot, in a reflection on how "warheads are like pieces on a chessboard—they inscribe the rules of the game in things which then acquire a material existence of their own," concludes that in international politics, "material things can take on a symbolic life of their own" (2010b, p. 301). In all my interviews with Chinese diplomats, textual objects were always present. A non-Chinese envoy comments that "the Chinese are very professional and well-prepared. They always come with the necessary notes and research documents" (Interviewee 59, personal communication, June 19, 2017). In two different interviews with Chinese diplomats, a thick file brought along for the meeting was never used but was conspicuously present, its function supplanted by its symbolism. This can be counterproductive sometimes. One Chinese interlocutor told me, "Our diplomats read from prepared remarks to the outside world a lot of times. We do not give the right remarks to make people believe [our positions]. They are not making people believe in them, creating some difficulties" (Interviewee 61, personal communication, June 27, 2017).

Next, the institution's history is consistently foregrounded through recurrent socialization of inhabitants into its history and ethos. One Chinese diplomat states: "To understand us [MOFA], you need to read the history of our Communist Party" (Interviewee 11, personal communication, July 1, 2017). This reinscription and valorization of the past are symptomatic of the broader clarion call to "not forget the glorious achievements of the Party" (*bu wang chuxin* 不忘初心). This also means that history (of MOFA and broader "Chinese history") regularly flows through MOFA's diplomatic practices. "A lot of what is going on in the South China Sea is driven by history, by China's perception of itself as a 'victim.' That's how you see the 'victim mentality' coming up. Chinese MOFA's actions can be seen like this too," comments a Chinese respondent (Interviewee 61, personal communication, June 27, 2017).

Deaths of former diplomats are an opportunity for MOFA to memorialize and entrench the "traditions" and "ethos" of the institution. For instance, at the memorial service of Wu Jianmin, a diplomat's elegy for him observed that his car accident was due to his work ethic—the long work hours he kept, well into the night, his obligation to the motherland, and his heavy sense of duty (Sina News, 2016). Another diplomat—Li Shengjiao—was also memorialized a year after his death in 2017 when Chinese diplomats and officials came to remember his deeds, especially his diplomatic achievements in international maritime law and boundary demarcation issues (*South China Morning Post*, 2018a). Zhou Enlai, China's former premier and first foreign minister, is arguably the most memorialized diplomat. His death and birthday (*dan chen* (诞辰) are often high-profile ministry benchmark dates, with top diplomatic officials delivering evocative, heart-felt eulogies. For example, in 2008, at the 110th "birth anniversary" of Zhou, the then-ambassador to North Korea delivered a speech dedicated to him, saying that his "alarming abilities allowed him to immensely contribution to China's diplomacy." He further noted that Zhou "was the founder and pioneer of diplomacy and the Foreign Ministry in China and he dedicated his life to world peace. Thus, his memory and legacy are a precious asset to the Ministry" (Liu, 2008, para. 2). This theme was repeated in 2018 at Zhou's 120th "birth anniversary." State-sponsored publications highlighted his frugality, while Xi Jinping gave a heartfelt speech praising his diplomatic contributions (Xi, 2018).

These efforts to routinely glorify deceased diplomats[20] are solidarity-building institutional rituals that help to physically, socially, and materially fix in memory the personal diplomatic histories of MOFA actors. A PRC envoy told me: "This is a good opportunity for officials and MOFA itself to remember these important people." When pressed on the benefits of such commemoration, he commented: "It is important for any organization to know its roots. Especially when we are doing important work for the country" (Interviewee 51, personal communication, August 1, 2018). Another consequence of this aspect of MOFA's habitus is that its agents are inclined to refer to history and to situate current issues in historical context, giving (rightly or wrongly) the impression that Chinese diplomacy is, in the words of several diplomats, "traditional." Indeed, as Ingram reveals (2009, p. 424), an institution's habitus is a product of its "history and experiences"; its current and previous inhabitants; and its preserved, performed, and iterated stories and traditions. An Oceanic envoy remarked, "When you have diplomats behave like that, you cannot but wonder whether they have a mind of their own" (Interviewee 62, personal communication, June 25, 2017).

One consequence of this reliance on historical knowledge is that, as one non-Chinese diplomat told me, "The Chinese [MOFA] have remarkable memory. They will be able to look through their files and can cite precisely what you said in the 1950s. They keep detailed records of everything you say, and this can be easily referred to. I have personally experienced this. They pull out things I have said before many years ago!" (Interviewee 63, personal communication, July 19, 2017). Similarly, in response to a question posed by a journalist on a trip organized by Taiwan to take foreign media to disputed islands, MOFA spokesperson Hua Chunying said: "I noticed this is the third time you asked. First, at an earlier press briefing, second, after the *lianghui* when you asked Foreign Minister Wang Yi and now you ask again" (AP Archive, 2016).

The persistent allusion to history among MOFA diplomats serves as a justificatory mechanism for many of its diplomatic practices. According to one Western diplomat, his Chinese colleagues "never seem to be able to think that they can do any wrong. They frequently remind us that China is a victim of history" (Interviewee 48, personal communication, June 24, 2017). Additionally, from the press briefings, whenever "controversial" questions (such as the SCS disputes or human rights issues) are brought up, spokespersons frequently state, "The international community agrees" or "This is the correct historical view of the international community"[21] to show the moral correctness of their stance. In SCS disputes, for example, assertive appeals of historical moral rightness have increasingly become commonplace (M. Li & Loh, 2015). In this way, history and accumulated beliefs and routines become institutional background knowledge.

Political Loyalty

In 2009, at the Eleventh National People's Congress Standing Committee, a law governing diplomats abroad, People's Republic of China Diplomatic Missions in Foreign Countries Act, was introduced (Zhongguo Xinwen, 2009c). This is the first-ever legislation on diplomats in modern China. Significantly, it switches the sequence between diplomats' "rights and obligations" (*quanli he yiwu* 权利和义务) to "obligations and rights" (*yiwu he quanli* 义务和权利). The government stressed that this switch was meant to prioritize obligations expected of diplomats before their personal rights. Article 8 of the legislation stipulates (in the first section) that diplomats must be loyal to the country and its people. The third section obliges personnel to be faithful to their duties and to work hard, while the sixth says diplomats must be obedient and compliant, must have work discipline, and, notably, must not resign while stationed abroad (Zhongguo Xinwen, 2009b).[22] The characters for "loyalty" (*zhong* 忠) appear no less than three times in the legislation and can be seen as a move to discursively augment loyalty, obedience, and duty.[23] Indeed, admission of applicants into MOFA rests not only on academic credentials but also on one's political persuasion: Clause 4 of Article 6 in the legislation notes that a prerequisite for overseas diplomats is one's "political quality and character"—a synonym for political fealty and allegiance. This piece of legislation is also important to show how the diplomatic field's shift toward greater discipline paralleled the broader "assertive turn" in China in 2009 that has been observed by scholars. More significantly, this legislation underscores how such structural shifts were already taking place before Xi Jinping took power in 2012. A respondent affiliated with MOFA says: "If we were to choose, we would choose someone who would make great contributions to China. Of course, the number one [criterion] is loyalty (*zhong cheng* 忠诚) and then, second, personal contribution—meaning sacrificing yourself and working through midnight" (Interviewee 36, personal communication, July 4, 2017).

This emphasis on political loyalty means that students who have studied international relations or social sciences abroad—even in prestigious universities—may find it difficult to enter MOFA because, in the words of a Chinese diplomat, "their educational experience overseas may contradict our ideology" and "it may have some issues with what the organization stands for. This time [when they are abroad] is particularly sensitive, as they are very impressionable" (Interviewee 64, personal communication, July 3, 2017). A Chinese envoy who had studied in another Asian country told me candidly: "First, it is rare that this [overseas education] can happen. Because of my studies there, *I am actually ranked lower in the ministry* compared to someone who studied in China. In fact, I am trying to move to another ministry or state-owned enterprise that is more cosmopolitan" (Interviewee 78, personal communication, July 11, 2018).

Institutional Discipline and Self-Regulation

One new rule flowing from the legislation governing overseas diplomats is the raising of the minimum age (from eighteen to twenty-three) for diplomats posted overseas (Zhongguo Xinwen, 2009a). This is functionally useful, as older personnel tend to have more academic credentials and longer work experience (Zhongguo Xinwen, 2009b). Another consideration, not officially articulated, is that older candidates are more mature politically and less susceptible to "dissenting views from host countries, particularly those of Western-liberal societies" (Interviewee 33, personal communication, July 5, 2017). A longer gestation period also allows more training and inculcation in the values and culture of the institution.

This alignment carries over into Chinese diplomats' personal lives. An Oceanic diplomat explains how PRC diplomats are "professional, intelligent, and clearly very disciplined, but when we go out for lunch, dinner, and drinks [with them], they always see these informal social gatherings as official events" (Interviewee 62, personal communication, June 25, 2017). One Chinese respondent similarly says that "Chinese culture for diplomacy is very careful—there's a saying that "there are no 'small things' in diplomacy" (*waijiao wu xiao shi* 外交无小事), so the [Foreign] Ministry must be very careful as a lot of small things can be amplified. They must be disciplined across all levels" (Interviewee 65, personal communication, July 31, 2017). The notion that "discipline" is a requirement and a pervasive trait may seem like an uninteresting point because all diplomats are expected to be professional and disciplined. Nonetheless, many restrictions are unique to China, to the extent that Chinese diplomats are expected to surrender their personal passports, have their movement restricted such that they cannot go on vacations, and submit to rules preventing their resignation. This was not always the case. A European diplomat reminisced how he had been able to meet his Chinese counterpart for weekly tennis sessions in the late 1980s and early 1990s (Interviewee 63, personal communication, July 19, 2017). A Chinese public servant shared with me an anecdote of how "insulted" he had felt when he asked his friend from MOFA out for lunch: "This is a friend I knew very well because we had gone to university together. So I really felt insulted when he said he could only meet me if he brought along a friend. I am not even a foreigner!" (Interviewee 66, personal communication, July 17, 2018).

The focus on discipline creates conditions where Chinese diplomatic assertiveness is keenly felt at the individual level because of the tight sticking to scripts, norms, and practices. That is to say, the institutional habitus disciplines MOFA actors to conform to prevailing diplomatic practices. Such discipline (together with the increase in resources and capital) has given rise to a perceptible increase in diplomatic assertiveness through microaggressions in diplomatic encounters and in assertive diplomatic discourse.[24] Indeed, several non-Chinese interviewees chorus the "feeling" that Chinese diplomats are displaying more confidence and are willing to display this publicly and privately. When quizzed on what this assertiveness entails, several interviewees point to their "confidence" and sometimes "arrogance." A diplomat sums this up: "It is not just [confident] behavior but also their demeanor, communication, and how meetings are arranged" (Interviewee 39, personal communication, July 19, 2018).

A source close to MOFA remarks: "Of course they [MOFA] must conform and be that way [assertive], they cannot do it any other way" (Interviewee 44, personal communication, September 1, 2017). It is certainly valid to say that the three aspects of MOFA's institutional habitus could apply in some way to other foreign ministries or state organizations. Nevertheless, Chinese MOFA differs in important ways from the foreign ministries of other countries. For example, MOFA's institutional habitus prevents its officials from speaking their minds and creates a reluctance to engage in one-to-one meetings with others. This is not what we would normally associate with diplomats. A Southeast Asian respondent puts it this way: "They are not flexible, a lot of them are linguists and not diplomacy trained, and they do things that go by the book. It means that part of that [training] is from linguistics. This has consequences for their worldview and ability" (Interviewee 35, personal communication, June 25, 2016).

From the interviewee's comments above, we can perceive how the adherence to discipline hinders smooth diplomatic interaction. Nevertheless, these practices appear to MOFA personnel just to be matters of common sense (which is a product of their group habitus). Indeed, in chapter 3 I wrote about how Chinese interlocutors justify their practices as "natural" outcomes or as "how things are done." What is more, actors themselves often attribute the nature of their diplomatic practices to how the organization has affected them.[25] One former diplomat told me: "You get numb to what you're doing. But we are not robots [*jiqi ren* 机器人] blindly following. When you are in the organization, you must and will believe" (Interviewee 54, personal communication, April 27, 2018).

As evinced above, we see individual habitus entangled with the institutional habitus in at least two ways. First, the history of the institution brings to bear its weight and exerts an influence on the individual habitus of PRC diplomats so that even "backstage" (see Goffman, 1959), there is little deviation from the "front stage."

Individual practices thus get disciplined publicly and privately as institutional scripts, history, and practices take precedence. Relatedly, while individuals are never completely without agency, mutual surveillance, legislative restrictions, requirements for political discipline, and selective hiring indicate a high degree of conformity across diplomats. This suggests that the institutional habitus has a greater influence over the inhabitants' habitus than the reverse. In sum, beyond the general importance of history, loyalty, and discipline, the diplomatic practices here show that while these practices are conditioned by the institutional habitus, their very enactment also reinforces the very structure that structures them.

MOFA's Identity Effects

How does understanding foreign ministries' habitus help us study identity? My contention is that foreign ministries play a critical role in giving content to a state's "actorness" and identity. I also suggest that a gap between MOFA's self-perception and others' perceptions of China's state identity emerges as an effect of the regulative and self-disciplining habitus of MOFA. If we take state identities to have both an internal and an external dimension, then the "external" dimension of state identities and its "actorness" obtain primarily from its foreign ministries.

While the importance of national and state identity is well acknowledged (Wæver et al., 1993, p. 22), the meaning of *identity* is debated. Scholars sometimes rely on state identity in their studies as something given and self-evident, without properly conceptualizing and constructing it (Callahan, 2006). Realists generally consider state identities as fixed, unchanging "billiard balls" à la classical realism (Waltz, 1979).[26] And liberalists, though seeing states as more complex intertwined entities, still view them as "solid" substances, with countries as actors managing their own affairs within formally demarcated territories (Keohane & Martin, 2003). It is in social constructivist literature that scholarship on identity is the richest and challenges the rationalist, materialist understandings of identity (Epstein, 2010, p. 328). Nevertheless, the constructivist project still leaves some theoretical gaps. Berenskoetter explains: "Much of the constructivist literature focuses on the 'Me' and leaves the 'I' undertheorized; that is, it focuses on how a sense of Self is defined in relation to other states in the international system with little consideration of internal sources of identity formation" (2014, p. 266).

Subotic and Zarakol further suggest that "because most IR scholarship brackets off domestic-level processes from scrutiny, it is often assumed that state identity is a given" and add that domestic "sources of identity (e.g. nationalism) are conceptualized as if they manifest themselves independently of international relations" (2012, p. 919).

This problem arises because the "internal" and the "external" tend to be studied in isolation. That is to say, not enough care is given to the dynamic interplay between the external and internal sources of identity supplied by institutions, like foreign ministries, that have clear internal-external facets.

Brubaker and Cooper also point out that constructivist studies of state identity are "an uneasy amalgam of constructivist language and essentialist argumentation" (2000, p. 6). Ringmar (1996, p. 452), for his part, flags the importance of the act of interpreting state identity: "While a state may consist of all kinds of bureaucratic structures, institutional mechanisms and other body-like organs, it is—as an entity endowed with an identity—necessarily at the mercy of the interpretations given to it through the stories in which it features." Phrased differently, interpretations and perceptions of state identity are critical to the construction of that very identity. In any event, we have no deep understanding of how foreign ministries influence a state's identity and image. Hence, this chapter complements existing accounts that locate domestic forces/institutions as an important source of state identity by showing how foreign ministries play a decisive role in informing states' external identity through their diplomatic practices and interactions with other diplomats. The interpretation of "foreign ministry"—through the organizational institutional habitus—is iterative and ongoing (albeit relatively durable). Therefore, the aspect of state identity under inquiry here does not fall into the "substantialist trap" (see Bucher and Jasper, 2017); nor does it commit the error of being so mercurial (or wholly relationally attained) that, being "everywhere," it becomes analytically inoperable (Brubaker & Cooper, 2000, p. 1).

In teasing out the link between foreign policy and state identity, Ashizawa shows how "identity functions as a source of a state's foreign policy," arguing that a state's identity creates preferences that, in turn, shape the country's foreign policy inclinations (2008, p. 595). State identities, he writes, "are observed in the way policymakers (therefore, persons) conceive of them, while they think they are acting as an agent of their state. Further, and as a common practice, actions undertaken by those policymakers on behalf of their states are observed as their state's foreign policy actions" (2008, p. 575).

Additionally, according to Tilley, *national identity* (internal) includes "formative history, ethnic components such as dress and language, and ideas about the collective political values" while *state identity* (external) refers to "qualities symbolically ascribed to the state by elites, meaningful to the international community and understood to determine the state's foreign policy orientation" (2003, pp. 46–47). Here I am concentrating on state (external) identity and how others in the world perceive this. This is important because there is a disjuncture between Chinese self-perception and others' perceptions of China's identity and image (see. e.g., D. Loh, 2017). Earlier, I explained how MOFA's habitus compels it and its agents to perform certain diplomatic practices in a fashion that also performs assertiveness. These diplomatic practices, for their part, form the materials upon which China's external identity is constructed and perceived by the self and others. In this case, the study concretizes the relational nature of identity (see also Hagström, 2015, p. 123) by showing how perceptions of China form from "the other." As Morozov and Rumelili say about the relationality of identity, "The Self can never be the sole author of its identity, and 'Self-centred' analyses of European identity are simply overlooking the ways in which external/spatial Others, such as Russia and Turkey, are shaping European identity in different ways" (2012, p. 29). In focusing on the discursive practices of "the Other," they zoom in on how Russia and Turkey, despite their subaltern status, have been able to influence articulations of what it means to "be" Europe. Contrarily, while there is certainly an exercise of discursive agency by other diplomats in the Chinese case, Beijing has, so far, fended off these attempts. In diplomacy, this self-other discourse arises out of diplomatic interactions most acutely and is the focus of inquiry here. Indeed, perceptions arising from private (and public) diplomatic encounters filter upwards and outwards, to the public, in at least two ways.

First, it is not uncommon (in fact, it is increasingly common) for non-Chinese diplomatic officials to speak about their diplomatic engagements with China to public audiences including the media, academics, and students. Non-Chinese diplomats told me, for instance, that they regularly met with scholars and reporters to give their candid views or answer media queries.[27] This information, particularly from the media, in turn, streams outward, informing public discourse on China. A 2019 Bloomberg report on China's diplomats captions this dynamic: "Foreign diplomats in Beijing say that the behavior of Chinese officials has become far more aggressive and assertive in private meetings in recent years. Their discussions have become more ideological, according to one senior foreign envoy, who described the behavior as a strong sense of grievance combined with increasing entitlement about China's international role and rights" (Bloomberg News, 2019, para. 8).

Second, the perceptions formed from these diplomatic interactions contribute to the "background knowledge" from which policymakers infer Chinese behavior. By reporting their findings to their capitals, diplomats generate authoritative country-specific knowledge and recommendations (see Neumann, 2012). This knowledge, for its part, feeds into the overall milieu from which states' leaders determine policies and sets the stage for how they interact with China. More recently, China's "aggressive" Twitter diplomats (chapter 5) have attracted considerable international attention, with analysts and officials imputing China's "wolf warrior" tendencies from their diplomatic tweets and magnifying China's supposedly "aggressive" identity. In sum, public and private diplomatic interactions play a decisive role in understanding and "producing" China.

In interviews, actors from other countries frequently take the behavior of these diplomats to represent China's diplomatic behavior and identity. A Western diplomat reveals: "China's diplomacy is getting increasingly assertive and also not very transparent. We can see this from their diplomats here when we deal with them" (Interviewee 67, personal communication, August 2, 2017). A Southeast Asian diplomat describes China as "definitely assertive, for sure. Some people call this assertive; some people call this a shift and a change. The quick answer is that they are stronger. They can increase diplomatic influence. China has a bigger international influence in the last five years—it is the *MOFA PRC pushing and driving it*" (Interviewee 68, personal communication, August 1, 2017).[28]

Yet another envoy underlines how Chinese diplomats are increasingly practicing "microaggressions," particularly over the SCS issue. While acknowledging that "China" is more than MOFA, he nonetheless adds, "The ministry's actions feed into China's increasingly assertive behavior on the world stage; their diplomatic behavior reflects that" (Interviewee 47, personal communication, August 31, 2017). Another East Asian diplomat recounts how difficult it is for him to get access to Chinese diplomats and how such difficulty "will affect how we deal with China" (Interviewee 5, personal communication, July 27, 2017). Observe how clearly these personal experiences supply the broader feelings and perceptions about "China," Chinese foreign policy, and Chinese diplomacy. One Chinese source comments (on Philippines' decision to bring its territorial dispute before the Permanent Court of Arbitration in 2013): "China's diplomacy and military is 'too rough' in its response toward the Philippines. It is not a good way, and surely the Philippines will respond in their own way" (Interviewee 10, personal communication, June 27, 2017). Furthermore, a Chinese interviewee says: "When Xi entered the PSC in 2007, these changes slowly happened. This brought about a shift into a Chinese foreign policy characterized by a recognition of China's power and capability. This sort of thinking then permeated the scholarly community and MOFA. So there is an effect there. But we think that other scholars and countries misunderstand our new confidence as some sort of assertiveness" (Interviewee 64, personal communication, July 3, 2017).

In the comments above, the mismatch between self-perceived confidence and an assertiveness perceived by others is clear. Speaking on behalf of the diplomatic community writ large, a non-Chinese diplomat opines:

> I think the diplomatic community here certainly share a sense that the Chinese diplomats are getting more confident, or assertive if you prefer. We talk about these things because we share information with close partners, and across the board it is uncanny how our experiences are similar. To your question, yes. Obviously, how they behave and what we observe them doing matter

in forming perceptions. They are not the only people we interact with. Our different desks have different sectors they reach out to. But MOFA is definitely the key institution. (Interviewee 68, personal communication, August 1, 2017)

The concatenation of domestic actors and the emergence of national identity in the Chinese context have not gone unconsidered. Whiting indicates how China's "national identity emerges in how the policy-making elite perceives and articulates the image of China in its relationship with the outside world" (1995, p. 296).[29] Moreover, the institutional habitus enforces discipline and self-regulation that foreclose the establishment of deep interpersonal relations with other diplomats from other countries. This gives rise to perceptions of "coldness" and inaccessibility and adds to the mystification of China.[30] It echoes Brown's (2017, p. 25) reflection that Chinese diplomats speak from "clear formulae and agreed postures that are trotted out" and that this practice "gives the impression of Chinese foreign policy being produced by a coldly calculating and highly rational machine . . . immune to human emotions."

In that connection, diplomatic interviewees from other countries frequently lament the difficulty in getting the Chinese diplomats to "open up" and form friendships. While acknowledging their professionalism and organizational discipline, some build ties with "informal" diplomatic interlocutors from other ministries, scholars, and Party organs because they perceive MOFA to be economical with information, ironically undermining MOFA as an unintended consequence (Interviewee 35, personal communication, June 25, 2016; Interviewee 30, personal communication, May 10, 2018). One Western diplomat underlined this difficulty: "It is difficult to get them into a room. When we do meet, they are pleasant enough, but they stick to the official line and don't say much. There is general reluctance on their part. I think that is true for most Chinese bureaucracies. We do our best to share information, but there is little reciprocity" (Interviewee 21, personal communication, July 1, 2017). This "accessibility problem" encountered by some Western countries was corroborated by a Commonwealth diplomat who shared in some detail how, "in 2010–2014, the Americans were having difficulties accessing Chinese diplomats. Even when some meetings took place, they [Chinese] refused to give name cards, making the Americans wonder if they were spooks and if China was not interested in engaging at all!" (Interviewee 75, personal communication, November 16, 2018). Yet another diplomat told me: "The Chinese are difficult to understand. They self-censor as well. It is difficult to negotiate with MOFA people or persuade them because they do not appear singularly. They are always accompanied by others so they can keep watch [on each other]. I have not met any really open official in my many years dealing with them" (Interviewee 69, personal communication, July 9, 2017). And a Chinese academic with close links with MOFA confided to me:

Chinese diplomats don't like to interact, especially with international scholars. They are afraid of using English, especially those whose English is not so
good. Sometimes when they do interact, they do so to push a point or say certain things. Sometimes, this does not leave a good impression on other academics. I know because I myself sometimes don't have a good impression of
our own MOFA when they interact! (*laughs*) (Interviewee 32, personal communication, July 11, 2017)

A Chinese diplomat rejected this characterization when I put it to him that
others had problems "being friends" with them. Nevertheless, he was unable to explain why others held this persistent view of Chinese practitioners (Interviewee 77,
personal communication, November 16, 2018). What is evinced here is that other
countries (through their MOFA and officials) impute China's diplomacy and its identity through its diplomatic agents—it is how others construct their view of Chinese
behavior and identity. While it is true to say that this is the case for other countries'
ministries of foreign affairs, given the general lack of access to information, many
officials can get glimpses of China's identity only through these official channels. One
Western envoy told me: "I speak to scholars to try and get multiple views, but that is
mainly because MOFA doesn't like speaking to us! I think if their MOFA opened
up, it would do for them and China a whole world of good! For its image, diplomacy,
transparency, and so on" (Interviewee 67, personal communication, August 2, 2017).

In contrast, a diplomat whose country enjoys multiple channels of communication puts it this way: "Many countries have problems [understanding China]. For
us, we speak not only to them [MOFA] but also to their Party organs, think tanks,
businesses, and scholars consistently. We have good access" (Interviewee 37, personal
communication, June 24, 2016). In other words, the key to more precise interpretations of China, broadly speaking, is accessibility. Recalling my discussion in chapter 2
on MOFA's implementing capacities, one can also construe MOFA's rising influence
from its ability to access the leaders of other countries. One non-Chinese diplomat
elaborates on this point: "The Chinese ambassador has direct access to the prime
minister in this country. And he will only speak to junior ministers and above. Such
access, of course, lends him and the ministry some arrogance because not all diplomats have this privilege. As far as I know, in most countries, because of China's importance and because of the diplomats' requests, Chinese ambassadors have very good
direct access to host countries' ministers and key leaders" (Interviewee 75, personal
communication, November 16, 2018).

MOFA, as the main interface of access, controls (by design or otherwise) how
others perceive the state. I hasten to add that I am not alleging that MOFA is the
only source of China's state identity or that there are no internal contestations of its

identity (see Abdelal et al., 2006). Also, I do not purport to capture the "essence" of Chinese state identity. Indeed, it is important to acknowledge the consequential identity effects of the myriad of nonstate actors such as the flows of tourists, students, businesses, and so forth (Mahler, 2000) and the role of substate actors that are traditionally missed in studies of Chinese state identity. The point here is simply to highlight the substantial yet underacknowledged role of MOFA's role in constructing China's identity—a process that is rarely systematically theorized and scarcely empirically detailed, even as MOFA's important identity effects are recognized (e.g., Gries, 2005). Put simply, diplomatic encounters and foreign policy discourses engendered by diplomats have important identity effects.[31]

In sum, the emphasis paid to the assertive quality of China by non-Chinese diplomats helps fuel the broader identity structures of China. Johnston, in his book on China's socialization, insists that it matters a great deal, "when explaining state behavior, how small groups, even individuals, are socialized through social interaction with other small groups and individuals in other states (and non-state entities)" (2008, p. xv). One East Asian envoy's experience drives home this point (Interviewee 76, personal communication, June 25, 2016):

> My ambassador has never met China's foreign minister. Two weeks before he was about to leave for his new posting in Europe, he received a surprise phone call from him, asking to meet him. He was so angry! Absolutely furious! He saw this as an insult because he [China's foreign minister)] obviously knew our ambassador didn't have the time to meet as he was moving posts. *We could see how their international relations and diplomacy were going to play out.*[32]

Here a particular capacity to coordinate—access to the ministry and the minister, and the manipulation of schedules and accessibility—is clearly brought to the foreground. The frequent, everyday interchanges between international diplomats are not neutral, insignificant moments; they are politically productive interactions that decisively intervene in the making of China's diplomacy and state identity. Just as we can map out the habitus of an individual only through its practices, we can only, in a parallel move, identify the institutional habitus through its institutional practices and objects, namely the presence of intervening materials, collectively enacted practices, and the history, ethos, and values of the organization. This is what I have sought to do by illustrating the consequentiality and pervasiveness of preprepared documents, of organizational rituals such as the memorialization of the deceased, and the ubiquity of history that permeates the material and nonmaterial elements of the organization.

Conclusion

Institutions are not merely aggregations of individuals because they adjust and correct individual behavior in multifarious ways (e.g., Rogowski, 1999; Bendor & Hammond, 1992). As an interstitial entity—straddling the "state" and the individual "agent"—the organization is a fertile field for studying IR and state identity. Focusing on MOFA, this chapter makes the case for understanding organizations through their institutional habitus in IR. In that regard, I suggest three conditions that a habitus may develop: synergistic habitus and mutual socialization; the presence of a meaningful field for expression; and historical stability.

Through the Chinese example, I have shown the effects of MOFA's institutional habitus. Whereas the habitus of an individual resides permanently with her, the habitus of an institution must be repeatedly sustained to sediment. In MOFA it is maintained in three ways—iterative reinscription of institutional memory and invocation of history; recurrent displays of fealty to the president; and organizational and personal self-regulation and discipline. Thereafter, I explained that MOFA is a critical institution in forming perceptions of China. I suggested that the gap between Chinese self-perceptions of "assertiveness" and other diplomats' perceptions arises from the disciplining and regulative capacities of MOFA and the broader diplomatic field.[33] Johnston states how "Chinese leaders' sensitivity to the international image made them responsive" to international opprobrium and expectations (2008, p. 79; see also D. Loh & Loke, 2023). Being, quite literally, the front stage of this image, MOFA, not least through its press briefings, is the *first and usually only* institution that responds to such interactions. MOFA's relevance and importance in managing and projecting China's image and identity cannot be overstated.

Having explored the practices, sites, and institutions of Chinese diplomacy, I turn to Twitter to explore its materiality in relation to Chinese diplomacy. I argue that Chinese diplomats' Twitter forays are an extension of its recent energetic diplomacy and that they gesture at the (new) ways diplomatic power is exercised and understood.

FIVE

China's Twitter Diplomacy

#Taiwan is part of #China. No attempts to split China will ever succeed. Those who play with fire will only get themselves burned. Period.

AMBASSADOR CUI TIANKAI, July 12, 2019, Twitter[1]

Appreciate #JamesCurran & @FareedZakaria vision & objectiveness. Big doesn't mean threat. Giant panda more dangerous than bald eagle? KungFu Panda adored by all. ONLY THERAPY for dangerous #Chinaphobia: Openness & Inclusiveness.

MOFA SPOKESPERSON'S OFFICE, December 12, 2019, Twitter[2]

Starting from around 2019, China started to use Twitter to convey its diplomatic messages and activities: the number of official Chinese diplomatic Twitter accounts multiplied to over eighty in 2020 compared to an initial seventeen in October 2018 (*The Economist*, 2020).[3] Significantly, a study on Chinese Twitter diplomacy found that PRC envoys on Twitter are now exercising "less restraint, discretion, and caution than might typically be expected from Chinese officials who speak in public or post on social media" (A. Huang & Wang, 2019, p. 3000). This chapter builds on earlier discussions of Chinese diplomatic assertiveness and sheds light on the ways Beijing has conducted diplomacy through Twitter and the consequent implications. How have social media—specifically Twitter—changed the conduct of diplomacy vis-à-vis "face-to-face" diplomacy? How does Chinese assertiveness manifest and circulate through Twitter?

To answer these questions, the chapter first surveys current studies on social media diplomacy and shows how Chinese Twitter diplomacy remains understudied despite its current widespread use and international attention. Next, through a qualitative analysis of some Chinese diplomatic tweets—from Zhao Lijian, Hua Chunying, and Zha Liyou—I suggest that China's Twitter diplomacy produces two interconnected effects in relation to diplomatic assertiveness: amplification of existing discourses and the exercise of discursive power. Finally, extending the discussion in the preceding chapter, I examine preliminary reactions to Beijing's Twitter diplomacy and explain how PRC's Twitter diplomacy extends Chinese assertiveness to the online sphere.

There is no shortage of studies examining the link between diplomacy and social media (e.g., Seib, 2012; Bjola, 2015; Duncombe, 2017). Importantly, these analyses observe how foreign ministries of all stripes must now grapple with the effects of social and digital technologies on diplomacy. Bjola (2015, p. 4), for one, posits that social media "can be described as nothing less than a revolution in the practices of diplomacy." Moreover, the use of social media by practitioners "change[s] practices of how diplomats engage in informational management, public diplomacy, strategy planning, international negotiations or even crisis management" (2015, p. 4). Focusing on Twitter, Duncombe's research on US-Iran negotiations (between 2013 and 2015) found that the social networking application played a decisive role in constructing and addressing legitimacy concerns for both sides—culminating in the successful 2015 nuclear deal. Like Bjola, Duncombe observes how social media are "changing the space within which diplomacy unfolds" (2017, p. 546), even as she underlines how scholarship on "state-to-state diplomatic engagement through social media remains underexamined" (2017, p. 549). Also concentrating on Twitter, Manor and Pamment (2019) investigate the politics of "diplomatic prestige" through the platform. They suggest that international actors accrue diplomatic prestige through the "strategic management" of Twitter activities. Paying attention to Israeli's Twitter diplomacy during the 2014 Gaza War, Manor and Crilley (2019, p. 68) argue that foreign ministries today have an added role as media producers: "MFAs are now media actors that produce and circulate their own media content directly to social media audiences and adopt media logics in their daily operations."

These scholars' contributions to enriching our understanding of social media and diplomacy notwithstanding, they seldom go "beyond American and European case studies" (Spry, 2019, p. 95), echoing a similar charge I make concerning the practice-theoretical literature on foreign ministries. Despite its growing importance, we still do not have a proper understanding of China's diplomacy on Twitter. What is more, predominant analyses of China's foreign affairs—surveyed in chapter 1—tend to remain either at the structural, global level or at the domestic levels. Social media, and in particular Twitter, in no small part owing to its relative novelty, seldom figure in academic discourses of China's IR. This omission is all the more significant given that Chinese diplomats have received "written instructions" from President Xi to "show more fighting spirit," authorizing them to take the battle over diplomatic narratives onto Twitter (Zhai & Yew, 2020). In response to claims of assertive tweeting by its diplomats, MOFA insists that diplomats will continue to "resolutely safeguard" national sovereignty, adding that "if we are attacked, we will certainly counterattack" (Zhai & Yew, 2020). Practitioners, for their part, have elaborated on the principle of this diplomatic "fighting spirit." Hua Chunying, former spokesperson, called on diplomats to better "grasp the microphone" and to "clearly express China's position and attitude" (*Taipei Times*, 2019, p. 6). Likewise, in November 2019 China's then foreign minister urged MOFA diplomats to show "fighting spirit" in the international arena (Ruwitch, 2019). In the next month, the official Twitter account of the Spokesperson's Office of MOFA was registered (even though its first Tweet was only sent in February 2020).

The literature on Chinese foreign policy lags in understanding the reciprocities between diplomacy and social media. There are a few exceptions, however. One is Bjola and Lu's study on Weibo and Chinese diplomacy. Through a comparative analysis, the authors found that actors like Japan, the US, and the EU creatively leveraged Weibo to directly engage with the Chinese public. Three processes were found to be at play: "digital agenda-setting, digital presence-expansion and digital conversation-generating," where each factor "speaks to an important dimension of exerting influence: message content, informational reach and mode of engagement with the audience" (2015, p. 72). Another study is A. Huang and Wang's (2019, p. 3000) analysis of Chinese Twitter diplomacy, which concludes that tweets from Chinese diplomatic agencies conveyed "Chinese political views in a pluralistic way," "used hashtags purposefully," and "interconnected to form an online narrative." Others have used quantitative tools to make sense of China's Twitter activities. Alden and Chan (2021), for instance, conducted a "hashtag" analysis to assess the topics on which China desires to "influence the conversation" (2021, p. 7). They found that during the Covid pandemic, the hashtag #Covid19 was by far the most used, producing positive narratives on China's pandemic management by Chinese diplomats. The authors suggested that Beijing was "utilising the Twitter to shape the emerging debate on a given topic" (2021, p. 10), thereby underlining the current prominence of Twitter in representations of China's foreign policy signaling.

Adding to this literature, I have conducted interviews and a qualitative, granular analysis of the tweets of Zhao Lijian, Zha Liyou, and Hua Chunying—widely seen as diplomatic "wolf warriors" who are the most striking exemplars of Chinese assertiveness (D. Loh, 2020b; Landale, 2020; Hille, 2020a)—to show how discursive power and diplomatic assertiveness are reproduced and represented in the online sphere. As case examples (Levy, 2008, p. 4), these act as a synecdoche for Chinese Twitter diplomacy, furnishing broad insights into an emerging phenomenon. Such a reading, which is sensitive to contexts behind the snide and sometimes undiplomatic language used, is well suited to identify themes that emerge across their Twitter activity and the ways in which others perceive such diplomacy.

The Case of China's Twitter Diplomacy

There are three distinctive reasons why the PRC's Twitter diplomacy is intriguing and important to examine. First, the adoption of Twitter for diplomacy is relatively new. Hua Chunying, MOFA's spokesperson and the director general of the Department of Information, joined Twitter only in October 2019 and sent out her first tweet in February 2020. This exactly parallels the timeline of the MOFA spokesperson's official Twitter account. For China, this is a "huge departure" from more conservative offline diplomatic messaging both in forcefulness and in sheer volume. Research by the German Marshall Fund "suggests there has been a 300% increase in official Chinese state Twitter accounts over the last year, with a fourfold increase in posts" (Landale, 2020, para. 19).

Second, China's Twitter diplomacy is noteworthy as China's diplomats grapple with and push the boundaries of what is acceptable (or not) to domestic and foreign audiences. Consequently, we sometimes see experimentation turning controversial as diplomats wrestle with what the standards of "appropriate" conduct on Twitter are and what diplomatic styles are palatable to international/domestic audiences.[4] China's Twitter diplomacy is also exceptional given that Twitter is banned domestically. The fact that MOFA can legitimately use a forbidden tool—conducting "exceptional" practices—reveals not only the prominence of MOFA but also the hierarchical structure of the diplomatic field that I charted in chapter 3. This point cannot be overstated because, compared to other state and Party organs, MOFA is the first and remains one of the few state-sanctioned users of Twitter.

Finally, China's Twitter diplomacy is different from that of other international diplomatic Twitter actors with regard to the "forcefulness" of diplomatic messages. While assertive Twitter diplomacy is not restricted to China, there is strong prima facie evidence that the PRC is most prolific in this regard. To be sure, a principal motivator of the PRC's Twitter diplomacy is to enable criticism of Western politicians, media, and/or governments (e.g., Toosi, 2019; Sharma, 2020). This is not surprising, as a key directive from Xi is for his diplomats to take the fight abroad to defend China's image. In the main, Chinese Twitter diplomacy warrants further investigation to address the "dearth of empirical studies" on "how social media facilitate" or hinder interstate dialogue and how they figure in broader debates of representations of Chinese assertiveness (Duncombe, 2017, p. 546).[5] This chapter identifies two processes at play—the amplification of discourse and the exercise of discursive power. These, I argue, extend existing communicative practices but also prefigure new forms of diplomatic communication, power, and control.

China's Exercise of Discursive Power

In China, there is a lively public discourse concerning China's discursive power (*huayu quan* 话语权) (G. Zhang, 2011). Concretely, this Chinese formulation of discursive power emphasizes the *right to know, the right to express views*, and the *right to participate* in international affairs. Discursive power, Zhang adds, is a definitional or "meta power": the ability to decide on the rules of the (international) game. Gregory (2018, para. 10) adds that this emphasis on discursive power is animated by domestic concerns—"China has historically put a greater emphasis on a government's discursive legitimacy than the West, emphasizing that things must be named correctly (*mingzhen*) for them to be talked about sensibly (*yanshun*)." Indeed, this echoes Bourdieu's notion of "symbolic power." For Bourdieu, symbolic power involves the "production of common sense or, more precisely, . . . the monopoly over legitimate naming" (1989, p. 21), which more or less captures the meaning of *mingzhen yanshun* (名真言顺). In appropriating the right to impose and legitimize names, categories, and what "common sense" entails, discursive power works similarly to symbolic power, which is "the power to produce and to impose the legitimate vision of the world" (Bourdieu, 1989, p. 20). Indeed, as I demonstrated throughout the chapters, better-positioned players in the field reinforce existing rules of the game—which are then taken as legitimate or commonsensical for participants.

Incremental increases in discursive power, for the Chinese, are attempts to exert their symbolic power—to have a say in defining, naming, and categorizing the structure of international relations and to impose views "of legitimate divisions" (1989, p. 22). Xi Jinping has described the "international discursive order" as one where "the West is strong, and China is weak" (*xiqiang wo ruo* 西强我弱). He has articulated China's desire to grow its discourse power and has demanded stronger efforts to improve China's "right to speak" in order to make this possible (Xi, 2020). Taking instruction from these understandings, I conceptualize discourse power as the public and private capacities to authoritatively articulate and define policy positions across various international issues. MOFA's discourse power, through Twitter, represents its ability to project Chinese narratives and stories further, faster, and more effectively than what it could before.

The notion of a Chinese discursive power is not lost on China watchers. Bill Bishop (cited in Toosi, 2019, para. 6), for example, notes that the Chinese leadership "feel like their international discourse power is significantly smaller than it should be." Zhao (2016, p. 1), for her part, suggests that "China places more emphasis on discursive power than other states." What is more, Twitter is not just a means to exercise diplomatic discursive power internationally. Domestically, China's Twitter diplomacy also serves as a mark of distinction (Bourdieu, 1984) as officials' nationalistic tweets recirculate and frequently go viral on Chinese social media. Twitter usage thus sets MOFA and its inhabitants apart from others in that it is an "accreditation" that others cannot access. Recall chapter 2's discussion on power and how an attentiveness to practices and processes of diplomacy helps recast notions of power in IR. MOFA's use of Twitter, much like its scheduling, implementing, and advising functions, increases its influence and manifests and contributes to China's assertiveness. In this connection, China's diplomatic activities on Twitter bring this aim into sharp relief.

First, in its ability to use Twitter, MOFA has, quite literally, *distinguished* itself from other state organs and ministries. Local societal norms and regulations are thus "suspended" to serve diplomatic ends. How does this special dispensation allow MOFA to exercise power? According to a non-MOFA Chinese official (Interviewee 66, personal communication, December 15, 2019), "It is quite clear they are allowed to do this and there is a need for them to do this. Their work requirements are such that Twitter allows them to speak up and speak for China. Only MOFA are uniquely positioned to do that." A Chinese reporter observes, "Twitter is quite new to MOFA, on the whole. The fact is, they have made this 'official' and use it so consistently now. I think this makes it clear that they are different and *speaks to their current rank*" (Interviewee 82, personal communication, May 2, 2020). That MOFA is allowed to use Twitter—something generally forbidden—serves as a cachet distinguishing them from the other, secondary diplomatic players listed in chapter 3. Put differently, it validates MOFA as the authorized vehicle to transmit, discuss, and articulate China's foreign policies. MOFA and others are constantly (and visually) reminded of this distinction as MOFA diplomats respond to and tweet prolifically, raising the profile of MOFA at home and abroad. China's Twitter diplomacy thus goes some way to showing that MOFA, far from being sidelined, is in fact, at the forefront of realizing Xi Jinping's most important international goals. A PRC diplomat adds that their Twitter diplomacy is "due to the nature of MOFA's job. It is MOFA's job to speak and engage with the outside world; it is natural, then, that we do this. Of course, this also parallels China's foreign policy and diplomacy's importance. After us, other departments will follow and will learn from our experiences" (Interviewee 70, personal communication, November 10, 2019).

Similarly, a former Chinese diplomat (Interviewee 7, personal communication, November 11, 2019) reckons that engaging in diplomatic Twitter performances is "good" because "it adds to their [China's] discursive power, and also shows the increasing openness and strength of China's diplomacy that is much needed right now." This "discursive power" is also referenced by a MOFA-affiliated scholar. He states that Twitter use represents a "positive desire to expand our discursive power, and diplomats' tweets can be seen primarily through this lens" (Interviewee 83, personal communication, May 9, 2020). He adds, "This is a natural step to take in response to the Western media's bias, and one major reason is to push back directly against faulty and inaccurate reporting on China!"

This sort of discursive power generally entails the display of both "attack" and "defense," as seen in a May 8, 2020, tweet by Hua (2020d) that garnered 715 "retweets" and almost four thousand "likes." In response to Washington's calls for an independent investigation of the coronavirus outbreak, it declares, "The #US keeps calling for transparency [and] investigation. Why not open up Fort Detrick [and] other bio-labs for international review? Why not invite #WHO [and international] experts to the US to look into #COVID19 source [and] response?" Another tweet by Hua (2020c), responding to accusations of China's ill intent behind its "mask diplomacy" amid the pandemic, highlights this defensive-offensive dynamic as well: it maintains that China has simply chosen to "reciprocate kindness and help others to the best of our ability." In a jibe at detractors of China's "mask diplomacy," the Chinese diplomat suggests that those "badmouthing China" would rather the country "stand by and turn blind to others' suffering." Such tweets are often visually arresting, since images can be added, and are often laden with emotive language, in contrast to traditional closed-door diplomacy with regard to managing disputes and disagreements. To an important extent, being able to show anger, disagreement, and dismay publicly is important to Chinese diplomats. Many diplomats themselves believe that it befits China's current might and power.

A PRC envoy notes that what we are seeing now is a "harmonization of Twitter activities." He explains:

> In the past, usually only diplomats and embassies in big powers had a Twitter account. I believe it was the one [Chinese consulate] in San Francisco that opened it first. Now we want to reach everywhere, and in every country there is. Of course, this shows our reach and capabilities because it is not just Twitter, but this adds onto our Facebook, online and offline media, and physical activities of our diplomats overseas. (Interviewee 70, personal communication, November 10, 2019)

As noted in chapter 2, after MOFA set up the spokesperson system, China's Ministry of National Defense followed suit with MOFA's guidance— representing a new type of facilitating and advising power unique to MOFA. The accumulated experiences of MOFA's Twitter engagement similarly add to MOFA's advising repertoire. Thus the decision of the International Liaison Department of the Communist Party of China, an important diplomatic actor, to open a Twitter account in April 2020 was impelled in no small part by MOFA's successful and high-profile use of Twitter

(Interviewee 82, personal communication, May 2, 2020). Hu Zhaoming, spokesperson of that department, sent out its maiden tweet in the same month the account was set up, urging political cooperation among 230 international political parties against the Covid-19 pandemic (Z. Hu, 2020). The PRC's Twitter activities are of course not the only representation or outcome of China's bid to both increase and display its discursive power, but Twitter diplomacy is now an increasingly important conduit for representations of China's assertive foreign policy.

In sum, China's Twitter diplomacy has increased its discursive power in two main ways. First, it gives Chinese diplomats greater and quicker awareness of what foreign actors are saying about China. Consequently, where they previously could not intervene directly (or were simply not aware), they are now able to engage with others almost instantaneously. This was evinced by Hua Chunying's almost immediate responses to perceived slights by Washington via the social networking platform. For example, it took less than a day for her to strike back at then acting director of national intelligence Richard Grenell for his barely concealed barb about the Chinese government and "untrustworthy" 5G vendor Huawei (Hua, 2020a). Likewise, Hua dismissed, on the very same day, the US Department of State's tweet that "Huawei and other Chinese state-backed tech companies are Trojan horses for Chinese intelligence," calling it "worst selling fiction." She then pointed out alleged hypocrisy on the part of the White House: "How about #CryptoLeaks scandal and Snowden stories?" (Hua, 2020b). Such a rapid response would not have been possible through MOFA's daily press conference, as this is a question-directed interaction with a time lag. Also, as is observed elsewhere, Twitter allows international actors to establish a "direct link of communication with foreign audiences in order to obtain their support," and this is superior to "traditional methods of dissemination including pamphlets and radio broadcasts" since it makes possible instantaneous communication (T. Jones & Mattiacci, 2017, p. 741).

Second, Chinese capabilities, professionalism, and "care" can get a very public airing among foreign and domestic audiences. This, in effect, projects China's diplomatic nous to the world. A respondent observes: "Using social media like Twitter is one good example to show [China's power [and competence]. In Singapore's case, I think the Chinese embassy in Singapore has been very active on Facebook, sharing things from their coronavirus efforts. They are posting very regularly to share how many masks they donate and to demonstrate their outreach efforts' capabilities. This allows them to showcase their resources" (Interviewee 81, personal communication, April 20, 2020).

Certainly, the Chinese embassy in Singapore reached out directly to Chinese citizen-workers during the pandemic to provide medical supplies (D. Loh, 2020a). Such practices were replicated elsewhere. In Manchester, UK, the Chinese embassy distributed 12.7 tonnes of supplies to Chinese students, including herbal medicine, masks, and disinfectant wipes (Kwan, 2020). Not only "exceptional" acts of diplomacy but also "ordinary" diplomacy, when properly publicized and narrated, reinforces the diplomatic discursive power that China craves. Zha Liyou's tweets have displayed the embassy's ability to help in consular matters. In one instance in 2019, Zha was "*@ mentioned*" by someone seeking assistance for two Chinese nationals in India. He was able to respond directly, publicly, and very quickly: "We have requested personnel to assist. The two Chinese tourists will go to FRO⁶ for certain procedures. Friends familiar with FRO should also help" (Zha, 2019). Thus displaying the power to mobilize, act, and corral resources is an act of diplomatic power. While this publicity could have been created through traditional forms of media, a contact stresses how "social media and Twitter in particular make these [acts] highly visible, shareable, and quick; this makes the message even more powerful" (Interviewee 79, personal communication, December 28, 2019). As such, the amplification of Chinese-sanctioned discourses is part of the process to "authoritatively articulate and define" matters concerning China's own rise and its politics.

The Amplification of Discourse

One discernible effect of China's Twitter diplomacy is that it has afforded MOFA another vehicle to extend and promote state-sanctioned narratives. What was previously considered the domain of state-controlled media is now also a core function of embassies and diplomats as they take on the role of "media producers" in the age of social media (Manor and Crilley, 2019). Twitter presents itself as a low-economic-cost option to broaden the reach of China's messages to more overseas audiences. This contrasts with China's Weibo and WeChat accounts, which have limited global reach owing to the censorship exerted over them and the limited number of non-Chinese users (Y. Lin, 2019). By contrast, Twitter diplomacy enables the courting of foreign audiences. Indeed, an interviewee who worked in the media industry told me that "China's Twitter diplomats can engage and speak directly to other citizens abroad, something that WeChat did not previously allow" (Interviewee 81, personal communication, April 20, 2020).

A Chinese scholar explains how the voice of the foreign ministry has increased considerably because of Twitter:

> For MOFA, they are showing their attitude alongside the official take, but in a much more intimate way. So, we see MOFA's Twitter or any related Chinese diplomats' Twitter posts to be more robust in terms of the language and to be provoking, emotionally. It feels like you are hearing somebody talking to you. So, the benefit here is to get rid of the stereotype that MOFA people or

Chinese diplomats are dull, boring, and robotic figures. They have certainly raised their profile domestically, compared to others. (Interviewee 79, personal communication, 28 December 2019).

One MOFA contact told me that Twitter facilitates the spread of official messages to its overseas citizens and the sizable group of noncitizens overseas who are ethnic Chinese. Indeed, the courting of overseas Chinese (*huaqiao* 华侨) has ramped up under Xi (D. Loh, 2023), and social media are one tool that allows direct access to them. This MOFA contact explained that Twitter "gives diplomats more leeway to speak than before. You can say this is a level up in terms of telling China's story. Definitely in telling China's story and messages in a new way. This will only increase, further befitting our big-power status" (Interviewee 83, personal communication, May 9, 2020). A Southeast Asian journalist who reports mainly on Chinese politics observes a growing "flexibility" of Chinese diplomats in their Twitter activities:

> They can now say the things that MOFA was not able to say before on other, more formal occasions. Twitter's public image as a social media platform can allow MOFA to insinuate a lot of things, throw out a lot of strong words, and provoke a lot of sentiments. It gives diplomats more flexibility, and they are being more flexible in the sense that *they can now say more things than before because of Twitter.* (Interviewee 81, personal communication, April 20, 2020)[7]

Thus the use of Twitter for diplomatic communication on Twitter means that China's voice is being projected louder, faster, and more conspicuously, while the profile of MOFA is raised. Indeed, a Chinese media source states that even as Twitter helps project China's diplomacy abroad, it is simultaneously playing to domestic audiences: "If Chinese envoys gave a friendly, cooperative impression, it might not go down well with the Chinese people. So we see how Chinese diplomats have hardened their diplomacy since 2012" (Interviewee 82, personal communication, May 2, 2020). He adds that "if China's diplomats tried to secure peaceful relations through compromise, it would not go down well with the Chinese people. This is the reason Chinese diplomacy has hardened in the past five years. This is perceived as increasing China's power through its power to speak." To be sure, Zhao Lijian himself clarifies how Twitter acts as a "weapon" to counter "negative narratives." Twitter, he insists, "allowed Chinese diplomats to tell the true picture" (B. Smith, 2019, para. 15).

Twitter, then, has amplified diplomatic narratives in two major ways. First, it has empowered Chinese diplomats to reach more people, at home and abroad. Domestically, Twitter has expanded China's reach to netizens who regularly scale the great "Firewall" by presenting a competing (and compelling) alternative to Western sources. Internationally, Twitter can better reach three main audiences: (1) overseas

Chinese,[8] (2) Chinese citizens living abroad, and (3) the domestic audiences of other societies. A Chinese scholar based in Guangdong told me, "Beijing is aware that many overseas Chinese, including international students from China, are able to get access to Twitter. So it is a struggle to win the heart of the Chinese diaspora, broadly speaking" (Interviewee 79, personal communication, December 28, 2019). Such maneuvers are different from those of traditional Chinese media and Chinese-inflected social platforms, which have limited reach vis-à-vis Twitter.

Second, because of the quick-fire nature of Twitter and the increasing propensity of Chinese diplomats to react with hostility over perceived slights and criticisms, the volume of diplomatic messages has increased, in tandem with every Twitter interaction. The consequence is that the discursive amplification increases China's discursive power. Indeed, China's Twitter diplomacy has incited new forms of communication practices that are more contingent, flexible, and innovative. A Western media contact recounts his experience communicating with Chinese diplomats on Twitter:

> I reach out to them in their DMs [direct messages], and, surprisingly, some of them actually respond and speak to me on Twitter DMs. Those that respond tend to be the more active ones. Yes, they are responsive, and this kind of instantaneity is rather new. They also respond to my tweets—defending or criticizing tweets deemed to be critical of China. Again, this sort of rapid response was not seen before and is enabled by Twitter. (Interviewee 80, personal communication, March 30, 2020)

This presents a deviation from prior practices (the reliance on the fax machine mentioned earlier comes to mind), where attempts to reach diplomats directly and in an unsolicited fashion were often met with silence.

In the main, China's various Twitter diplomatic activities coalesce to form particular strands of narratives that China seeks to promote. A. Huang and Wang (2019, p. 3001) term this a "timid polyphony": "Public diplomacy practitioners have relative freedom to choose strategies and content for daily communication, permitting wide use of timid polyphony on Twitter. Timid polyphony is the use of diverse voices and perspectives to demonstrate and endorse government initiatives. Using hashtags, mentions, and time-phased information releases, Chinese diplomats could devote single tweets to particular aspects of China stories but link tweets across the network to form a narrative."

A Southeast Asian respondent comments that it is "evident that Chinese diplomats are getting more and more involved in Twitter." He notes how Twitter allows Chinese diplomats to extend their defensive posture abroad and in multiple virtual-geographic areas: "More often than not, they have been taking a more defensive approach when tackling posts on Twitter and are seemingly using it as a tool to defend actions by the Chinese government. They now see the value of Twitter and are using it to hopefully sway Westerners and people in general to support their actions and not reject their ideals in multiple areas through their Twitter network tied to their embassies" (Interviewee 81, personal communication, April 20, 2020).

Twitter diplomacy thus spreads and amplifies existing diplomatic discourse but also produces *new communicative practices* that were not previously available to diplomats. The instantaneity and spontaneity increasingly extended to diplomats demonstrate this clearly. An editor for a major media organization recounts his experience interacting with Chinese diplomats and compares it to his exchanges with them in a pre-Twitter setting:

> A few things strike me as odd about Chinese diplomats on Twitter. One, they start with the ability to veer from script. Having watched for many years Chinese diplomats recite precisely the same "correct" answers to queries, it is strange to see diplomats speak off script at all to foreigners in any venue. Two, the variation in their rhetoric, feistiness, ability to be rude . . . even to politicians and other public figures . . . suggests they have been *given an incredible amount of discretion in exercising "discourse power."* Three, and this is something I had noticed before the recent Covid-19 shenanigans about the US Army, they are increasingly using Kremlin-style tactics, amplify[ing] fringe propaganda . . . that appears aimed to sow doubt about the truth and divisions in society, particularly in America. (Interviewee 80, personal communication, March 30, 2020)[9]

Thus a shift brought about by the Twitter platform and its usage by diplomats has allowed more flexibility in diplomatic messages. Noticeably, the enlargement in Chinese diplomats' communication repertoires has not only amplified diplomatic messages/messaging but also incited an accompanying increase in China's (and MOFA's) discursive power.

Resistance Within and Without

This section reviews the resistance engendered by China's Twitter diplomacy. As mentioned in the previous chapter, even the staff of an organization like MOFA are not monochromatically compliant and disciplined, as the exercise of power is never frictionless. I will first discuss the international reactions before broaching domestic resistance. Internationally, China's Twitter diplomacy has given rise to a negative label for its diplomats that has gained international notoriety—"wolf warriors."[10] But regardless of how Twitter diplomacy may be received by international audiences, it appears that imperatives of obtaining a good reception domestically weigh heavily on the minds of diplomatic practitioners. As one prominent Chinese scholar (Interviewee 84, personal communication, November 22, 2019) told me: "One aspect of China's discourse or discursive power, particularly of using 'dirty conspiracy' against another, won't improve China's power and influence. The international effect might be the opposite, although it might play well in some circles domestically, which may be what matters more, at times."

Indeed, various opinion polls indicate that China's purported abrasiveness (online and offline) has created a difficult diplomatic environment for itself. A 2020 survey by the ISEAS-Yusof Ishak Institute showed that 71.9 percent of Southeast Asian elites worried about China's growing economic influence (ISEAS, 2020, p. 15). Of potentially greater concern to Beijing was the fact that 60.4 percent of respondents had "no confidence" or "little confidence" in China to "do the right thing" in global affairs and contribute to world peace (ISEAS, 2020, p. 43). Almost identically, the 2022 iteration of the same survey saw 58.1 percent as having "little" or "no confidence" in China doing the "right thing" (ISEAS, 2022, p. 42). Additionally, a Pew research poll conducted in 2021 saw a median of 69 percent from the publics of seventeen countries as having an unfavorable view of China, which was a "historic high" (Silver et al., 2021). Such disapproving views are increasingly prompted by China's diplomatic assertiveness (D. Loh, 2020b). In Europe, countries have not taken kindly to China's diplomatic conduct, which grates on sensibilities and violates notions of decorum. France, for example, summoned the Chinese ambassador, Lu Shaye, "to express its deep disapproval about Chinese diplomats' claims that France had left its older citizens to die" over the coronavirus (Wintour, 2020). And Germany openly detailed how it had rejected requests by Chinese diplomats to portray China's coronavirus fight in a more positive light (S. Lau, 2020). François Godement, senior adviser for Asia at the Paris-based Institut Montaigne, says: "You have a new brand of Chinese diplomats who seem to compete with each other to be more radical and eventually insulting the country where they happen to be posted. They have gotten into fights with every northern European country with whom they should have an interest, and they have alienated every one of them" (Erlanger, 2020, para. 7).

What is noteworthy here is that this discursive power has political consequences. For instance, it is not often known that when China's Twitter diplomacy intensified in 2019, Twitter was actively giving support to Chinese officials by setting up and "verifying their accounts and training them on how to amplify messages, including with the use of hashtags" (Banjo & Frier, 2019). In fact, Twitter sold ads "to Chinese state media companies that used them to push the narrative that Hong Kong protests were orchestrated by foreign forces and angry mobs unrepresentative of the city's majority"

(Banjo & Frier, 2019, para. 14). The complex dynamic above underscores the multiplicity of actors, foreign and domestic, public and private, that coalesce, wittingly, or not, to reproduce and contest Chinese discursive power.

China's abrasiveness on Twitter is sometimes controversial even within MOFA itself. On March 12, 2020, Zhao tweeted a disproved conspiracy theory that America was behind the Covid-19 outbreak. "It might be US army who brought the epidemic to Wuhan," the Foreign Ministry spokesman said, and questioned further in his tweet the (lack of) transparency of Covid-19 data in the US: "When did patient zero begin in US? How many people are infected? What are the names of the hospitals?" Subsequently, he went so far as to declare that Washington owed China an explanation (L. Zhao, 2020).

This message was retweeted 7,600 times and received over 15,400 likes—showing the reach that such diplomatic messages can achieve. But this bold display of diplomacy did not go unchallenged internally and caused some disquiet, with one diplomat doubting how effective and useful such statements on Twitter were for the conduct of Chinese diplomacy (*Straits Times*, 2020a). China's ambassador to the United States, Cui Tiankai, rebuked Zhao and distanced himself from such claims by calling them "crazy." He reiterated his stance in an interview later, saying, "That was my position then and it's my position now. . . . This is the job for the scientists to do, not for diplomats, not for journalists to speculate. Because such speculation will help nobody. It is harmful" (Swan & Allen-Ebrahimian, 2020). Older diplomats such as Cui and others at MOFA see such incautious displays of power as unhelpful to diplomacy—hinting at an age-based cleavage. The emergence of "wolf warrior" diplomats who are prepared to "attack and defend first" has "caused a rift with the old foreign policy establishment, amid worries that increasingly assertive rhetoric could put the country on a dangerous collision course" (*Straits Times*, 2020a, para. 5). Older diplomats also resent these newer diplomats' showy and public conduct of diplomacy, which they themselves never got to enact. What is remarkable is that "such public differences are rare among Chinese officials who are famous for their ability to stick closely to the Communist Party's official line" (Martin & Li, 2020, para. 4). Alden and Chan suggest that the diplomatic leadership wanted to "rein in such ambassadors while still retaining the benefits that 'wolf-warrior' diplomacy provides" (2021, p. 11)—a difficult balancing act, to say the least.

As a former director of the CCP's propaganda department observes, "This is the first time since 1949 that the 'new hawks' have the power to reshape China's diplomatic policy" (*Straits Times*, 2020a, para. 4). To be sure, the uneasiness caused by Zhao's tweet was expressed only by a minority, since these practices were pushed by Xi himself. In fact, Zhao's return to MOFA headquarters caused quite a stir, as "a group of young admirers at the ministry gathered at his office to cheer his return"

(*Straits Times*, 2020a, para. 2). A scholar affiliated with a think tank under MOFA adds: "Zhao and other Twitter diplomats are viewed positively. It would be wrong to say that he is very aggressive. Zhao Lijian has character and is not your cookie-cutter diplomat that China is filled with. Generally speaking, his diplomatic tweets and actions have been met with wide support and approval in MOFA and in Chinese society" (Interviewee 83, personal communication, May 9, 2020).

In response to questions on his tweet, Zhao said that it was "a reaction to some US politicians stigmatizing China a while ago" and that it "reflects the anger of many Chinese people about this stigma" (*Straits Times*, 2020b, para. 3). Externally, Zhao's abrasiveness has given offense to other countries. To commemorate Thanksgiving Day on November 30, 2019, he sarcastically tweeted—with an attached photograph of then US president Donald Trump holding out a plate of food to US soldiers—his special gratitude toward Washington for "squandering trillions of dollars" in war-torn countries such as "Afghanistan, Iraq, Libya, [and] Syria" (L. Zhao, 2019).

As noted earlier, China's Twitter diplomacy has met with "some amount of hostility from the West" (Interviewee 77, personal communication, November 6, 2019). When Zhao was the deputy chief of mission in Pakistan, he defended China's human rights record and the presence of detention camps in Xinjiang by tweeting: "If you're in Washington DC, you know the white never go to the SW area, because it's an area for the black & Latin [*sic*]. There's a saying 'black in & white out,' which means that as long as a black family enters, white people will quit, & price of the apartment will fall sharply" (H. Wu, 2019, para. 12).

This prompted a swift backlash, with former US national security adviser Susan Rice (2019) calling Zhao a "racist disgrace." Zhao fired back, replying that Rice herself was "racist," "disgraceful," and "disgusting" (Marlow & Li, 2019). When quizzed on Zhao's tweets, Geng Shuang, the PRC spokesperson, did not directly respond (Austin & Smith, 2020). Both tweets from Zhao were subsequently deleted after they captured international media attention, indicating that Zhao had overstepped his authority and taken his defense (and attack) too far. A diplomat suggested likewise: "He has overstepped some lines. This was a little too much and got the attention of lots of people and the media too. Also, how does this help the Chinese ambassador to the US in his job?" (Interviewee 77, personal communication, November 6, 2019). Such assertive Twitter diplomacy is repeated elsewhere. Zha Liyou, the consul-general of the PRC in Kolkata, often personally replies to critical tweets from unnamed accounts. One of these was an undiplomatic tweet by him in response to an online troll on February 16, 2020: "You speak in such a way that you look like part of the virus and you will be eradicated just like virus. Shame on you" (Zha, 2020b). Another melee took place in the same month, with Zha (2020a) branding the Twitter user as a "cold blooded" person who should either "go to any hospitals to help" if he or she was "even half of a doctor or nurse" or should "consult a mental health expert." In another instance, Zha again used threatening language to a troll: "If it were not for efforts by my government, you won't have time sitting here defaming China" (2019).

In fact, a quick search for Zha's "replies" on Twitter throws up plenty of such hostile engagements with trolls, and he is not alone in such engagements. In any event, it is clear that Zhao's (and others') diplomatic forays on Twitter are met with the blessings of top leadership. An interviewee from the media observes: "I should note I don't think when Zhao tweets like that he's freelancing. I believe the decision to spread anti-American disinformation like that is a high-level matter." Furthermore, he says, "The tweets/retweets are less important in and of themselves than what they seem to represent: officially sanctioned aggression or hostility" (Interviewee 80, personal communication, March 30, 2020). Across the board, similar exchanges have been observed. One contact discloses how tweets by Zhao, Zha, and others "does not resonate for the English-speaking world. That is not to say there is no value. There certainly is, but what they are doing is making their bosses happy and making the Chinese people who read English happy. But let me remind you that not every Chinese citizen agrees with their action" (Interviewee 81, personal communication, April 20, 2020).

Most importantly, PRC diplomats' online activities and propaganda efforts, including Twitter, have entered their overall work performance appraisals (D. Loh, 2020b). This, as a consequence, incentivizes diplomats to take to Twitter. As an added effect, there is now an unspoken competition among them to outdo each other in the quest to be more patriotic and perform diplomacy more assertively.

Conclusion

It is clear from the present analysis that China's Twitter diplomacy has had mixed results. This tracks with a similar trend in its offline diplomacy, highlighted in previous chapters. A thread that runs through the online and offline worlds is that Chinese diplomats are empowered, encouraged, and incentivized to be more assertive in their diplomacy—even as this sometimes proves costly to China's image and reputation (see Pu, 2019). A Chinese diplomat told me, "We have to remember that MOFA does certain things not only for the outside world but for China itself. People in China see our activities with pride and see these as befitting a major power, they support us. We will carry on with activities that are supported and correct" (Interviewee 70, personal communication, November 10, 2010). From that perspective, it is clear that diplomats constantly take into account, preempt, and adjust to the domestic audience's reactions when performing diplomacy.

It is also important to bear in mind that MOFA's Twitter diplomacy is but part of an increasingly complex and sophisticated repertoire available to Chinese diplomats in their broader bid to achieve national interests and generate discourse power. Within the field of diplomacy, Twitter is fast emerging as a tool that denotes "status," and in the eyes of these diplomats, the more competent they are at practicing Twitter diplomacy, the more quickly they accrue social and diplomatic capital. In that respect, the impact and importance of Twitter diplomacy for more traditional registers of diplomacy should not be underestimated. This new form of diplomacy is "hugely consequential," as one media contact told me. He also noted: "As China succeeds in getting its diplomats more of a following, whether that is via bots or other forms of inorganic promotion, it becomes even more consequential. Zhao Lijian's 'U.S army-Wuhan' tweets got massive exposure and seem to have provoked Trump and Pompeo to place stress on 'Chinese virus' and 'Wuhan virus,' leading to an escalation in tensions that hurt chances for real cooperation, however slim they may have been" (Interviewee 80, personal communication, March 30, 2020).

In this chapter, through a broad appraisal of China's Twitter diplomacy and an analysis of Hua's, Zhao's, and Zha's Twitter activities, I tease out three principal effects of this diplomatic practice. First, Twitter has empowered Chinese embassies and diplomats to expand their diplomatic reach and messages so as to boost their discursive power, understood here as the public and private capacities to authoritatively define and articulate policy positions across various international issues.[11] This power, and the visibility of this power, means they are now able to respond to slights, criticisms, and insults much more quickly and collectively. This reinforces more traditional forms of diplomacy to employ similar styles and content in diplomatic narratives as they shift from offline to online worlds. In practical terms, the volume and presence of PRC diplomats and their discourses have increased significantly with the proliferation of official Twitter accounts.

Second, Twitter diplomacy is a manifestation of both China's status as a risen/rising power and its growing assertiveness. Twitter diplomacy thus acts as a tool for wielding and exercising that power. It augments diplomats' domestic position: by using "the forbidden" in legitimate ways, Twitter diplomacy acts as a hallmark of distinction. PRC envoys can exhibit their capabilities and strengths to a wider audience and on much quicker timelines. This "mediatization" and promotion of diplomatic nous gives China greater flexibility and power to fashion the narratives and stories they desire to tell and is a critical constituent of China's discursive power. Twitter also enables diplomatic interlocutors, on the authorization of the president, to pursue a course of diplomatic communication that is sometimes hostile and often assertive—especially when reacting to criticism. While smaller powers may eschew such diplomatic practices because they are "undiplomatic" breaches of decorum and may cause diplomatic problems, China has the capacity to "get away" with them even as they generate some reputational costs.

Finally, Twitter diplomacy is met with resistance from within and without. While this practice reinforces diplomacy in various ways, it simultaneously undercuts traditional diplomacy by narrowing spaces for dialogue, cooperation, and compromise, mirroring similar criticisms of China's offline diplomacy. While some within MOFA, and some local diplomatic actors, are dismayed by this brand of diplomacy, they remain the minority and have little influence to substantially affect current Twitter diplomatic practices. Indeed, China's foreign minister has defended MOFA's "wolf warrior" diplomats, saying that China diplomats will defend against "smears" and "hit back" to defend "national honor" (W. Wu, 2020).

Externally, Chinese diplomatic practices have, sometimes, eroded traditional diplomatic relations of friendship, camaraderie, and cooperation, redefining, in various ways, what decorum and appropriate conduct of diplomacy signify. This has resulted in pushback from some international actors against perceived assertive diplomacy, but has not resulted in significant reflection. This chapter also considered how social-technological products like Twitter have compelling political effects on their human users. In doing so, it shows the verity of Pouliot's reflection that in international relations, technology and material objects make human actors "do things they would not have done otherwise" (2010b, p. 294).

CONCLUSION

Representations of Assertiveness and "Wolf Warriors"

Practices are the "fundamental constituent" of social reality (McMillan, 2018, p. 1) and the "gluon" of international relations (Adler & Pouliot, 2011b, p. 10). They are what makes "relations" in international relations possible. While the practice approach has reinvigorated diplomatic studies in Western imaginaries, it has yet to be put to productive use to investigate Chinese diplomacy and its international politics. Drawing on the practice-theoretical toolkit, I asked these questions: How is China's assertiveness represented, and what are its concrete manifestations? Why has Chinese behavior on the international stage been increasingly *evaluated* by different international actors and publics as assertive? How do other state actors construct and understand Chinese foreign policy behavior? Ultimately, this analysis seeks to properly locate the role and impact of MOFA in contemporary Chinese foreign policy (2009–2020).

Interpreting MOFA and Diplomacy in China

The main empirical findings for the period from 2009 to 2020 are (1) MOFA's representational role has become more pronounced as it intervenes and represents Party and state across various domains; (2) Chinese diplomacy has become increasingly assertive, albeit in an incremental way; (3) MOFA exercises considerable influence through its counseling, implementing, and coordinating competencies; (4) official perceptions of China's identity are derived, frequently, from MOFA; (5) Twitter diplomacy has reinforced offline assertiveness and extended it to the online sphere as China seeks an extra vector to generate discourse power. These conclusions may seem straightforward at first glance, but they complicate (and add to) traditional understandings of Chinese diplomacy and foreign policy.

First, by linking diplomacy at the national and international levels to the micro-level practices of human and institutional actors, I challenge state-centric views of China as "acting" and "doing" diplomacy with a view that is firmly practice based and representational. State-centric scholarship, underwritten by the preponderance of realist accounts, often bases analysis on a monolithic China. In contrast, I demonstrate how the "making" and performance of diplomacy start from seemingly innocuous practices of diplomats and secondary diplomatic actors who are simply discharging their work duties. In complex struggles and cooperation for institutional and personal resources, diplomats are increasingly predisposed toward using a suite of assertive diplomatic practices during their everyday dealings with others.

These microaggressions/assertiveness filter upwards to "make" Chinese diplomacy. For instance, non-Chinese diplomats frequently comment in interviews that "China is assertive" and state explicitly that Chinese assertiveness influences, at a strategic, national level, how their own country reacts to China. Indeed, for non-Chinese diplomats, *an assertive Chinese diplomat is an assertive China*. Neumann recalls the difficulties of accessing Chinese diplomats "backstage" to get at what they privately think (2012, pp. 126–127). The line between backstage and front stage is so blurred that they often become one personification in which the Chinese diplomat is MOFA, and MOFA is the diplomat. MOFA and its diplomats have come to assume the representational role of China. And this is not restricted simply to international affairs: it is also evidenced through MOFA's interventions in various domains, such as military affairs, economic affairs, and issues of domestic governance (CGTN, 2020).

What is more, as chapter 2 highlights, important domestic actors such as the PLA are acknowledging MOFA's ascendancy and ceding discursive control over issues traditionally under the PLA. While it is correct that more agencies, institutions, and state organs are intervening in external affairs as the PRC's foreign policy footprint grows, the literature misses how MOFA is raising its competencies and profile while boosting its overall coordinating role. In most foreign ministries (particularly those of liberal regimes) and international organizations, one would expect the presence of strong personalities, where individual charm, skill, and competency are readily apparent (Bode, 2018; Adler & Pouliot, 2011a, p. 18). Contrarily, Chinese diplomacy deemphasizes "personalities"; Party leaders are wary of personality politics, as the emergence of such characters could potentially compete with the core leadership (Interviewee 70, personal communication, July 10, 2017).[1] Even so, we are witnessing the rise of highly visible online performances from diplomats such as Zhao Lijian and Hua Chunying that are officially sanctioned by the political leadership, as chapter 5 points out.

Relatedly, claims of MOFA's weakness in the literature are inflated. The ministry has in fact, expanded materially and symbolically and commands significant material and symbolic capital. While MOFA's direct foreign policy–making powers are debated, they are not insignificant, as the literature typically suggests. MOFA can apply influence through counseling top leadership, implementing policy, and coordinating the efforts of other actors. What is more, Chinese diplomatic assertiveness raises the profile of MOFA internationally and domestically, with positive consequences for its influence. Domestically, current Chinese diplomatic practices align with (and drive) Beijing's attempt to gradually reframe for international society China's former narrative of itself as victim, a project that fits well with both public opinion and the intentions of the top leadership, even as it still opportunistically mobilizes these narratives for nation building and to apply pressure to other countries to extract compliance (see Weiss, 2014). Second, MOFA's assertiveness means other domestic institutions have come to mimic their diplomatic practices—particularly their assertive practices. For instance, the International Liaison Department established its own official Twitter account, following in MOFA's footsteps, to increase its own outreach and profile. Meanwhile, China's Ministry of National Defense (MND) sought MOFA's advisory help in starting its first-ever regular press conference in 2011. In sum, MOFA is discursively and practically speaking on and intervening in a myriad of issues that it previously did not. These processes are disregarded by most scholars working in Chinese politics. Yet I found that the performances and practices that come with advising and implementing are politically consequential. MOFA has a monopolistic hold on country-specific and international affairs knowledge through its 276 embassies, consulates, and missions.[2] Notably, China overtook America in 2019 to have the most diplomatic outposts in the world (Lew, 2019). MOFA provides geopolitical information to the government on overseas projects (such as the BRI), and such data is usually taken as authoritative. While the possibility of rejecting its advice always stands, in practice this happens rarely, if at all.

When government officials and provincial leaders make the decision to meet (or not to meet) foreign leaders, they almost always seek advice from MOFA. While the ultimate decision rests with the top-level officials themselves, they seldom go against the counsel of the ministry because doing so would be risky in terms of bringing undue attention to oneself (Interviewee 70, personal communication, July 10, 2017). Here is an empirical illustration: during a period of tension between a Southeast Asian country and China in 2016 and 2017, MOFA advised high-level state and Party officials not to meet with equivalently ranked visiting officials but to send their deputies or lower-level officials instead. This was not a decision taken by the PSC but one in which MOFA clearly exercised its *capacity to counsel* (Interviewee 37, personal communication, August 3, 2018).[3] This capacity is closely wedded to MOFA's IR knowledge production capabilities. As the central arbiter of IR knowledge and information, MOFA can influence which knowledge and/or information matters, how it matters, and how such information/knowledge is put into practice.

In the execution of diplomatic activities, MOFA can also appropriate and strategically deploy its *capacity to implement*. As mentioned in chapter 2, a Southeast Asian diplomat revealed that MOFA had disinvited the Philippines from several ASEAN functions in the aftermath of Manila's decision to refer maritime areas under dispute with China to the PCA. Again, the decision was not a direct order but rather a move initiated by MOFA itself (Interviewee 29, personal communication, August 17, 2017).

MOFA's third capacity is its *coordinating* functions. One sees MOFA playing a central role in facilitating issues ranging from the Doklam standoff to the SCS disputes, even bringing companies to heel, as it seeks to perform its duties.

MOFA's control of these three levers—levers that are not normally registered in the literature—shows a degree of influence that has not been acknowledged before. One Chinese MOFA source notes: "Top leadership is giving greater authority to MOFA and greater freedom. This is a natural spillover of China's greater role [in world politics]" (Interviewee 60, personal communication, July 9, 2018). Such claims were increasingly common in my conversations in 2017 and 2018, compared to the previous years. Instructively, in 2017, former MOFA spokesperson Li Jianying observed that Chinese diplomats today have "greater flexibility in expressing themselves" and also more "latitude" than before, even as this is not unfettered (J. Li, 2019).

In chapter 3 I indicated how an increase in resources and a shift in the diplomatic field have emboldened MOFA and its diplomats. Xi's move to centralize control of diplomacy through the Central Foreign Affairs Commission (CFAC) with Yang Jiechi as its director shows MOFA's heightened profile and its importance to Xi and the Communist Party's legitimacy.[4] Significantly, in creating CFAC, Xi abolished the Central Leadership Group on Maritime Rights and Issues and announced that "all maritime rights and sovereignty issues will now be coordinated, promoted and implemented" by CFAC (Xinhua, 2018), further accenting the coordinating functions of diplomacy and the representational role that diplomats increasingly adopt. This does not necessarily endow diplomats with decision-making powers. Nevertheless, it allows them to act more assertively and coherently. I reiterate that recasting the aforementioned functional capacities—not as apolitical and politically neutered but as imbued with social productivity and power—would have been possible only with a practice-sensitive approach attuned to the daily "doings and sayings" of a diplomat's work. A case in point would be a diplomat's retelling of how a high-level PRC envoy ranked others. In a casual lunch meeting at her residence, her Chinese counterpart was asking other diplomats: "How many people do you have at your China desk?" and "How well staffed is it?" Strikingly, "He proceeded to rank and classify others based on how well resourced their respective China desks were" (Interviewee 75, personal communication, November 18, 2018).

This anecdote hints at three things. First, it shows the importance of micro-level diplomatic interactions for state-to-state diplomatic relations. Second, it signifies how international hierarchies of societies can be (re)produced in contingent and emergent ways. Third, it tells us how MOFA's assessments of others are not necessarily made in a systematic and organized fashion. This is of particular importance since MOFA is one of the main contributors of country assessments.

In chapter 5, I showed the increased influence of Chinese diplomats in greater detail by demonstrating how Twitter diplomacy cements Chinese diplomats' legitimacy and importance at home. Twitter diplomacy is, in no small part, impelled by Chinese society's desire for greater diplomatic activism but is also, more importantly, enabled and supported by the political leadership. Notably, policymakers see Twitter as a key tool in expanding China's "discursive power," allowing diplomatic interlocutors to fight back and attack hostile elements in highly visible and instantaneous ways. All in all, while it may be true that MOFA does not match up to the stature of its American or European counterparts, it is inaccurate to claim that it has little influence in China's international or even domestic affairs.

Chinese diplomatic practices are driven not only by more instrumental or normative considerations but by practical logics. This practical sensibility is informed by and drawn from what Pouliot calls *practical knowledge*, the "stock of unspoken know-how learned in and through practice and from which conscious deliberation and action become possible" (Pouliot, 2008, p. 270). One Southeast Asian envoy, in recalling his interactions with former Chinese diplomats, divulged how they had "definitely changed" in their interactions with him and in their worldviews after they left MOFA. To explain how their views had become more moderate, he added, "They were not simply pretending when they were diplomats, it was just *what they had to do*" (Interviewee 37, personal communication, August 3, 2018).[5] Chinese diplomats and secondary diplomatic actors can exercise discretion and nuance, as I have repeatedly emphasized, their decisions on how and when to do so are motivated not just by cost calculation or what is seen as correct social behavior but rather by considerations of what appears practical to them in a given context. In her work on practice theory and authoritarianism, Glasius tells us, "People do not obey an isolated dictator out of pure fear, or collaborate with him out of pure greed or hunger for power. They develop common understandings of how things are done within their social context, whether they are true believers in the government's legitimation narratives, or just pragmatists, or somewhere in between" (2018, p. 524).

In short, practitioners conduct their activities on a level of practicality. As one Chinese interviewee told me when I quizzed him about the contradictory stances MOFA diplomats had presented on different occasions—in some ways assertive to

ASEAN and in others very flexible and cooperative—he explained: "There is no contradiction. We can only do what is possible with our resources and what is realistic and right in the [differing] situations" (Interviewee 70, personal communication, July 10, 2017). This practical sense is largely induced by diplomats' individual habitus and MOFA's institutional habitus, as I discussed in chapter 4.

As Pouliot has noted, "Far from automatically or deterministically leading to a specific practice, habitus simply inclines or disposes actors to do certain things" (2008, p. 274). Accordingly, while we see a general propensity toward assertive displays across the diplomatic field, this is contingent on the social field. By bringing the focus back to what diplomacy actually entails and by studying practitioners and diplomats who are "doing" it, a relationalist approach informed by Bourdieu and PT enables us to empirically see how Chinese diplomacy and diplomatic outcomes are, paradoxically, the stability of and struggles over practices in the field.

The Study of China through the Practice Approach

This book extends practice theory and Bourdieu's sociology beyond their typical geographical concentrations by applying them to a non-Western imaginary. But more than simply applying theory to a different context, the segue to specifically engage in non-Western areas is a political move, for PT to be self-aware of its own limit and potential. In that way, I add to the theoretical enterprise in three distinct ways: emphasizing material objects' agency vis-à-vis diplomacy; gesturing at the change-inducing potential of transversal fields; and highlighting the conceptual utility of institutional habitus.

First, I underscored the ineluctable role of material objects in practices. Within the PT literature, while there is some focus and recognition of "nonhuman" actors (see Pouliot, 2010b; Nicolini, 2012, pp. 171, 174; Barad, 2003; Latour, 2005), most studies are about human individuals, practices, and agency. I add to these contributions by demonstrating the ways in which the material interacts with and produces practices. Fax machines, WeChat accounts, institutional documents, Twitter activities, the staging of daily press briefings, and physical infrastructure are not mere additives but crucial sites for the analysis of Chinese diplomatic practices themselves. It is vital to acknowledge how "practices are partly constituted by and always embedded in material arrangements" (Shove et al., 2015, p. 274; see also Schatzki, 2010, p. 130). The following paragraphs on the material architecture of MOFA's press briefing room will highlight this point, particularly regarding infrastructural/material arrangements.

The structure of the room where MOFA press briefings are held (the "Blue Hall") is functional and comes equipped with the latest audiovisual setup.[6] Seats for journalists are arranged in a slightly curved fashion facing the central rostrum, where the spokesperson stands over the crowd. Seats at the back are arranged for visitors, who can pose no questions and take no photographs while the press briefing is ongoing. This is usually policed by a staff member. The distance (both physical and literal) from the stage mutes these visitors as passive observers rather than active participants. Chairs for visitor-observers are also distinct from those of the media in their more basic form, likely out of cost concerns but also, nonetheless, helping establish and sustain a stratum at the site; nonofficial individuals are mere transient, inconsequential observers (figures 3 and 4).

FIGURE 3. Journalists' desks in the MOFA press briefing room, July 2, 2018.

FIGURE 4. Side view of the press briefing room, July 2, 2018.

The spokesperson of the day enters the rostrum through a side door on stage and exits it (usually) as hastily and confidently as he or she arrives, always bearing a thick binder of notes (figures 5 and 6). This is frequently referred to when answering questions. On two occasions, the spokesperson conversed with me and fellow visitors. In another instance, one spokesperson left without acknowledging our presence, aided by the ease of entry and exit. In those moments when we interacted, it was made clear by their minders and our organizers (informed also by the material and immaterial "atmosphere"), that the meeting was allowed purely out of the spokespersons' largesse.

"Controversial" questions are often asked during the regular press briefings, for instance, those relating to Tibet, Taiwan, and human rights. In one session where I was present, a question on Liu Xia[7] was asked, and this earned a stern rebuke.[8] When I checked the official WeChat account of MOFA,[9] that particular question had been scrubbed. Outside the Blue Hall is an "international press center," and to its right are well-stocked bookshelves with books ranging from official MOFA publications to Xi Jinping's *The Governance of China* that visitors can take for free (figures 7 and 8).

The books are all, unsurprisingly, state-sanctioned publications. Thus, like MOFA's press briefings and its actors' practices, the assemblage of physical arrangements in the Blue Hall amounts to an attempt to partake in transparency and present information, albeit within clearly bounded confines. In this brief description, one sees how the material interacts with discursive human practices:

> *Discursive practices are specific material (re)configurings of the world through which local determinations of boundaries, properties, and meanings are differentially enacted. That is, discursive practices are ongoing agential intra-actions of the world through which local determinacy is enacted within the phenomena produced. Discursive practices are causal intra-actions*—they enact local causal structures through which one "component" (the "effect") of the phenomenon is marked by another "component" (the "cause") in their differential articulation. (Barad, 2003, pp. 820–821)[10]

Here, through the specific ensemble of the material and the discursive, human practices come together to enact a particular, local conduct of diplomacy. The deletion of controversial questions, the assortment of preselected free books (some of which are sold at bookstores), and the persistent material presence of the "binders" (which serve a symbolic purpose besides its functional utility) are some examples of how nonhumans interact with humans to produce and sustain practices. In making clear the differences between corporate practices and "agent-centered" practices, I also crystallize the constitutive nature of the material for practices and, consequently the importance of the material to the conduct of diplomacy itself (Dittmer, 2016).

Second, in my analysis of the diplomatic field in China, I introduced the concept

FIGURE 5. Geng Shuang, one of three then current spokespersons, holding the "binder," July 1, 2017.

FIGURE 6. Hong Lei, twenty-fifth MOFA spokesperson, who served from 2010 to 2016, with an assistant holding his "binder," July 2, 2016.

FIGURE 7. International Press Center, July 2, 2018.

FIGURE 8. Bookshelves near the International Press Center, July 2, 2018.

of "transversal disruption" to show how fields, as structures, have a bearing on other overlapping and related fields. Particularly, I examined how the (local) Chinese diplomatic field disrupted the transnational diplomatic field, showing how abrupt change need not be brought on only in moments of crises "when the old habitus does not 'fit' the field, is not (yet) adapted to the new Doxa" (Kerr & Robinson, 2009, p. 833) or when "dispositions become dysfunctional and the efforts they make to perpetuate them help to plunge them deeper into failure" (Bourdieu, 2000, p. 161). In contrast to Bourdieu, sudden changes need not be crisis centered and enclosed within the field; they can also occur in and at points *where fields overlap.*

In the cases under inquiry in this book, instances were observed where Chinese diplomatic actors were able to disrupt and successfully change certain field rules of the transnational diplomatic field. In chapter 3, I discussed how Chinese interlocutors in the track-2 diplomatic field were able to elicit shifts in both material (through the written constitution of the track-2 organization) and symbolic (through the shunning of Taiwanese participants) field rules. Even so, Chinese actors still wanted to operate legitimately within that transnational logic and to legitimize their goals under that logic. When I asked a Chinese academic (who was in the original track-2 Chinese delegation) about this incident, he told me, "This is the correct outcome, but we were prepared to discuss and see what the others wanted. We cannot be forcing our ideas alone" (Interviewee 74, personal communication, July 23, 2018).

Such endeavors, however, are not always successful. This can be seen in the transnational ASEAN diplomatic field, where China has played an increasingly influential role and has sought to recast ASEAN rules and norms, particularly the "noninterference" principle. Chinese envoys have persistently, both publicly and privately, tried to get ASEAN to remove references that may paint China in a negative light, including statements on the SCS disputes, land reclamation activities, and the PCA tribunal's award favoring the Philippines. In this transnational field, the omission and presence of SCS statements[11] reflect the struggle over the *doxa* and the stakes of the ASEAN-China field. For instance, SCS references were either omitted or adulterated in the years 2012, 2016, and 2017, while in the years 2013–2015 and 2018–2020 the usual language was included regarding "concerns on the land reclamations and activities in the area, which have eroded trust and confidence, increased tensions and may undermine peace, security and stability in the region" (Ministry of Foreign Affairs Singapore, 2018). These battles challenge the "naturalized understandings of how a particular field functions and which resources or types of capital are valuable within it" (Senn & Elhardt, 2014, p. 320).[12] Indeed, in trying to change the stakes and the field rules governing what can be said, what ought to be said, and what must not be said, Chinese diplomats are trying to regulate proper utterances and discourses, thus blending China's local operative logic into the transnational field. Such practices sometimes provoke negative responses from others. For instance, China's assertive brand of diplomacy brought into the Twittersphere has elicited sharp reactions from other countries, with many criticizing and questioning China's aggressiveness or assertiveness. The negative label "wolf warrior diplomacy" has also entered public consciousness, dealing some reputational damage to China (D. Loh, 2020b).

Third, I "upscaled" habitus through the notion of *institutional habitus* to study MOFA. The treatment of habitus in this book is not an aesthetic procedure but a major operation. By translating it upwards, I provide a dynamic rendering of organizations against a static, one-dimensional view of "organizational culture" (Özbilgin & Tatli, 2005, p. 864). With this notion, one can better study processes of reproduction and change as they are grounded in history and can place the institution as an actor in its own right, capable of exerting influence not only on agents within but also actors outside the field. To an important extent, studying the institutional habitus of MOFA brought greater depth to my analysis of the organization. Certain strands of its institutional disposition stand out: political fealty, discipline, and an emphasis on history. These tendencies have clear effects on the conduct of Chinese diplomacy. For instance, actors in MOFA take personal discipline and self-regulation seriously, and this sometimes proves inimical to diplomacy. I gave an example in chapter 3 where what was hoped to be a friendly, private dinner turned officious when the invited PRC diplomat brought his colleague along to take notes. MOFA "acts" too, through its spokesperson, various diplomatic actors, and press releases in both the material and symbolic forms, generating corporate practices. The continued reliance on fax machines for communication is seen as "strange" (Interviewee 28, personal communication, August 29, 2017) and, adds one interviewee, "shows how cold, impersonal, and strict MOFA is" (Interviewee 27, personal communication, June 17, 2017).

Beyond the inhibitory effects that MOFA's habitus can have on diplomacy I maintain that only after having undergone a proper appraisal of MOFA's habitus can one arrive at a better understanding of China's identity. Thus I draw attention to how diplomatic agents and MOFA's practices are enabled (and disabled) by its habitus and how diplomatic activities that arise from these practices form the ingredients that construct China's state identity. As the official ministry in charge of diplomacy and foreign affairs—in other words, its international relations—MOFA, quite literally, makes China's identity on the world stage. While some non-Chinese diplomats continue to claim that MOFA is weak and insipid, they nevertheless still rely on MOFA to "produce China." This has practical effects for state-to-state relations because these officials submit reports to their governments, which in turn help to formulate their respective China policies.[13]

Methodological Challenges and Innovations

It is germane at this point to consider some of the challenges of the PT approach in studying China's politics, with a specific focus on obtaining and accessing diplomatic practices in the Chinese case. I relied heavily on "third-party" non-Chinese diplomatic interviews to augment "direct" Chinese diplomatic interviews. Accessing practices this way has several benefits. With third-party interviews, I could get at a more "objective" perspective of practices as they appear to others (without discounting that these actors carry their own biases as well). Like "expert interviews" (Bogner et al., 2009), third-party interviews draft people who have expertise on Chinese diplomatic practices. This entailed securing interviews with non-Chinese diplomats based in China who had a working relationship with Chinese interlocutors. I also conducted field interviews with journalists, Chinese scholars, and government officials who had had direct interactions with Chinese diplomats. What at first seemed to be a round-about way to grasp Chinese diplomatic practices proved to be valuable. Even in cases where subject accessibility is unproblematic and plentiful, utilizing third parties is useful in teasing out practices that actors themselves may not be able to articulate (Pouliot, 2008, p. 270). It can also help validate more "primary" means of accessing practices that have been uncovered earlier.[14]

Additionally, practices that would otherwise be hidden and invisible can be rendered visible by these subsidiary interviews. That is to say, Chinese diplomats, like any other diplomats, may wish to hide, exaggerate, or not reveal certain practices and issues and carry with them potential bias (Adler-Nissen, 2014, p. 204). Speaking with others who have had actual dealings with Chinese diplomatic practices can tease out some of these practices and, in many cases, nuance what is presented by Chinese interlocutors. One simple example is the observation by several non-Chinese diplomats that the Chinese are very bureaucratic, more so than most foreign ministry officials they have dealt with, in a way that sometimes hinders candid discussions. At any rate, this formalized and bureaucratic quality is not readily accepted by the Chinese subjects themselves. What is more, suggesting the idea of "diplomatic assertiveness" and specific practices of such assertiveness to Chinese diplomatic interviewees commonly provokes a spirited justification and defense of these practices. And this defense itself adds a valuable dimension to the understanding of diplomatic practice and how MOFA and its agents cope with criticism.

Direct observation is one of the best methods to access practices, as it allows one to see and document the practice as it is performed (Bueger & Gadinger, 2014, p. 85). But it is also well recognized that direct observation is not always possible (Pouliot, 2016, p. 276). To that end, qualitative interviews are the preferred surrogate method of approaching practices (Adler-Nissen, 2016, p. 97). Adler-Nissen advocates for a two-stage interview strategy (which this research generally follows), with the first being an open, almost exploratory interview stage focused on the "everyday knowledge of the informants" and, building on the initial stage, the second, more substantive phase, which "reflects the analytical framework" (Adler-Nissen, 2014, p. 205). In my case, even when my access to Chinese diplomats was granted, the interviews tend to be short, sterile affairs.[15] Indeed, getting close to official Chinese diplomatic contacts can be a protracted process. Thus, in addition to third-party interviews, *public performances* of actors can be used much more to uncover practices.

Within the PT universe, there is an inclination toward studying "closed-door" and exclusive arenas, principally through participation and observation. These intimate sites are often privileged at the expense of more public expressions of practices. However, there is value also in studying public expressions of practices. This means making use of the full registry of actors' practices under study in the public domain— drawing on every available public source related to the actor(s) in question. For my research, besides third-party interviews, I used two other sources: *video footage* and *textual sources*. Hence, I used writings by contemporary diplomats to understand diplomatic discursive practices. What themes were repeated? What did their writings reveal about Chinese diplomacy and diplomatic practices? Concretely, one can leverage diverse sources such as Twitter, online question-answer sites,[16] public video clips, and fiction[17] as extra entry points to assemble practices. In the case of video sources, I examined press conferences involving diplomats and diplomatic meetings, paying careful attention to participants' gait, gestures, tone, script, and, where possible, the *scripting of their script*. The emphasis on the body and the "nonverbalized" is central to Bourdieu's construal of habitus (see chapter 2). It is natural, then, to read the gait, bearing, and verbal/body language of Chinese diplomatic agents and the reactions of others to these as indicators of the agents' social positions in the field, accessed through a close observation of these body demeanors. As Bueger and Mireanu put it (2014, p. 134), "Participant observing is a sensory technique of recording what can been seen, smelled and heard. It is an interpretative device."

Practically speaking, analyzing the embodied and nonverbal adds an extra layer to Chinese diplomatic practices that, while complicating them, also compelled me to think more deeply about the nondiscursive dimensions of practices and what their sources and practical effects are. While I do not construct the habitus of specific diplomats, the empirical analysis of different bodies across various domains allows one to subsequently "zoom out" from the specific to the abstract. This enables theorization about the general dispositions of Chinese diplomats and the ministry more broadly (see Pouliot, 2016, p. 278; 2007). Relatedly, practice theorists can make use of the latest technologies to access practices. In China's case, MOFA established an official WeChat account in January 2018 that users can "follow" to directly receive news and information on MOFA and China's foreign policy (Chi, 2018). Additionally, since 2019, Chinese diplomats have intensified their Twitter activities. These new interfaces provide new vectors for data collection and analysis on the Chinese diplomatic field and practices (despite being "distanciated") in real time and in novel ways.

Finally, practices gleaned from "material documents such as architecture, houses, or city design can give important clues about a prevailing practice, since they have been designed for use and enable certain types of behaviour" (Bueger, 2014, p. 402). Objects cannot "exist" outside of social practices, and once they are interpellated with practice, they acquire a materiality that not only receives meaning but gives meaning to people and practices (Pouliot, 2010b). Neumann, to take an example, highlights the significance of objects like the champagne glass and the pinstriped suit in the presentation of self and of practices that flow from these materials in diplomatic circles (2012, pp. 97–98). Indeed, ways of doing things are often "inscribed" into an artifact, implying that the research process can be "initiated by a detailed study of an artefact followed by the observation of how it is used and an interpretation of which practices are inscribed in it" (Bueger, 2014, p. 397). Besides physical infrastructure, one can pay attention to the presence of documents. These include "electronic (e-mails, PDF files, or Word documents), piles of loose or stapled paper, soft cover and hardcover documents or even illustrated books. Documents are artifacts that are shipped, flown or sent around the planet via post or electronic media." They are important because "physically disconnected sites—an office around the corner, an office in a different continent and time zone, a library, an archive, or assemblies and court rooms—become connected by documents" (Bueger, 2014, pp. 398–399).

Relatedly, I considered documents (not just their content but, in some ways more important, their symbolic presence, as in the case of binders of notes at press briefings) and the stories that MOFA tells. I considered the architecture of MOFA's headquarters, material and immaterial settings, and locations where meetings with Chinese officials took place and their "social atmosphere."[18] How was the meeting arranged? How long did officials allow the meeting to run? What questions did they ask and solicit? That said, I am mindful not to make claims based solely on one of the abovementioned modalities. On its own, each should serve as a validator and supplement—but the aggregation of a robust data-gathering framework with multiple sources (one that is open to innovation but rigorous) is most powerful in allowing for the gathering and subsequent analysis of practices.

What Is Different about Chinese Diplomatic Practices?

Many of the observations on Chinese diplomatic practices presented here are not unique to China. Indeed, they can be said to be general diplomatic practices seen in most foreign ministries—as is the case with the general need for discipline across foreign ministries and in diplomats' behaviors.

Yet although certain sets of general diplomatic practices are widely shared within the diplomatic community, variations exist within these sets. I suggest two types of variations: differences in quality and differences in intensity. By *differences in quality*, I refer to practices that are present only in the PRC.[19] For instance, in this book, I point to legislation that forbids diplomats stationed abroad from resigning and requires that all diplomatic personnel must be Party members. I also reveal that Chinese diplomats often cannot meet with others individually. And it is uncommon for diplomatic recruiting practices to emphasize language training over IR knowledge, and ideological loyalty over competency (Bloomberg News, 2019). As for *differences in intensity*, any diplomat is expected to be disciplined and hardworking and to place state interests before self. Nonetheless, Chinese diplomats are displaying these traits more pronouncedly and much more intensely—even at the expense of breaking international and regional diplomatic protocols and norms. I observed, for example, how the ethos of discipline is so absorbed by MOFA actors that it crosses into their personal lives.

We also see the general practice of "advancing state interests" take on more extreme forms. Examples abound of how Chinese diplomats are blocking statements unfavorable to China (D. Loh, 2018b), physically preventing diplomats from speaking out against the PRC (Doherty & Davidson, 2018), disrupting "anti-China" academic activities (Lloyd-Damnjanovic, 2018), and scolding other diplomats and reporters publicly (Buckley, 2016). Also, as I suggest in chapter 5, China is rather different from other nations in using Twitter to conduct very pointed displays of diplomacy, consistently and in large volumes. Thus, while all diplomats are expected to guard and promote their national interests, MOFA diplomats perform some practices more intensely than others and are also more prepared to breach diplomatic decorum and mount "exceptional" or "inappropriate" practices.

PT and the Study of Chinese Diplomacy

Taken together, what consequences does practice theory hold for IR and the study of Chinese diplomacy? In IR, this study adds to a proliferation of works that counteract IR's "unfortunate habit of treating social dimensions of international interactions as negligible" (Zarakol, 2011, p. 241). A practice orientation is well suited to critically recast and rethink "traditional" IR concepts in three ways that earlier sections of this book have also alluded to: change and stability; power; and the nonhuman/material.

In understanding change and stability, PT argues against explanations of innovation and transformation brought about either by structural changes or by entrepreneurial agents who initiate changes to the system. Rather, a PT approach looks at practices as a potential force for both change and the status quo. Thus small changes in practices can be incremental and can engender broader structural, systemic changes—a "change in practice through practice" (Hopf, 2018, p. 692; see also Bouris & Fernández-Molina, 2018). In chapter 1, I underlined how others overwhelmingly saw a "sudden" change in Chinese assertiveness from 2009 onwards and again in 2019 when Chinese diplomats ramped up their Twitter presence. Yet this change was not actually sudden. It was a result of practices that additively took on a more diplomatically assertive tenor as MOFA increasingly came to speak and act on behalf of other domestic actors. These practices "streamed out" from MOFA to the secondary players and thus were encouraged to the point where they became natural or simply "a way of doing things"—an unarticulated sensibility of what works.

I then highlighted how fields themselves can incite change in two ways. First, in chapter 3, I showed how shifts in the field, particularly over stakes and incentives, brought about an attendant change in the practices of the actors within it. Thus, when Xi initiated several small but significant moves to provide for an enlarged foreign policy congruous with that of a major power, the diplomatic field, somewhat synchronously, underwent changes to its stakes and incentives. Xi's call for greater *biao tai* (表态) or "ritualistic declarations of loyalty" across the board (Lam, 2018, para. 10) reified *biao tai* as a stake to be competed over—who could display the most fealty to Xi and the Party. In 2019 Xi also called for greater fighting spirit to be shown in diplomacy, both online and offline. In the immediate aftermath of this call, Chinese diplomats' Twitter accounts and tweets proliferated (Ruwitch, 2019). Seen in the broader context of diplomatic change where there was a turn toward greater political discipline and diplomatic assertiveness, this was not surprising or sudden but a result of incremental shifts in the diplomatic landscape. In sum, Bourdieu's sociology and PT can show new pathways of studying and understanding change and stability in China's IR.

The concept of power can also profit from more thorough engagement with the practice approach, as others such as Adler-Nissen and Pouliot (2014) and Guzzini (2013, pp. 93–106) have shown. In chapters 2, 3, and 5, I illustrated how power, conceived through forms of "capacity" or "competency," begets significant diplomatic effects. Moving against prevailing interpretations of power, I underlined how considerable leeway remains open to diplomats and MOFA in their implementing, coordinating, and advising functions. These functional capacities allow space for discretionary and bounded exercise of influence and power in the diplomatic sphere.[20]

Thus, while MOFA does not ordinarily have decision-making powers, its exercise of competencies has significant and far-reaching effects on China's diplomacy. Also, Twitter diplomacy raised MOFA's profile as diplomats increasingly turned to Twitter to advertise their consular expertise and skills in rendering assistance to Chinese citizens needing help. This had the effect of illustrating the influence and competency of its embassies and diplomats in protecting Chinese interests. In the previous chapters, I consistently emphasized how MOFA increasingly represents China, across various fields, to the outside world. This heightened role is made possible through the top leadership's delegation and greater investment of resources in MOFA. PT can offer an account of power that is processual, representational, and based on the possession and exercise of competencies.

Finally, a practice-sensitive account of diplomacy allows us to grasp both the human and the material.[21] PT can cast new light on how the human and the material coproduce diplomatic practices—a point I stressed at the start of this chapter. Human-material (and "more-than-human") intercourse will find increasing importance as diplomacy gets progressively complex and reliant on new technologies such as big data and artificial intelligence (AI), to name but a few. This is particularly relevant here, since MOFA has already turned to AI for strategic input (S. Chen, 2018). To that end, I furnished examples of material-human interchanges that sustains certain practices. For example, MOFA's introduction of a WeChat account supports its communicative practice of controlling information flows through the scrubbing of "sensitive" questions in the application. My investigation of China's Twitter diplomacy also underlined how technological tools have impelled new articulations of power and play a decisive role in the construction of the "assertive diplomat." By taking earnestly the material/nonhuman and by problematizing the human/nonhuman dichotomy, PT can help IR better study diplomacy and technology and the associated manifold, still-developing implications.[22]

To readers of Chinese foreign policy, this serves as a corrective to state-centric, predominantly realist understandings of China's rise and its place in the international system. This research calls for further attention to the "everyday" practices and practitioners of Chinese diplomacy. It expands the analytic range of what is traditionally considered as "significant" in Chinese foreign policy—beyond simply the state and various state/Party-sponsored institutions. It demonstrates the theoretical importance of studying the practices of actors within MOFA and the broader non-Chinese diplomatic community within China. Furthermore, it signals the consequentiality of various diplomatic actors, such as think tanks, scholars, retired officials, and the media, and, the material, such as architecture, documents, and social media accounts, to the study of Chinese diplomacy.

Since this book borrows key concepts from Bourdieu for its analysis, it seems apt to pay homage and to close the book with an eponymous quote:

> As soon as we observe (*theorein*) the social world, we introduce in our percep-
> tion of it a bias due to the fact that, to study it, to describe it, to talk about
> it, we must retire from it more or less completely. This *theoreticist* or intellec-
> tualist bias consists in forgetting to inscribe, into the theory we build of the
> social world, the fact that it is the product of a theoretical gaze, a "contem-
> plative eye." A genuinely reflexive sociology must avoid this "ethnocentrism
> of the scientist" which consists in ignoring everything that the analyst injects
> in his perception of the object by virtue of the fact that he is placed outside of
> the object, that he observes it from afar and from above. (Bourdieu as cited in
> Wacquant, 1989, p. 34)

It is perhaps only through the importation of a conscious and deliberate reflexive gaze to our everyday lives that we can break with existing practices and perceptions and, in doing so, bring more clarity and understanding to our analysis of Chinese international politics.

Instances of the PRC's Cooperative and Assertive Behavior in Southeast Asia

In tables 2 through 13 I list instances from 2009 to 2020 that show Chinese assertiveness and cooperation in Southeast Asia. Per my operationalization in this book, acts of "assertiveness" are those that involve imposing or threatening to impose costs to police or guide behavior, which would cause anxiety and concern to countries, while "cooperation" would refer to activities that aim to promote goodwill and reduce anxieties. In that sense, the assertive activities listed below would have elicited a negative response and the cooperative practices would have elicited a positive response. These activities span the military, economic, nontraditional security, cultural, and diplomatic domains.

TABLE 2. Cooperative and assertive behavior, 2009.

Date	Assertive	Cooperative
March 17	China's largest fishery administration vessel, *China Yuzheng 311*, begins patrolling the SCS, with Foreign Ministry spokesperson stressing that China has indisputable sovereignty over it.	
April 1		China and Vietnam sign protocol on science and technology cooperation.
April		China announces the establishment of a USD $10 billion "China-ASEAN Investment Fund" underwritten by the Chinese government to invest in Southeast Asia.
April 14	China sends naval ships for the largest-ever SCS patrol.	
May 7	China submits the "nine-dash line" map to the United Nations.	
May 13	China formally asks the UN not to consider Vietnam's maritime boundary declaration, with Chinese Foreign Ministry spokesman Ma Zhaoxu saying that it infringes on China's sovereignty.	
October 29		China signs the Joint Action Plan for Strategic Cooperation, a five-year agreement with the Philippines, to deepen cooperation in all fields.
November 11		China and Malaysia sign five agreements expanding cooperation in trade and investment, especially in the financial services sector.
November 18		China and Vietnam sign a land boundary demarcation agreement on their 1,300 km land boundaries.
December 28		China signs the Chiang Mai Initiative Multilateralization Agreement, in which it is the largest contributor to a USD $120 billion reserve currency fund.

TABLE 3. Cooperative and assertive behavior, 2010.

Date	Assertive	Cooperative
March	A high-ranking Chinese official reportedly asserts that China's claims in the SCS are a "core interest" during a meeting with two senior Obama administration officials, Jeffrey A. Bader and James B. Steinberg.	
June 26		China and Cambodia sign cooperation agreements on road and bridge infrastructure.
August 5	China launches live-fire naval drills in the SCS, focusing on anti-missile attack drills.	
August 27	A Chinese submarine plants the national flag deep on the floor of the SCS.	
October 29		Chinese troops help in evacuation of Vietnamese near the China-Vietnam border river Beilun in Dongxing in disaster wrought by Typhoon Son-Tinh.
November 3	Chinese foreign minister Yang Jiechi hits out at the US and other countries in the Seventeenth ASEAN Regional Forum as an "attack" on China after eleven out of twenty-seven countries express concerns over the SCS.	
November 4	China's Marine Corps holds live-fire naval exercises in the SCS with 1,800 troops and more than 100 ships, submarines, and aircraft.	
November 10		China and Indonesia sign cooperation agreements worth USD $6.6 billion covering areas such as finance, energy, electricity, and agriculture.
November 18		The PLA and the Singapore Armed Forces kick off their second joint counterterrorism training exercise ("Cooperation 2010").
November 24		China and the Philippines sign a new air rights deal that would significantly increase flights between the two countries.
November 26		China and Laos sign a security cooperation pact to further develop their comprehensive, strategic, and cooperative partnership.

TABLE 4. Cooperative and assertive behavior, 2011.

Date	Assertive	Cooperative
January 6		China announces a plan to invest USD $1.51 billion to build a "China City Complex" in Bangkok, trading in Chinese-made goods, including garments, ornaments, and household items.
February 25	A Chinese missile frigate orders three Filipino fishing vessels to leave contested maritime waters under the threat of gunfire. Three rounds are fired that land near the vessels.	
April 11	The Philippines' largest naval vessel, *Gregorio del Pilar*, is engaged in a standoff with two Chinese maritime surveillance ships in Scarborough Shoal.	
April 26		China and Indonesia ink a memorandum of understanding on development of industrial technology, with the Chinese ready to invest in relevant industrial fields in Indonesia.
May 11	China imposes a unilateral fishing ban in the SCS directed toward Vietnam.	
May 25	Chinese patrol boats cut the cables of a Vietnamese ship conducting an underwater survey in the SCS.	
May 26	Three Chinese maritime patrol boats confront a Vietnamese oil vessel operated by the Vietnamese state-owned energy company PetroVietnam.	
July 20		China and ASEAN agree on guidelines to govern behavior in the disputed SCS.
August 15		China and the Philippines sign a $60 billion, five-year trade development program.
September 29	A commentary in the state-controlled nationalist newspaper *Global Times* states that Singapore is participating in an arms race and calls for waging "tiny-scale battles" against Vietnam and the Philippines.	
November 18		The "China-ASEAN Maritime Cooperation Fund" is established; it is underwritten by China and valued at RMB 3 billion.
November 18		Ten vocational schools and centers are established in China to help "ASEAN countries develop human resources needed in economic and social development."
November 21		The China-Vietnam People Friendship Festival opens in Liuzhou in the Guangxi Zhuang region.

TABLE 5. Cooperative and assertive behavior, 2012.

Date	Assertive	Cooperative
April 20	Suspected Chinese hackers vandalize the website of the University of the Philippines, leaving the message: "We come from China! Huangyan Island is Ours."	
May 3	China imposes unofficial "economic sanctions" by restricting banana imports from the Philippines. More than half of the Philippines' banana exports goes to China.	
May 25		The first China-ASEAN Culture Ministers' Meeting is held in Singapore.
May 29		Chinese Defense Minister Gen. Liang Guanglie attends the inaugural China-ASEAN Defense Ministers' Consultation in Phnom Penh.
June		The China-ASEAN senior police officers' workshop is held in Zhejiang, China.
June 27	China's state-owned CNOOC invites foreign companies to tender for exploration rights that Vietnam claims infringe on its territories and blocs already licensed to America's ExxonMobil and Russia's Gazprom.	
July 3		A bilateral antiterrorism exercise ("Sharp Knife") between China and Indonesia commences in Jinan, China. This is the second such exercise thus far.
July 13	ASEAN fails to issue a joint communiqué for the first time in its history as Cambodia, widely acknowledged to be under the direction of China, frustrates the process.	
July 22	China formally establishes a military garrison at Woody Islands, part of the contested Paracel Islands.	
September 10		China hosts the 2012 China-ASEAN Seminar on the Protection of Intellectual Property Rights, Traditional Knowledge, and Genetic Resources in Beijing.
September 11		The inaugural China-Malaysia defense and security consultation is held in Kuala Lumpur.
September 27		A permanent mission to ASEAN is opened in Jakarta by the Chinese government.
November 21	China issues new passports that include its claimed SCS territorial map.	

TABLE 6. Cooperative and assertive behavior, 2013.

Date	Assertive	Cooperative
February 6		China and Malaysia launch their Second Joint Industrial Park in Qinzhou, South China.
March 26	A Chinese vessel opens fire on a Filipino fishing boat near the Paracel Islands, setting it alight.	
March 27	The Chinese navy conducts military exercises at the outermost limits of its "nine-dash line" in James Shoal.	
April 26	The Chinese Foreign Ministry claims that the Philippines is illegally occupying Chinese territories in the SCS.	
Late May	The PLA Navy uses ships from its three fleets to carry out a joint exercise in the SCS, the first such three-fleet exercise since 2010.	
June 6		China and Thailand pass a five-year plan (2014–2018) to strengthen marine cooperation.
June 7		China and Vietnam establish a naval hotline between China and Vietnam.
June 17		The Chinese Naval Hospital Ship "Peace Ark" docks at Brunei, offering free medical checkups to locals.
June 20		The Chinese send 110 personnel, including fifty sappers, to the inaugural ASEAN Defense Ministers' Meeting Plus Humanitarian Assistance and Disaster Relief and Military Medicine Exercise.
June 21		China and Vietnam establish a hotline to deal with "fishery incidents."
July		China and the Vietnamese Marine Police commence the Eighth Joint Maritime Fishery Patrol in the Tonkin Gulf.
August 5	Chinese foreign minister Wang Yi tells ASEAN that it should have realistic expectations and adopt a gradual approach to a proposed CoC.	

August 14	The Fourteenth Naval Escort Fleet—CNS *Harbin*, a frigate, CNS *Mianyang*, and CNS *Weishanhu*—visits Thailand.
October 18 –November 1	The Chinese PLA Navy holds large-scale, sophisticated military exercises called "Maneuver-5" in the Yellow Sea, East China Sea, and SCS—the first time the navy has conducted coordinated combat drills with all three PLA Navy fleets.
December 16	Chinese and Indonesian navies hold naval military exercises in the SCS. Additionally, it is announced that Indonesia intends to send pilots to Beijing for aviation courses.

TABLE 7. Cooperative and assertive behavior, 2014.

Date	Assertive	Cooperative
January 27	A Chinese vessel fires water cannons at Filipino fishermen in Scarborough Shoal.	
February 20	A Chinese naval flotilla conducts a three-week patrol that extends well beyond its claimed territories to the Lombok Straits in Indonesian waters.	
March 11		China announces that it will build the "China-ASEAN Ocean College" in Malaysia, utilizing the China-ASEAN Maritime Cooperation Fund.
May 2	China deploys an oil rig 120 miles from Vietnam's coast, sparking a diplomatic standoff between China and Vietnam.	
May 11		China and Cambodia agree to boost defense ties with China, increasing the number of scholarships offered to Cambodian military personnel to study in China.
May 27	A Vietnamese fishing boat is sunk after forty Chinese vessels "surrounded and rammed" it.	
June		China participates in the US-led Rim of the Pacific International Maritime Exercise (RIMPAC) for the first time. RIMPAC is the world's largest international maritime warfare exercise and regularly includes Southeast Asian states—Malaysia, Singapore, Brunei, Indonesia, and Thailand.
June 2		China and Malaysia sign a joint communiqué on trade development and the SCS, stressing the importance of maintaining peace, security, and stability as well as upholding freedom and safety of navigation in the SCS.
September 17		China and the Philippines sign a memorandum of understanding to promote and facilitate investment cooperation.
November 2		The Singapore Armed Forces and China's PLA start their third bilateral training exercise ("Cooperation 2014").
November 13		China pledges USD $480 million to help less developed members of ASEAN to reduce poverty.

TABLE 8. Cooperative and assertive behavior, 2015.

Date	Assertive	Cooperative
February 4	A Chinese ship rams into three fishing boats carrying twenty-nine Filipino fishermen at Scarborough Shoal.	
March 26	The PLA conducts a night live-fire drill at the China-Myanmar border of Yunnan.	
May 25		The Republic of Singapore Navy and China's PLAN conduct a new joint naval exercise.
May 31	A Chinese admiral from the PLA suggests that China may impose an Air Defense Identification Zone over the SCS.	
June 1	The military conducts live-fire land and air drills on the China-Myanmar border of Yunnan.	
June 8	A China Coast Guard vessel is found anchored in Malaysian waters at Luconia Shoals, prompting a diplomatic protest. Malaysia sends its navy and coast guards to the area.	
June 16		Beijing says it will stop land reclamation activities in the SCS.
September 15		China kicks off its first joint military drill with Malaysia with more than 1,000 Chinese troops involved—the largest ever between Beijing and an ASEAN country.
September 20	China completes construction of a runway on Fiery Cross Reef in contested territory with the Philippines.	
October 16		China hosts the inaugural ASEAN-China Defense Ministers' Informal Meeting in Beijing, where it proposes to hold joint training on the "Code for Unalerted Encounters at Sea (CUES)" and suggests setting up an "Asian" dispute settlement mechanism.

October 16	China fended off competition from Japan and signs an agreement with Indonesia for the construction of a USD $5.5 billion, 150 km high-speed railway.
October 16	China announces that it is willing to hold joint drills in the SCS on rules about accidental encounters at sea, search and rescue, and disaster relief with ASEAN nations.
December 13	Chinese navy holds a war drill in the SCS.
November 7	China announces that the third government-to-government project between China and Singapore will be located in Chongqing and will increase bilateral ties.
November 13	China, through Foreign Minister Wang Yi, holds high-level talks with his Philippine counterpart for the first time in six years.
November 15	Joint air exercises ("Falcon Strike") commence between China and Thailand.
November 18	A joint table-top exercise is held between China and Indonesia on Maritime Search and Rescue operations in Haikou, Hainan province.
November 21	China pledges infrastructure loans totaling $10 billion to Southeast Asian countries and proposes railway and production capacity cooperation.
December 1	China and Vietnam sign an agreement to resolve problems with border marker delineation and demarcation and to enhance cooperation in protecting and managing border markers.

TABLE 9. Cooperative and assertive behavior, 2016.

Date	Assertive	Cooperative
March	Indonesia summons the Chinese ambassador after a maritime standoff in the Natuna Sea.	
March 31	Malaysia summons the Chinese ambassador after encroachment by a large number of Chinese ships in Malaysian waters in the SCS.	
June	The ASEAN statement on the SCS at the ASEAN-China meeting is first issued and later retracted owing to pressure from China.	
July 16	ASEAN, under diplomatic pressure from China, fails to issue a joint statement on the rejection of Chinese territorial claims by PCA.	
August 19		China and Myanmar agree to restart talks and find a solution to the suspended Myitsone dam joint project.
September 27	China accuses Singapore of inserting the SCS issue at the Seventeenth Non-Aligned Movement summit in Venezuela, precipitating a chill in bilateral relations.	
November		China and Malaysia sign over USD $30 million worth of deals covering energy and rail infrastructure.
November 24	China seizes nine Singaporean armored vehicles in Hong Kong en route to Singapore from Taiwan.	

TABLE 10. Cooperative and assertive behavior, 2017.

Date	Assertive	Cooperative
January 5	Naval drills in the SCS are led by the Liaoning aircraft carrier.	
April 27	The Chinese military attempts to force away two Philippine planes that were carrying Manila's defense and military chiefs near a reclaimed island in the SCS.	
May 19		China and ASEAN "agree on a "framework" for the stalled CoC negotiations.
May 27	China's MOFA criticizes G7 Summit for having interfered in the SCS issue when a statement expressing concern was made.	
June 4	China lowers its participation and delegation size at the annual track-1 "Shangri-La" dialogue.	
June 17	China releases a video criticizing a India-Singapore naval exercise.	
November 12		Premier Li Keqiang proposes to start negotiations on a CoC with ASEAN at the ASEAN-China leaders' meeting.
November 14		ASEAN and China sign an agreement to sync the ASEAN connectivity program with China's BRI.
November 16		China and the Philippines sign fourteen deals ranging from transport to military aid worth around USD $21.6 million.
December 6	China summons Australia's ambassador and publicly scolds Canberra as the Turnbull government introduces foreign interference laws.	

TABLE 11. Cooperative and assertive behavior, 2018.

Date	Assertive	Cooperative
February 6		China and ASEAN agree to commence joint military exercises in 2018.
March 26	Chinese navy conducts live-fire drills in the SCS.	
April 9		Premier Li Keqiang announces plans to develop its "Silk Road" project with Singapore's development plans.
April 13	President Xi presides over China's largest-ever naval exercise in the SCS.	
May 21	China lands a heavy bomber on a disputed island in the SCS for the first time.	
June 2	PLA says China will put troops and weapons on islands in SCS and it has every right to do so.	
August 2		Agreement on the "Single Draft CoC Negotiating Text" is announced at an ASEAN-China meeting.
August 2		Inaugural ASEAN-China Maritime Exercise is conducted in Singapore.
August 4		China's MOFA lobbies ASEAN for joint military exercises.

TABLE 12. Cooperative and assertive behavior, 2019.

Date	Assertive	Cooperative
January 1	The China Academy of Sciences establishes an Oceanographic Research Centre on Mischief Reef.	
April 26		China kicks off naval drills with six countries in Southeast Asia on its east coast.
May 5		The biggest joint venture between Brunei and China in oil refinery and petrochemicals enters its production phase.
May 1		China offers to provide $1 billion yuan (USD $140 million) to Myanmar to support socioeconomic development.
June 12	Vietnamese fisherman Tran Van Nhan has his ship forcefully boarded by Chinese coast guards, and he and his crew are forced to surrender their harvest while being held against their will with electric prods.	
June 16	China Coast Guard vessel *Haijing 35111* harasses the Japanese rig *Hakuryu-5*, and up to seven other Chinese ships set out to join the standoff.	
July 1	China tests its first Anti-Ship Ballistic Missile (ASBM) in the South China Sea.	
July 12	Chinese survey ship *Haiyang Dizhi 8* reportedly enters waters near the Vietnamese-controlled Vanguard Reef, triggering a standoff.	
September 6		China pledges $169 billion to the Philippines for infrastructure projects.
September 13		China and Malaysia set up a joint dialogue mechanism to enhance cooperation and dialogue over the SCS.
October 1		China agrees to withdraw its survey ship *Haiyang Dizhi 8* from the Vanguard Bank after Hanoi officials express "profound displeasure" during the Eighteenth ASEAN–China Senior Officials' Meeting.
November 3		China pledges "long-term peace" in Southeast Asia and makes a commitment to conclude the CoC soon.
December 30	Indonesia lodges protests as China Coast Guard vessels allegedly intrude into the Natuna waters.	

TABLE 13. Cooperative and assertive behavior, 2020.

Date	Assertive	Cooperative
February 17	China's People's Liberation Army Navy vessel (Bow number 514) aims its gun control director toward the Philippine Navy's antisubmarine corvette BRP *Conrado Yap* at the Spratly Islands.	
March 1	The West Capella, a drill ship operated by London-managed Seadrill and contracted to Malaysia's Petronas, is repeatedly harassed by China Coast Guard ships near the Lala-1 oilfield block.	
April 18	The Chinese State Council approves the establishment of two districts in Sansha City. The eponymously named Xisha and Nansha Districts are responsible for administrative duties on the Xisha and Nansha Islands, respectively, and are part of the greater Hainan Province.	
May 29		China's ambassador to ASEAN, Deng Xijun, proclaims that China is ready to include ASEAN in its $2 billion Covid-19 aid assistance scheme.
June 9		China's Guangdong Fishery Mutual Insurance Association apologizes to the Philippines embassy in Beijing for a Chinese fishing boat's unintended collision with a Filipino fishing boat from Occidental Mindoro.
July 14	China's embassy in the United States accuses the US State Department of distorting facts and international law (including the UN Convention on the Law of the Sea) to "sow discord between China and other littoral countries in the South China Sea."	
August 26	China tests its second Anti-Ship Ballistic Missile (ASBM) in the South China Sea concurrently with the US annual naval exercise, as a potential show of force.	
September 2		The PRC's Ministry of Foreign Affairs' vice foreign minister Luo Zhaohui releases a statement reassuring ASEAN that ASEAN is pivotal to China and that China will continue its history of bilateral engagement to manage the disputes in the South China Sea.
October 22		Philippines and China sign a memorandum of understanding on jointly cooperating to harvest oil in West Philippines Sea. A commercial agreement between CNOOC and Forum Energy has yet to be ratified.

From the information above, it is clear that assertiveness in the military field is most salient. Nevertheless, assertive activities occur in other fields as well. In the diplomatic and economic fields, for instance, China has shown its assertiveness through unofficial sanctions or through the issuance of statements that cause anxiety and concern. Conversely, many cooperative activities take place in the security sphere as well. The data also exhibits how MOFA plays a key role in the SCS disputes. The above examples are not meant to be exhaustive but simply to point out how China's foreign policy demonstrates *both* assertive and cooperative behavior. The activities shown here underline multiple cooperative and assertive activities across all domains, by different parties, every year. Moreover, there are ongoing cooperative activities with disputant states and assertive behavior toward nonclaimant states.

APPENDIX B

Interviewee Profiles

Balancing interviewees' anonymity with transparency, I include a general institutional association in their profiles. Interviewees marked "CP" are Chinese primary diplomatic actors, those marked "MOFA-CP" are MOFA diplomats, and those marked "CS" are Chinese secondary diplomatic actors (see chapter 3).

Interviewee 1: Chinese diplomat based in England (MOFA-CP). Interviewed March 15 and November 20, 2016, London.

Interviewee 2: Senior Southeast Asian diplomat. Interviewed May 9, 2014, February 10, 2015, and July 11, 2018, Singapore.

Interviewee 3: Senior Southeast Asian diplomat. Interviewed July 10, 2018, Singapore.

Interviewee 4: Major general from the PLA (CP). Interviewed June 20, 2016, Beijing.

Interviewee 5: East Asian diplomat in Beijing. Interviewed July 27, 2017, Beijing.

Interviewee 6: Senior colonel from the PLA (CP). Interviewed July 29, 2017, Beijing.

Interviewee 7: Former MOFA diplomat and current think-tanker (MOFA-CP). Interviewed June 29, 2017, Beijing, and November 11, 2019, on WeChat.

Interviewee 8: Chinese diplomat (MOFA-CP). Interviewed June 2, 2018, Beijing.

Interviewee 9: CFAU student and MOFA aspirant. Interviewed June 25, 2016, and July 12, 2017, Beijing.

Interviewee 10: Scholar from CFAU (CS). Interviewed June 27, 2017, Beijing.

Interviewee 11: Chinese diplomat (MOFA-CP). Interviewed July 1, 2017.

Interviewee 12: Scandinavian diplomat. Interviewed June 27, 2018.

Interviewee 13: British reporter based in Beijing. Interviewed August 27, 2017, Beijing.

Interviewee 14: Former PLA officer and current government official (CS). Interviewed August 28, 2017, Shenyang, and July 1, 2016, Beijing.

Interviewee 15: Former PLA officer and current government official (CS). Interviewed August 28, 2017, Shenyang.

Interviewee 16: Senior colonel from the PLA (CP). Interviewed August 1, 2018, Beijing.

Interviewee 17: Major general from the PLA (CP). Closed-door conference, August 2, 2018, Beijing.

Interviewee 18: Senior colonel from the PLA (CP). Interviewed August 2, 2018, Beijing.

Interviewee 19: Chinese analyst from CIIS (CS). Interviewed August 3, 2017, Beijing.

Interviewee 20: Senior Southeast Asian diplomat. Interviewed August 1, 2017, Shanghai.

Interviewee 21: Western diplomat. Interviewed July 1, 2017, and August 2, 2016, Beijing.

Interviewee 22: Asian academic. Interviewed February 11, 2015, Singapore.

Interviewee 23: Senior colonel from the PLA (CP). Interviewed July 31, 2018, Beijing.

Interviewee 24: Southeast Asian diplomat. Interviewed August 15, 2017, Beijing.

Interviewee 25: Southeast Asian diplomat. Interviewed August 13, 2018, Singapore.

Interviewee 26: Chinese scholar in a Beijing-based university (CS). Interviewed July 25, 2018, Beijing.

Interviewee 27: Senior Southeast Asian diplomat. Interviewed June 17, 2017, Beijing.

Interviewee 28: Southeast Asian journalist and former diplomat. Interviewed August 29, 2017, Beijing.

Interviewee 29: Southeast Asian diplomat in China. Interviewed August 17, 2017, Beijing.

Interviewee 30: Southeast Asian government official. Interviewed May 10, 2018, and January 20, 2020, by email.

Interviewee 31: Southeast Asian journalist. Interviewed August 31, 2017, and July 19, 2018, Beijing.

Interviewee 32: Chinese scholar (CS). Interviewed July 11, 2017, Shanghai.

Interviewee 33: Chinese scholar whom the Chinese government consulted with (CS). Interviewed July 5, 2017, Shanghai.

Interviewee 34: Chinese scholar from a Beijing-based think tank (CS). Interviewed June 27, 2016, Beijing.

Interviewee 35: ASEAN official. Interviewed June 25, 2016.

Interviewee 36: Senior MOFA-affiliated scholar (CP). Interviewed July 4, 2017, and July 30, 2018.

Interviewee 37: Southeast Asian diplomat. Interviewed June 24, 2016, July 11, 2017, and August 3, 2018, Singapore.

Interviewee 38: Think-tanker and retired naval (senior colonel) officer (CS). Interviewed July 11, 2017, Beijing.

Interviewee 39: Western diplomat. Interviewed July 19, 2018, Beijing.

Interviewee 40: Chinese diplomat (MOFA-CP). Interviewed July 16, 2018, Beijing.

Interviewee 41: European diplomat. Interviewed June 27, 2016, Beijing.

Interviewee 42: Scholar from CFAU (CS). Interviewed August 13, 2017, Beijing.

Interviewee 43: Analyst from the Chinese Academy of Social Sciences (CS). Interviewed August 22, 2017, Beijing.

Interviewee 44: Analyst from a MOFA-affiliated think tank (CS). Interviewed September 1, 2017, Beijing.

Interviewee 45: Scholar from Peking University, affiliated with a Beijing-based think tank (CS). Interviewed July 31, 2017, Beijing.

Interviewee 46: Scholar and deputy director of a MOFA-affiliated think tank (CP). Interviewed July 30, 2017, Beijing.

Interviewee 47: Southeast Asian diplomat in charge of economic affairs. Interviewed August 31, 2017, Beijing.

Interviewee 48: North American diplomat. Interviewed June 24, 2017, Beijing.

Interviewee 49: Dean of a Chinese university (CS). Interviewed August 7, 2017, on campus, Beijing.

Interviewee 50: Scholar from a university in Beijing (CS). Interviewed June 23, 2017, Beijing, September 27, 2016, London, and March 25, 2018, Cambridge.

Interviewee 51: Chinese diplomat (MOFA-CP). Interviewed August 1, 2018, Beijing.

Interviewee 52: Vice president of a university (CP). Interviewed July 29, 2017, and July 28, 2018.

Interviewee 53: Scholar and former Chinese diplomat (MOFA-CP). Interviewed July 28, 2018, Beijing.

Interviewee 54: Former MOFA diplomat (CS). Interviewed April 27, 2018, Cambridge.

Interviewee 55: Academic based in Singapore. Interviewed February 26, 2015, Singapore.

Interviewee 56: Southeast Asian diplomat. Interviewed August 28, 2017, Beijing.

Interviewee 57: Scholar from Tsinghua (CS). Interviewed June 28, 2017, Beijing.

Interviewee 58: Southeast Asian diplomat. Interviewed September 3, 2017, Beijing.

Interviewee 59: East Asian diplomat. Interviewed June 19, 2017, Beijing.

Interviewee 60: Scholar in a MOFA-affiliated institution (CS). Interviewed July 9, 2018, Beijing.

Interviewee 61: Scholar from CICIR (CS). Interviewed June 27, 2017, Beijing.

Interviewee 62: Oceanic diplomat. Interviewed June 25, 2017, Beijing.

Interviewee 63: Senior European Union diplomat. Interviewed July 19, 2017, Beijing.

Interviewee 64: Chinese diplomat (MOFA-CP). Interviewed July 3, 2017, Beijing.

Interviewee 65: Scholar from Beijing Jiaotong University (CS). Interviewed July 31, 2017, Beijing.

Interviewee 66: Chinese public servant. Interviewed July 17, 2018, Beijing, and December 15, 2019, on WeChat.

Interviewee 67: Western diplomat. Interviewed August 2, 2017, Beijing.

Interviewee 68: Southeast Asian diplomat. Interviewed August 1, 2017, Beijing.

Interviewee 69: Western diplomat. Interviewed July 9, 2017, Beijing.

Interviewee 70: Chinese diplomat (MOFA-CP). Interviewed July 10, 2017, Beijing, and November 10, 2019, on WeChat.

Interviewee 71: Chinese scholar based in Singapore (CS). Interviewed September 12, 2017, Singapore.

Interviewee 72: European diplomat. Interviewed January 6, 2018, London.

Interviewee 73: Retired senior PLA officer who consults with the government (CS). Interviewed August 1, 2018.

Interviewee 74: Senior academic in a MOFA-affiliated think tank (CP). Interviewed July 23, 2018.

Interviewee 75: Senior Southeast Asian diplomat. Interviewed November 16, 2018, London.

Interviewee 76: East Asian diplomat. Interviewed June 25, 2016, Beijing.

Interviewee 77: Chinese diplomat (MOFA-CP). Interviewed November 16, 2018, London, and November 6, 2019, by email.

Interviewee 78: Chinese diplomat (MOFA-CP). Interviewed July 11, 2018.

Interviewee 79: Chinese academic (CS). Interviewed December 28, 2019, by phone.

Interviewee 80: American reporter from a global media outlet. Interviewed March 30, 2020, by email.

Interviewee 81: Southeast Asian journalist based in Beijing. Interviewed April 20, 2020, by email.

Interviewee 82: Chinese journalist (CS). Interviewed May 2, 2020, by email.

Interviewee 83: MOFA-affiliated scholar (CP). Interviewed May 9, 2020, by phone.

Interviewee 84: Chinese academic (CS). Interviewed November 22, 2019, by email.

Notes

Introduction

1. The terms *assertive diplomacy* and *assertive foreign policy* is often used by scholars to refer to the same phenomenon. See Ross (2013).

2. The vocabulary used in such analysis ("core interests," "national strategy," and so forth) reflects this penchant (e.g., J. Wang, 2011; Zeng et al., 2015).

3. The first MOFA press conference was held on March 1, 1983, with Qi Huaiyuan 齐怀远 as the first spokesperson (*Baijiahao*, 2023).

4. The "two meetings" are meetings of the National People's Congress and the National Committee of the Chinese People's Political Consultative Conference.

5. This references the military border dispute between India and China over China's construction of a road in Doklam in June 2017 (Blanchard, 2017).

6. A similar process can be traced back to the Qing dynasty in the late nineteenth century, when political reformers and revolutionaries actively constructed others' visions of "China" (Hayton, 2020).

7. This refers to the twin goals of a "moderately well-off society" by 2021 (coinciding with the one-hundredth year of China's Communist Party) and of a "fully developed nation" by 2049 (coinciding with the one-hundredth year of the People's Republic of China).

8. The top leadership is embodied by the seven-member Politburo Standing Committee (PSC), in which Xi Jinping is the "core" leader. The number of people in the PSC was nine before 2012 and had been as low as five members in the ninth PSC in 1969.

Chapter 1

1. Office of the Historian (1971).

2. The terms *foreign policy* and *diplomacy* are often used interchangeably in the literature. Although they are closely related, they are not identical (see Clinton, 2011). I take *foreign policy* to refer to a government's broad strategy in dealing with another nation and *diplomacy* to refer

to the practice of managing a country's international relations, principally by its foreign ministry. The focus of this book is on diplomatic practices and the effects that obtain from these practices.

3. See also Lynch (2009), Tang (2008), Cheng and Wang (2011), and Mearsheimer (2010).

4. Some scholars protest this development and go as far as to say they remain "unconvinced that it is a useful term analytically" (D. Chen et al., 2014, p. 180). Even so, there is little doubt that "assertiveness" is a construct used by political elites, scholars, and laypersons to explain Chinese foreign policy.

5. This is analogous to the Cabinet in most parliamentary democracies and is constitutionally the "executive body" and "the highest organ of state administration" (A. D. Barnett, 1985, p. 52).

6. Callahan explains how "China's citizen intellectuals are slightly different from the 'public intellectuals' found in more liberal societies. Citizen intellectuals have emerged in the shadow of state censorship that continues to shape modern Chinese thought" (2012, p. 621).

7. The belief that there is one legitimate ruler and that this legitimacy is mandated by the gods/heaven.

8. *Tianxia* translates to "all under heaven"—"a combination of nature, super-nature, and morality. Thus, it was not a mere material thing out there. It was more a cultural concept containing the system of morality, or the way of the heaven" (Qin, 2007, p. 329). The tributary system was a regional order in which entities paid regular tributes to imperial China in exchange for trade concessions and protection.

9. This is where "states are neither unitary actors of IR theory, expressing a 'national interest' or 'identity,' nor politically neutral, rationally designed, problem-solving instruments; rather, they are institutional ensembles that reflect and embed historically evolving social power relations" (Hameiri and Jones, 2016, p. 78).

10. Hameiri and Jones add "decentralisation to provincial governments and the incorporation of special administrative regions (SARs)" (2016, p. 82) to support their claims. Nevertheless, evidence indicates that the governments of both SARs are more aligned with the CCP than ever before. A main reason for the massive street protests (numbering over one hundred thousand participants) that took place in Hong Kong in September 2014 was perceived interference by the CCP in which the Standing Committee of the National People's Congress in mainland China would need to "pre-approve candidates to run for elections in the Hong Kong's Legislative Council—even if the candidates receive at least 1% endorsement by the electorate" (D. Loh, 2015, p. 118).

11. Through an analysis of successive generations of diplomats from 1949 to 1994.

12. *Substantialism* refers to the view of "substances (things, beings, entities, essences)" as "the units or levels of analysis and [the view] that they exist prior to the analysis" (Adler-Nissen, 2015, p. 290). See Adler-Nissen (2015, pp. 284–308) for a critique of IR scholars' preoccupation with substantialism.

13. Latour defines *actant* as "something that acts or to which activity is granted by others. It implies no special motivation of human individual actors, nor of humans in general. An actant can literally be anything provided it is granted to be the source of an action" (1996, p. 373).

14. "Grand theory" is understood as having "something to say on the international or global-structural level—that there is a logic or set of patterns at that 'level of analysis' that can be understood via particular theoretical assumptions" (Solomon & Steele, 2017, p. 3).

15. Where "different scientific methodologies generate different bodies of knowledge, each of which is internally justified in distinctive ways, but none of which commands unqualified universal assent" (Jackson, 2011, p. 210).

16. The most popular chat application in China.

17. Ding calls this behavior that "is mostly devoted to maintaining the bureaucracy's public image of responsiveness, benevolence, and effectiveness" (2022, p. 7).

18. In 2016 I spent six weeks in Beijing, China (from June to August), and one week, later that year, in Singapore; in 2017, I spent thirteen weeks in Beijing, China (from June to September, including field travels to Shanghai and Shenyang); and in 2018 I spent three weeks in Beijing, China (July to August), and one week (in August) in Singapore. After Beijing, Shanghai is arguably the next most important political center in China (with important foreign policy scholars, think tanks, and universities); hence my journey there in 2017. Relatedly, a trip to Shenyang (August 28, 2017) was prompted by interviews granted by former and current PLA members and government officials. Trips to Singapore were made based on securing interviews with Southeast Asian diplomats who had deep interactions with PRC envoys during their careers. I also tapped into existing networks to get access to Chinese PRC representatives in the United Kingdom, and these are reflected in interviews conducted in London in 2016 and 2018. Some interviews were conducted opportunistically in 2019. I conducted a round of virtual/phone interviews in January, March, and April of 2020, in a bid to understand China's Twitter diplomacy.

19. Emphasis added.

20. I am cognizant of the problems in reconstructing data *ex post* and was careful not to let the information—which was not collected in any systematic manner—speak more than it could or should. That said, these interactions formed an important part of my data-gathering process, as the practices I saw there spanned the period under study here.

Chapter 2

1. While by no means a scientific inquiry, a modest Lexis Nexis database search for news articles using the terms *China assertiveness* and *Chinese assertiveness* for the years 2019 and 2020 yielded news coverage that frequently referenced China's diplomats and its "wolf warriors." Comparatively, a search, using the same keywords, for the years 2007 and 2006 yielded markedly fewer references to MOFA.

2. *Capacity* is used here, broadly, to imply competencies and abilities that can be brought to bear in a field. This is not unlike Pouliot's rendition of Goffman's "sense of place," where this sensibility "stems from a stock of tacit know-how that is bound up in competent performance" (Pouliot, 2016, p. 74).

3. It may be valid to ask: Are there "nonrobust" displays of diplomacy? I suggest that Chinese diplomats' assertiveness that other parties internationally might regard as incompetent "overperformance" is viewed as a sign of competence at home (in the local diplomatic field) and that a failure to display that assertiveness would be regarded as incompetent "underperformance."

4. President Xi himself stressed the importance of the "harmonization of foreign policy" (*dui wai gongzuo de ji zhong tongyi* 对外工作的集中统一) and made apparent MOFA's coordinating role in consolidating foreign policy work.

5. I do not wish to exaggerate the "disdain" the PLA feel toward MOFA. Yet a nationalistic segment of the military has not been shy in scolding diplomats. For instance, upon hearing news of the death of respected former diplomat Wu Jianmin 吴建民, Dai Xu 戴旭—a well-known hawk and senior colonel and professor at the National Defense University—posted a statement on Weibo saying that Wu was "rude, arrogant, obtuse, and narrow-minded" (*wuzhi qie aoman wu li, xinxiong xia ai* 无知且傲慢无礼，心胸狭隘), while another message posted a few days later likened him to a lap dog (Dai, 2016).

6. Emphasis added. This comment also brings out MOFA's capacity to counsel well, by virtue of their proprietorship over "legitimate knowledge" in world affairs.

7. This supports You Ji's observation that MOFA retains control over China's "foreign affairs and daily diplomacy" in relation to the PLA (2014, p. 237).

8. Emphasis added.

9. From my interactions with CFAU students and faculty between 2016 and 2018, I have observed a widely shared sense that a MOFA job is desirable.

10. Bourdieu's ethnographic account of the Kabyle people is replete with observations like this: "His way of walking, that of a man who knows where he is going and knows he will arrive in time, whatever the obstacles, expresses strength and resolution, as opposed to the hesitant gait (thikli thamahmahht) announcing indecision, half-hearted promises (awal amahmah)" (1977, p. 94).

11. Somewhat ironically, he also said, "I think any person without prejudice or 'tinted glasses' would recognize such facts. Finger-pointing is not a proper way to treat guests" (Luo, 2016, para. 18).

12. Here I am drawing on my attendance at three live press conferences and my watching of more than sixty MOFA press conference clips from 2016 to 2018 on the Associated Press YouTube channel. The stiff body movement on stage and the often stern demeanor are quite plain to see.

13. Geng Shuang, Lu Kang, and Hong Lei.

14. Or, as Goffman puts it, the "frontstage" (1959, p. 78).

15. This was at a closed-door conference with Philippine, British, and Chinese diplomats (in London in 2016) discussing the SCS.

16. I do not use the term *backstage* here because even when diplomatic actors step off the literal stage or when the conference on the SCS ends, they are still performing, albeit less intensely.

17. Emphasis added.

18. They tend to use Hotmail or Gmail free accounts rather than official email addresses. See *Sociopolítica de Asia Pacífico* (2018).

19. I note that the Japanese are similarly known for their reliance on fax machines.

20. For instance, I received an email communication where a MOFA diplomat misspelled my name and made several grammatical errors.

21. Recall that in practices "competence" is performative and needs to be seen in its social context. Seen domestically, the Chinese diplomat's assertiveness was a competent act.

22. It must be pointed out that these practices can backfire. An example would be MOFA's purported "overreaction" to a tourist incident in Sweden when a Chinese family was refused accommodation because they had booked the wrong dates and the hotel was full. MOFA and the Chinese embassy "made solemn representations" to the Swedish government demanding a thorough investigation and asking for an apology (Zhuang, 2018, para. 11). This, in turn, was touted as part of a broader trend by China to "weaponize" tourism (Rees, 2018). In interviews, non-Chinese diplomats frequently cited Wang Yi's Canada visit and the Swedish tourist incident as examples of the overbearing, "bullying" nature of China's diplomacy and its diplomats (Interviewee 75, personal communication, November 16, 2018).

23. See Gherardi (2017) on "sociomateriality" and the ways materials are constitutive to practices.

24. In the Chinese case, the distinction between the "public" and "private" spheres is blurred because of the levels of discipline demanded, the presence of mutual surveillance, and the internalization of the institutional habitus.

25. The ruling by the Tribunal in The Hague was widely seen as a "victory" for the Philippines, as it concluded that there was "no legal basis for China to claim historic rights to re-

sources within the sea areas falling within the 'nine-dash line'" (Santos, 2016). The "nine-dash line" refers to China's expansive territorial claims in the South China Sea, which stretch as far as two thousand kilometers away from Mainland China and encompass 90 percent of the entire South China Sea (Z. Liu, 2016).

26. It was also Wang Yi who announced a "four-point consensus" with Brunei, Cambodia, and Laos on the SCS issue in April 2016, to the chagrin of others who saw this as an attempt to divide ASEAN (Ismail, 2016).

27. Emphasis added.

28. Emanuel Adler (personal communication, November 8, 2018) suggests that the emergence of a "competitor" CoP could contest dominant practices engendered by the preponderant CoP.

29. The NDRC formulates and implements national economic and social development plans.

30. Bo was commerce minister from 2004 to 2007 and is currently in jail for multiple corruption-related offenses.

31. This weapon's deployment in South Korea (in coordination with the United States) in 2017 raised bitter objections from Beijing.

32. See also Toh (2016), Si (2018), and X. Yang (2016) for examples of ASEAN-China events organized and coordinated by MOFA.

33. One major difference between China's MOFA and foreign ministries in liberal regimes is that MOFA personnel are expected to hold personal beliefs that align with the CCP since employees must be Party members. In contrast, in the United Kingdom, for example, it is not uncommon for government officials to personally disagree (sometimes publicly) with policies that they need to implement.

34. Such was probably the case with the threat made by senior Chinese diplomat Li Kexin to members of Congress in Washington that a US naval ship visit to Taiwan would mean war (Blanchard & Yu, 2017). This statement is unlikely to have been made without Beijing's assent.

35. It was also in 2010 that the press conference was moved to the present "Blue Hall," a room built for hosting conferences (Ministry of Foreign Affairs, 2011).

36. One source told a story in which a Chinese diplomat who was studying for a master's degree scolded a fellow student when the issue of Taiwan was brought up (Interviewee 37, personal communication, June 24, 2016).

Chapter 3

1. A version of this chapter was first published in D. Loh (2018a).

2. Here I am referring not to ontological distinctions but to scales of "going deep" and "zooming out" as a methodological device. Shove writes how a flat ontology "does not mean lacking in mountain ranges of inequality and power, nor does it mean being incapable of explaining how exceptionally uneven landscapes emerge and change—potentially via a full gamut of methodologies and empirical enquiries—it's just that there is a certain way of conceptualising what's going on." In other words, "We can finally have the cake (remain 'ontologically flat') and eat it after all (talk about transsituative phenomena)" (Shove, 2017, para. 14).

3. The use of the concept of "field" is common in French IR. I thank a reviewer for clarifying this.

4. It is appropriate to stress here that fields do not necessarily need a territorial substratum (although they can have one); rather, they are defined by a "stake at stake" and are "spaces of interaction and struggle" (Pouliot, 2016, p. 211).

5. The "power over other species of power, and particularly over their rate of exchange" (Bourdieu & Wacquant, 1992, p. 114).

6. From economic capital (taxation money) to cultural capital (building of monuments) in the Roman Empire, for example.

7. On this connection, see Julian Go's (2008) conception of "global field" in examining British and American empires.

8. Hysteresis exists when one's habitus gets "out of step" with the (new) environment. See Neumann and Pouliot's (2011) work on Russian agents experiencing hysteresis when entering the international diplomatic field.

9. Universities and think tanks are in themselves fields. These are universes worthy of study, but they are not my object of inquiry here.

10. My mapping here is similar to Glaser's "three concentric rings" visualization of Chinese foreign policy institutes and their influence (2012, p. 91). The difference, however, is that my conception of the Chinese diplomatic field is broader and I underline the relational nature of actors in the field.

11. Although I use the term *objective*, these were not coded in any way, nor were they derived from any dataset (no such publicly available data exists), and I relied on interviewees to get these indicators.

12. See China Foreign Affairs University (2018).

13. CFAU provides an "easy example" of how the identification of a secondary player works, but this is not always the case. Actors sometimes downplay or overplay their importance in the field, and they do not necessarily see themselves as entangled in the web of hierarchical relations. For instance, an interviewee from the "academic" category self-identified as an influential player (Interviewee 71, personal communication, September 12, 2017), yet analysis (whether he had published "influential" op-eds and obtained concrete "face time" with MOFA and PSC leaders) and third-party triangulation did not corroborate this account. In instances such as this, I had to decide whether to accept or reject the actor's self-identification. Within the diplomatic field of China, such examples are rare, and most secondary and primary actors have a keen sense of self-other awareness.

14. One MOFA diplomat (Interviewee 77), a former PLA officer (Interviewee 73), and two non-Chinese diplomats (Interviewee 75 and Interviewee 3).

15. Based on "a survey by questionnaire, carried out in 1963 and 1967–68, on a sample of 1,217 people" (Bourdieu, 1984, p. 13).

16. See Pouliot (2016, pp. 227–233) for an overview of his application of MCA and how its inductive, relational, and exploratory nature renders it well equipped for the study of field logics.

17. See Bernhard's article (2011) on the emergence of an EU policy field for an excellent example of a nonquantitative method of constructing and interpreting a field.

18. This took place during the 2018 International Studies Association convention's "Critical Security Studies Methods Café" on the "practice approach" in San Francisco.

19. Here we can see a tension between the desire to professionalize MOFA (chapter 2) and organizational inertia and resistance.

20. As always, there are exceptions. One Southeast Asian diplomat who enjoys a close relationship with his Chinese counterpart claims that they are able to meet one-to-one: "This is unusual, and I don't think others have that. Normally, we still have colleagues around, but we have met alone before" (Interviewee 37, personal communication, August 3, 2018).

21. I had work interactions with North Korean diplomats (in 2014), and they, too, turned up in pairs.

22. That said, Chinese scholars who have distinguished themselves and are close to the polit-ical center are allowed to skirt these travel limitations, as they are deemed more "trustworthy."

23. A famous Chinese liquor made from fermented sorghum and one of the main objects of Xi's ire in his anticorruption crackdown.

24. This was during a short meeting after the daily diplomatic press briefing in MOFA's headquarters in 2017.

25. Bo Xilai, Zhou Yongkang, Sun Zhengcai, Xu Caihou, and Guo Boxiong, to name but a few, are senior Party cadres who were purged in his anticorruption drive and who had no clear prior displays of loyalty. I am not equating failure to pledge loyalty as the reason for political purges but merely drawing attention to the importance of pledges and how they may bear on one's political future. It must also be noted that the political element in the anticorruption campaign runs "deeper than simply ensuring Xi's hold on power. It is, in fact, a fundamental tool to deliver sustainable one-party rule" (Brown, 2018, p. 9).

26. All four books on Chinese foreign policy that I got at no cost, in 2018, at MOFA's headquarters heavily feature Xi and his leadership (see also the Conclusion). For example, the MOFA-sponsored book *Big Power Diplomacy* (*Da guo wai jiao* 大国外交) (Bian Xiezhu, 2017) obtained there is fundamentally about Xi's words and thoughts, rather than a concrete, academic, exposition of China's diplomacy. This is typical of the other institutionally under-written books by MOFA and their increasing accreditation of Xi (e.g., Department of Policy Planning, 2018).

27. That is not to say that in the transnational diplomatic field the "stronger" power will always get what it wants. The outcome is not predetermined, as each field's participants engage in a struggle to either preserve or transform resources. Thus there is always a possibility for change "even under the most repressive 'totalitarian' regimes" (Bourdieu & Wacquant, 1992, p. 102). Alternatively stated, the possibility of challenging and transforming the field is always open to lower-placed actors (though seldom possible to enact in reality). See Bourdieu's anal-ysis (1984) on consumption patterns of the lower classes in this regard. Undoubtedly, the em-phasis on struggles can easily give rise to the impression that fields are nothing more than conflict-ridden spaces, an impression I have sought to balance in my discussion by underlining cooperative practices.

28. A case in point for the local diplomatic field would be the proliferation of think tanks in the Chinese diplomatic field, so much so that MOFA has come to consult and rely on them regarding some diplomatic issues. This entrance into the field was not obtained as a "natural" progression; it was fought for and negotiated, thus pushing the field borders. Bourdieu notes how borders themselves are a point of struggle as a stake within the field (Bourdieu & Wac-quant, 1992, p. 104).

29. Emphasis in original.

30. The importance of the track-2 arena as a microcosm of the larger diplomatic field is well explicated (Nan, 2005; Mapendere, 2005, p. 68). Besides, the Chinese never see track-2 or 1.5 as "unofficial."

31. This incident was recounted by two member states of the track-2 organization. I was also a member and participated in meetings of the track-2 organization.

32. Emphasis added.

33. These are not isolated examples. For instance, a 2018 study on Chinese interference on US campuses notes that "officials from the Chicago consulate contacted the University of Wisconsin-Madison sometime between 2010 and 2013 to complain that the university was hosting too many Taiwan-related events and too many high-profile people from Taiwan" (Lloyd-Damnjanovic, 2018, p. 52). In Spain, a similar incident at the University of Salamanca

played out where the Chinese embassy sent an email pressuring the school to drop a Taiwanese cultural event (Zheng, 2018).

34. There has been an explosion of "ASEAN-China" meetings, projects, initiatives, and ad hoc working groups. These include the ASEAN-China Cooperation Fund, the ASEAN-China Media Exchange Year, the China-ASEAN Environmental Cooperation Centre, ASEAN-China Cultural Cooperation, ASEAN Plus China Ministers Responsible for Culture and Arts, China-ASEAN Education Cooperation Week, the ASEAN-China Health Ministers' Meeting, the ASEAN-China Summit, the ASEAN-China Ministerial Meeting on Quality Supervision, Inspection and Quarantine, the ASEAN-China EXPO, and the ASEAN Defense Ministers Meeting Plus, among numerous other such ventures (ASEAN Secretariat, 2018).

35. Particularly from 33:00 onwards.

36. Formal rules include how meetings are conducted, the processes in drafting statements, and so forth. Informal rules would include ASEAN norms such as "consensus decision making" and "quiet diplomacy."

37. Many secondary ASEAN actors—including former secretary-generals and ASEAN officials—have commented on the issue, clarifying why "centrality," "credibility," and "neutrality" are important for ASEAN. These include former ASEAN secretary-generals Ong Keng Yong and Surin Pitsuwan, as well as former officials such as Bilahari Kausikan, Dr. Termsak Chalermpalanupap, and Dr. Marty Natalegawa, among others. See also *Myanmar Times* (2017).

38. This relates to my earlier discussion on the "Taiwan" issue, as Nauru and Tuvalu, as of this writing, are two remaining Pacific countries that have official diplomatic relations with Taiwan.

39. Another instance of such assertiveness was seen in the Asia-Pacific Economic Cooperation Summit, where Chinese diplomats tried to "barge into the office of Papua New Guinea's foreign minister to influence a draft communique from the international event," although MOFA has denied this account (Lee, 2018, para. 1).

40. "The 1MDB scandal" refers to the corruption allegations against former prime minister Najib Razak, who was accused of funneling around RM $2.67 billion (USD $700 million) from a state-owned company into his personal bank account (*The Guardian*, 2015).

41. This "assertive" view is sometimes supported by Chinese sources, but they profess different reasons. They commonly say that the Olympic Games in Beijing, the financial crisis of 2008, and the Obama "pivot strategy" have been reasons for China to react more assertively since 2008/2009 (Interviewee 57, personal communication, June 28, 2017; Interviewee 38, personal communication, July 11, 2017).

Chapter 4

1. A version of this chapter was first published as D. Loh (2020a).

2. For exceptions, see Hocking and Spence (2002), Neumann (2012), and Spies (2019). In any case, my contention is that the scholarship mostly sees foreign ministries as a variable to understand other IR phenomena. The literature seldom studies foreign ministries on their own terms, as an IR phenomenon itself.

3. Emphasis in original.

4. Wendt advances a "states-as-conscious-agents" hypothesis where he claims that consciousness is a "transaction between the mind and its environment" (2015, pp. 277–278). This view is far from consensual, as even the "state-as-person" argument (Wendt, 2004) remains

contentious (Kustermans, 2011; Epstein, 2010, p. 331), let alone the states-as-conscious-agents proposition.

5. That is not to deny that agents' practices can deviate from and challenge the organizational practices and habitus. On the other hand, the MOFA case here shows that agents' practices are wedded to MOFA's habitus, stretching into the private sphere and into transnational fields.

6. See Waltz's (1959) "three-level" images for understanding war through human nature, regime type, and international structure.

7. One implication of the concept of institutional habitus is that it can be further abstracted to the state level. Subotic and Zarakol posit "that modern states may be conceptualized as exhibiting attitudes similar to emotion because they represent collectivities shaped by narratives which in turn constitute a common habitus" (2012, p. 917). Also of interest here is Bourdieu's construal of habitus in the general sense, where agents share a relatively stable and "common," field-wide habitus. For instance, in his study of the French university field, he writes that teachers "were endowed, at every hierarchical level, with an academic habitus," and that such a habitus "causes the individual agent to realize the law of the social body without intentionally or consciously obeying it: in the absence even of any express regulation or any explicit warning, aspirations tend to adjust themselves to the modal *trajectory*, that is the normal trajectory for a given category at a given moment" (1988, p. 143). While I do not have the space to elaborate on a Chinese "diplomatic habitus," I suggest that one way this habitus gets "distributed," beyond the structure of the field itself as Bourdieu implies, is through key institutions like MOFA.

8. Such coercion can be exerted on the individual, as when parents send a child to a school that she dislikes, or on an organization, as when the organization is compelled to accept someone who is subpar because of a leader's insistence.

9. For instance, the individual can engage in foot-dragging or implement decisions slowly (Lipsky, 1980). A full exploration of how and under what conditions a conflicting habitus can emerge is an important topic but one that this book does not examine.

10. It needs to be said that I do not intend here to provide a definitive guide for identifying an institutional habitus but merely to offer guiding signposts to show how this can be done.

11. On this point, Bourdieu notes how a transformation in hiring practices led to an influx of new entrants to the French academic field. New entrants, whose dispositions were not aligned with the status quo, did not have the "patience" deemed suitable for promotion, and thus their entrepreneurial practices led to a change in how faculty were incentivized and promoted in the field (1988, pp. 156–158). See also Bode (2018) on reflective practices and the importance of agents' personalities in her work on human rights at the UN.

12. Emphasis added.

13. Emphasis in original.

14. Its institutional predecessor was the Central People's Government Ministry of Foreign Affairs (Zhongyang renmin zhengfu waijiao bu 中央人民政府外交部),which was set up in October 1949 (Ministry of Foreign Affairs, 2013).

15. Interviews with Chinese MOFA officials and non-Chinese diplomats throw up different figures ranging from four thousand to six thousand. An official report from 2009 put the figure at five thousand diplomats working overseas but noted that these were "from different ministries" and that under MOFA there were 2,500 diplomats working overseas (Zhongguo Xinwen, 2009c).

16. MOFA's staffing numbers need to be placed in context. The United States, for instance,

has around 13,000 employees (Wilkinson, 2017) while the United Kingdom had 4,591 in 2016 (Foreign and Commonwealth Office, 2018). Thus, even as the moves to improve MOFA's professionalism and staffing must be acknowledged (see C. Wang, 2022), it is worth pointing out that its size is relatively modest.

17. Emphasis in original. The stress on behavioral routines following from organizational memory is analogous to Bourdieu's idea of habitus animating practices (1984, p. 101).

18. Clips of its press briefings (from 2016 to 2018) were accessed on the Associated Press's YouTube channel. I watched over sixty MOFA press briefings.

19. Translation my own.

20. Others include the memorials for Luo Tianguang (Guang Ming, 2008); Qian Qichen—former foreign minister (Li Zhaoxing, 2017); and Wang Hairong (Ji Zhe, 2017).

21. Observed from MOFA's press briefings.

22. They are also legally required to keep MOFA apprised of any changes to their marital status (Yi, 2009).

23. This is spelt out as loyalty to the "motherland" and the Chinese people; loyalty to the constitution; and loyalty to duty.

24. See, for example, former ambassador Fu Ying's book *Seeing the World* (*Kan shijie* 看世界)—a collection of speeches—which repeatedly stresses that China is ready to contribute to a new global order (2018, pp. 8, 30). See also MOFA's own publication *China's Foreign Affairs 2018*, which notes the "strong leadership," "breakthroughs in diplomacy," and "confidence" of China's diplomacy (Department of Policy Planning 2018, pp. 49, 12).

25. A key contention here is that one may not be able to accurately access actors' practices by asking them for their own account. That said, actors' own rationalizations of their practices are certainly important. Indeed, such rationalizations and justifications, post hoc, are a practice in itself.

26. The delineations between realism, constructivism, and liberalism are often not so neat. An illuminating case in point is Mercer's (1995) study on anarchy and state identities. Using social identity theory on intergroup conflict, Mercer reaches the same conclusion as Waltz, that "states are a priori self-regarding" (1995, p. 251), thus supporting the Waltzian self-help anarchic thesis.

27. It might be obvious to state that diplomats might not be as candid when "going on record." Nevertheless, in recent years, we are seeing more non-Chinese envoys speak out publicly and privately to the media against the diplomatic behavior of the Chinese officials (e.g., Doherty & Davidson, 2018; W. Wu, 2017; Bloomberg News, 2019).

28. Emphasis added.

29. Although Whiting's description of "policy-making elites" focuses almost exclusively on Deng Xiaoping and PLA leaders, *policy-making elite* here refers to MOFA and its agents.

30. There are exceptions. One Southeast Asian diplomat whose country enjoys privileged access to MOFA says, "Friendship can be cultivated. Once you find an opportunity to do them a favor, they will remember and be grateful to you. It is possible to be friends and meet them one-on-one then" (Interviewee 37, personal communication, July 11, 2017). These examples remain rare.

31. I thank Vincent Pouliot for pushing me on this point.

32. Emphasis added.

33. I will also add that the negative perceptions of China's diplomatic practices and state identity get looped back to the PSC and diplomatic actors through internal reports, media reports, scholarly analysis, and direct feedback in interactions with other diplomats/officials.

The accuracy of these appraisals, however, is hampered by the tendency of Chinese bureaucrats not to report "bad news" to their superiors (Interviewee 59, personal communication, June 19, 2017). Moreover, as I argued in chapter 3, the filtered feedback does not challenge diplomatic actors' commonsense understanding of the world sufficiently for them to change their operating logic.

Chapter 5

1. Cui (2019)

2. Spokesperson (2019).

3. Twitter diplomatic activities are understood here as using the "like," "mention," "tweet," "retweet," and "reply" functions.

4. Such was the case for the forays made by Zhao Lijian, former MOFA spokesperson, into race politics in the US, which breached diplomatic decorum and generated international backlash, as discussed in the previous chapter. Ironically, his wife generated significant domestic backlash when she lamented how hard Zhao worked and complained on Chinese social media in 2022 about how he could not procure painkillers after getting Covid. Zhao himself was moved to be the deputy director of the Department of Boundary and Ocean Affairs in MOFA in 2023, which some analysts saw as an unofficial demotion.

5. A comparative analysis of China's Twitter diplomacy with other countries' Twitter activities could be a worthwhile endeavor but is outside the scope of this chapter, which is primarily concerned with investigating how the PRC's Twitter diplomacy affects its offline diplomacy and contributes to China's self-professed notions of discursive power.

6. Zha does not state what "FRO" stands for, but we can infer that it refers to part of the embassy.

7. Emphasis added.

8. While these ethnic Chinese do not hold Chinese citizenship, the Chinese state often claims some proprietorship over them and sometimes assumes fealty based on ethnicity (see Hayton, 2020, pp. 75–100). I have written elsewhere (D. Loh, 2023) that "in 2018, the 'Overseas Chinese Affairs Office' was transferred from [the] Chinese government to the Chinese Communist Party's 'United Front Work Department' and amalgamated under it. Also in 2018, China started issuing longer-term 5-year visas to overseas ethnic Chinese so that it is easier to 'return home' as long as you had 'one parent, grandparent or ancestor.'"

9. Emphasis added.

10. "Wolf warrior" diplomacy is referred to by a scholar as the "offensives by Chinese diplomat [sic] to defend China's national interests, often in confrontational ways" (Zhu, 2020, para. 3).

11. Even though my operationalization of discourse power has public and private dimensions, this chapter is centered on its public (state-led) dimensions.

Conclusion

1. This is not to say that an individual's competency and skills do not matter in China's case. They certainly do, but they are often deemphasized.

2. The official foreign affairs website (Ministry of Foreign Affairs, n.d.) states 169 embassies, as it does not add consulates and missions to its tally. They also have an "Office of the People's Republic of China to the State of Palestine" that functions as a de facto embassy.

3. Pouliot conceptualizes "diplomatic power" in multilateral fields at the UN as technical expertise possessed by national missions that is brought to bear in diplomacy (2016, p. 200). In

a similar way, in the "local" diplomatic field in China, practitioners' usage of their capacity to counsel generates important status effects for MOFA and for China's diplomacy in relation to how China perceives others.

4. Wang Yi was promoted to director of the Central Foreign Affairs Commission in 2023 and was also promoted to the twenty-four-member Politburo in 2022, even though he was past the customary retirement age of sixty-eight. Qin Gang took over the reins of foreign minister to replace Wang at the end of 2022 but Qin himself was abruptly replaced by Wang in 2023 as foreign minister. As of October 2023, this meant that Wang concurrently held the roles of director of the Foreign Affairs Commission, foreign minister, and member of the twentieth Politburo, making Wang one of the most powerful foreign ministers in recent times.

5. Emphasis added.

6. The MOFA headquarters itself is somewhat new—completed only in July 1997 (Ministry of Foreign Affairs, 2000).

7. Liu Xia is the wife of Liu Xiaobo, a human rights activist and Nobel Peace Prize laureate. She was placed under unofficial house detention after the death of her husband. She was subsequently freed and flew to Germany on July 10, 2018 (Kuo, 2018).

8. One journalist recalls how, out of frustration with an absence of Xi Jinping–related news in 2016, he asked at a press briefing, "Is Xi Jinping still alive?," shocking everyone. His boss was "scolded by MOFA" and was told clearly that questions like this could never be posed again. This interviewee also told me that MOFA reacted sensitively to Xi-related news in journalists' reports and would call their offices whenever such news items appeared to "put pressure and dissuade negative coverage" (Interviewee 28, personal communication, August 29, 2017).

9. It publishes the questions and answers from its press briefings there.

10. Emphasis in original.

11. The main struggle over the references to China takes place at the semiannual ASEAN Summit attended by the heads of state of the ten ASEAN countries and the annual ASEAN Foreign Ministers' Meetings.

12. Grenfell also notes how "*doxa* is understood as comprising field-specific sets of beliefs that inform the shared *habitus* of those operating within the field" (2008, p. 125).

13. A few countries do draw on multiple sources for information—the military, nondiplomatic Party members, and provincial government—but this is not the norm, and most countries still rely, principally, on MOFA.

14. One site where I sought potential contacts with mixed results was LinkedIn. It was useful in setting up interviews with non-Chinese diplomats and some Chinese scholars but I was not successful in getting official contacts.

15. In some instances, MOFA respondents and MOFA-affiliated scholars would react strongly to my questions on purported Chinese assertiveness or perceptions that China might be "bullying" some ASEAN countries. On a few occasions, interviewees began to lecture me.

16. In this connection, I used Zhi Hu (知乎zhihu.com), a question-and-answer site, to seek contacts with and interact with supposedly Chinese diplomats. Although data from this site was not eventually used in this book, as there were obvious problems with verifiability, it was useful in bringing out background information on diplomats' practices and in constructing their lifeworld.

17. A good example is Shindo's (2018) use of two (semi-) fictional novels written by an anonymous Japanese bureaucrat to draw out "petty sovereigns'" practices. Shindo demonstrates how the novels can "resist" sovereignty and the governmentalizing endeavors of the state.

18. On "atmospheres" and practices, Reckwitz says, "People are affected by atmospheres

arising from the sets of relations of atefacts, as well as from other people, groups or practices" (2017, p. 123).

19. I am aware that these practices may also be shared with other authoritarian regimes, but they certainly differ from "Western" diplomatic practices.

20. There is certainly a space for improvisation and strategy within what is made possible by the habitus. Bourdieu himself talks about an actor's agency and "his or her capacity for invention and improvisation" (1990a, p. 13). See also Bourdieu and Wacquant (1992, pp. 132–135).

21. Though there are distinctions between material objects (e.g., rocks), material arrangements (e.g., architecture), nonhumans (e.g., worms), "more than humans" (e.g., sunlight), and "quasi-objects" (e.g., HIV virus), I can only broach the differences here because of space constraints.

22. A qualification to be made here is that not all strands of social practice theory consider the nonhuman as capable of "acting," but most sufficiently consider that material to be important to practices (although they differ on *how important* it is). Also, while I have focused here on material, nonhuman technology, I am not making equivalences between "material," "nonhuman," and "technology"—these are different albeit related concepts.

References

Abdelal, R., Herrera, Y. M., Johnston, I. A., & McDermott, R. (2006). Identity as a variable. *Perspectives on Politics, 4*(4), 695–711.

Åberg, J. H. (2016). A struggle for leadership recognition: The AIIB, reactive Chinese assertiveness, and regional order. *Contemporary Chinese Political Economy and Strategic Relations: An International Journal, 2*(3), 1125–1171.

Abrahamsen, R., & Williams, M. C. (2011). Privatization in practice: Power and capital in the field of global security. In E. Adler & V. Pouliot (Eds.), *International practices* (pp. 310–332). Cambridge University Press.

Acharya, A. (2006). Will Asia's past be its future? *International Security, 28*(3), 149–164.

Adler, E. (2019). *World ordering: A social theory of cognitive evolution.* Cambridge University Press.

Adler, E., & Pouliot, V. (2011a). International practices. *International Theory, 2*(1), 1–36.

Adler, E. & Pouliot, V. (2011b). International practices: Introduction and framework. In E. Adler & V. Pouliot (Eds.), *International practices* (pp. 3–35). Cambridge University Press.

Adler-Nissen, R. (2011). On a field trip with Bourdieu. *International Political Sociology, 5*(3), 327–330.

———. (2014). *Opting out of the European Union: Diplomacy, sovereignty and European integration.* Cambridge University Press.

———. (2015). Conclusion: Relationalism or why diplomats find international relations theory strange. In O. J. Sending, V. Pouliot, & I. B. Neumann (Eds.), *Diplomacy and the making of world politics* (pp. 204–308). Cambridge University Press.

———. (2016). Towards a practice turn in EU studies: The everyday of European integration. *Journal of Common Market Studies, 54*(1), 87–103.

Adler-Nissen, R., & Pouliot, V. (2014). Power in practice: Negotiating the international intervention in Libya. *European Journal of International Relations, 20*(4), 889–911.

Albrecht, H., & Koehler, K. (2018). Going on the run: What drives military desertion in civil war? *Security Studies, 27*(2), 179–203.

Alden, C., & Chan, K. (2021). *Twitter and digital diplomacy: China and COVID-19*. LSE Ideas. https://www.lse.ac.uk/ideas/Assets/Documents/updates/LSE-IDEAS-Twitter-and-Digital-Diplomacy-China-and-COVID-19.pdf

Allard, T., & Munthe, C. B. (2017, July 14). *Asserting sovereignty, Indonesia renames part of South China Sea*. Reuters. https://uk.reuters.com/article/uk-indonesia-politics-map/asserting-sovereignty-indonesia-renames-part-of-south-china-sea-idUKKBN19Z0YU

Allison, G., & Halperin, M. H. (1972). Bureaucratic politics: A paradigm and some policy implications. *Theory and Policy in International Relations, 24*, 40–79.

Allison, G., & Zelikow, P. (1999). *Essence of decision: Explaining the Cuban missile crisis* (2nd ed.). Pearson P T R.

Andrews-Speed, P. (2012). *The governance of energy in China: Transition to a low-carbon economy*. Palgrave Macmillan.

AP Archive. (n.d.). *Welcome to AP archive* [Video]. YouTube. https://www.youtube.com/channel/UCHTK-2W11Vh1V4uwofOfR4w

Areddy, J. (2016, June 20). Indonesian warship fires on foreign fishing boats in South China Sea. *Wall Street Journal*. https://www.wsj.com/articles/indonesian-warship-fires-on-foreign-fishing-boats-in-south-china-sea-1466350384

ASEAN Secretariat. (2018, August). *Overview of ASEAN-China dialogue relations*. ASEAN. http://asean.org/storage/2012/05/Overview-of-ASEAN-China-Relations-August-2018_For-Website.pdf

Ashizawa, K. (2008). When identity matters: State identity, regional institution-building, and Japanese foreign policy. *International Studies Review, 10*(3), 571–598.

Atkinson, W. (2011). From sociological fictions to social fictions: Some Bourdieusian reflections on the concepts of "institutional habitus" and "family habitus." *British Journal of Sociology of Education, 32*(3), 331–347.

Austin, H., & Smith, A. (2020, March 13). *Coronavirus: Chinese official suggests U.S. Army to blame for outbreak*. NBC News. https://www.nbcnews.com/news/world/coronavirus-chinese-official-suggests-u-s-army-blame-outbreak-n1157826

Autesserre, S. (2014). *Peaceland: Conflict resolution and the everyday politics of international intervention*. Cambridge University Press.

Ba, A. (2009). *Renegotiating East and Southeast Asia: Region, regionalism, and the Association of Southeast Asian Nations*. Stanford University Press.

Baijiahao. (2023, March 4). *Ruhe cong xinwen fabu dong zhongguo lianghui?* Baidu. https://baijiahao.baidu.com/s?id=1759435987373960935

Baliga, A. (2016, July 26). China thanks Cambodia for efforts to water down ASEAN SCS statement. *Phnom Penh Post*. http://www.phnompenhpost.com/national/china-thanks-cambodia-efforts-water-down-asean-scs-statement

Banjo, S., & Frier, S. (2019, August 21). *Twitter helps Beijing push agenda abroad despite ban in China*. Bloomberg News. https://www.bloomberg.com/news/articles/2019-08-21/twitter-helps-china-push-agenda-abroad-despite-ban-in-mainland

Barad, K. (2003). Posthumanist performativity: Toward an understanding of how matter comes to matter. *Gender and Science, 28*(3), 801–831.

Barnes, B. (2001). Practice as collection action. In T. R. Schatzki, K. K. Cetina, & E. V. Savigny (Eds.), *The practice turn in contemporary theory* (pp. 25–36). Routledge.

Barnett, A. D. (1985). *The making of foreign policy in China: Structure and process*. Westview Press.

Barnett, M. (2002). *Eyewitness to a genocide*. Cornell University Press.

Bendor, J., & Hammond, T. H. (1992). Rethinking Allison's models. *American Political Science Review, 86*(2), 301–322.

Berenskoetter, F. (2014). Parameters of a national biography. *European Journal of International Relations, 20*(1), 262–288.

Bernhard, S. (2011). Beyond constructivism: The political sociology of an EU policy field. *International Political Sociology, 5*(4), 426–445.

Bian xiezhu. (2017). *Da guo waijiao.* Renmin chuban she.

Bicchi, F. (2014). Information exchanges, diplomatic networks and the construction of European knowledge in European Union foreign policy. *Cooperation and Conflict, 49*(2), 239–259.

———. (2016). Europe under occupation: The European diplomatic community of practice in the Jerusalem area. *European Security, 25*(4), 461–477.

Bicchi, F., & Bremberg, N. (2016). European diplomatic practices: Contemporary challenges and innovative approaches. *European Security, 25*(4), 391–406.

Biernacki, P., & Waldorf, D. (1981). Snowball sampling problems and techniques of chain referral sampling. *Sociological Methods and Research, 10*(2), 141–163.

Bigo, D. (2011). Pierre Bourdieu and international relations: Power of practices, practices of power. *International Political Sociology, 5*(3), 225–258.

Bisley, N. (2011). Biding and hiding no longer: A more assertive China rattles the region. *Global Asia, 6*(4), 62–72. https://www.globalasia.org/v6no4/feature/biding-and-hiding -no-longer-a-more-assertive-china-rattles-the-region_nick-bisley

Bjola, C. (2015). Introduction: Making sense of digital diplomacy. In C. Bjola & M. Holmes (Eds.), *Digital diplomacy: Theory and practice* (pp. 1–10). Routledge.

Bjola, C., & Kornprobst, M. (2018). Why and how to study diplomacy? In C. Bjola & M. Kornprobst (Eds.), *Understanding international diplomacy* (pp. 1–10). Routledge.

Bjola, C., & Lu, J. (2015). Social media and public diplomacy: A comparative analysis of the digital diplomatic strategies of the EU, U.S. and Japan in China. In C. Bjola & M. Holmes (Eds.), *Digital diplomacy: Theory and practice* (pp. 71–89). Routledge.

Blanchard, B. (2017, July 3). *China says India violates 1890 agreement in border stand-off.* Reuters. https://www.reuters.com/article/us-china-india-idUSKBN19O109

Blanchard, B., & Yu, J. M. (2017, December 11). *China, Taiwan spar over Chinese diplomat's invasion threat.* Reuters. https://www.reuters.com/article/us-china-taiwan-usa/china -taiwan-spar-over-chinese-diplomats-invasion-threat-idUSKBN1E506A

Bloomberg News. (2017, March 8). *China uses annual congress to tout Xi's global leadership role.* https://www.bloomberg.com/news/articles/2017-03-08/china-uses-annual-congress -to-tout-xi-s-global-leadership-role

———. (2018, February 7). *As U.S. culls diplomats, China is empowering its ambassadors.* https://www.bloomberg.com/news/articles/2018-02-07/as-u-s-culls-diplomats-china-is -empowering-its-ambassadors

———. (2019, March 6). *Diplomatic outbursts mar Xi's plan to raise China on the world stage.* https://www.bloombergquint.com/global-economics/diplomatic-outbursts-mar-xi-s-plan -to-raise-china-on-world-stage

Bode, I. (2018). Reflective practices at the Security Council: Children and armed conflict and the three United Nations. *European Journal of International Relations, 24*(2), 293–318.

Bode, I., & Kalsrud, J. (2019). Implementation in practice: The use of force to protect civilians in United Nations peacekeeping. *European Journal of International Relations, 25*(2), 458–485.

Bogner, A., Littig, B., & Menz, W. (2009). Introduction: Expert interviews—an introduction to a new methodological debate. In A. Bogner, B. Littig, & W. Menz (Eds.), *Interviewing experts* (pp. 1–13). Palgrave Macmillan.

Bondiguel, T., & Kellner, T. (2010). The impact of China's foreign policy think tanks. *BICCS Asia Paper, 5*(5), 1–32. https://www.files.ethz.ch/isn/159102/wp213_abb.pdf

Borneo Post. (2018, February 24). BN govt will not allow attempts to sabotage M'sia-China ties—Najib. http://www.theborneopost.com/2018/02/24/bn-govt-will-not-allow-attempts-to-sabotage-msia-china-ties-najib/

Bourbeau, P. (2017). The practice approach in global politics. *Journal of Global Security Studies, 2*(2), 170–182.

Bourdieu, P. (1977). *Outline of a theory of practice.* Cambridge University Press.

———. (1984). *Distinction: A social critique of the judgment of taste.* Harvard University Press.

———. (1986). The forms of capital. In J. G. Richardson (Ed.), *Handbook of theory and research for the sociology of education* (pp. 241–258). Greenwood Press.

———. (1988). *Homo academicus.* Polity Press.

———. (1989). Social space and symbolic power. *Sociological Theory, 7*(1), 14–25.

———. (1990a). *In other words: Essays toward a reflexive sociology.* Stanford University Press.

———. (1990b). *The logic of practice.* Polity Press.

———. (2000). *Pascalian meditations.* Stanford University Press.

———. (2014). *On the state: Lectures at the College de France, 1989–1992* (P. Champagne, R. Lenoir, F. Poupeau, & M-C. Riviere, Eds.). Polity Press.

Bourdieu, P., & Wacquant, L. J. D. (1992). *An invitation to reflexive sociology.* University of Chicago Press.

Bouris, D., & Fernández-Molina, R. (2018). Contested states, hybrid diplomatic practices, and the everyday quest for recognition. *International Political Sociology, 12*(3), 306–324.

Bower, E. Z. (2012, July 20). *China reveals its hand on ASEAN in Phnom Penh.* Centre for Strategic and International Studies. https://www.csis.org/analysis/china-reveals-its-hand-asean-phnom-penh

Brandt, J., & Schafer, B. (2020). *How China's "wolf warrior" diplomats use and abuse Twitter.* Brookings Institute. https://www.brookings.edu/techstream/how-chinas-wolf-warrior-diplomats-use-and-abuse-twitter/

Branigan, T. (2012, November 15). Xi Jinping: The "big personality" taking charge in China. *The Guardian.* https://www.theguardian.com/world/2012/nov/15/xi-jinping-big-personality-china

Breslin, S. (2009). Understanding China's regional rise: Interpretations, identities, and implications. *International Affairs, 85*(4), 817–835.

———. (2010). *Government-industry relations in China: A review of the art of the state* (CSGR Working Paper 272/10). Centre for the Study of Globalisation and Regionalisation, University of Warwick. http://goo.gl/rox4p4

———. (2013). China and the South: Objectives, actors and interactions. *Development and Change, 44*(6), 1273–1294.

British Broadcasting Corporation. (2020). *Australia demands China apologise for posting "repugnant" fake image.* https://www.bbc.com/news/world-australia-55126569

Brown, K. (2016). *CEO, China: The rise of Xi Jinping.* I. B. Tauris.

———. (2017). *China's world: What does China want?* I. B. Tauris.

———. (2018). The anti-corruption struggle in Xi Jinping's China: An alternative political narrative. *Asian Affairs, 49*(1), 1–10.

Brubaker, R., & Cooper, F. (2000). Beyond "identity." *Theory and Society, 29*(1), 1–47.

Bruk, J. (2016, June 15). *In Chinese foreign minister's outburst, a test for Trudeau*. Open Canada. https://www.opencanada.org/features/chinese-foreign-ministers-outburst-test-trudeau/

Bucher, B., & Jasper, U. (2017). Revisiting "identity" in international relations: From identity as substance to identifications in action. *European Journal of International Relations, 23*(2), 391–415.

Buckley, C. (2016, June 2). China's foreign minister castigates Canadian reporter for rights question. *New York Times*. https://www.nytimes.com/2016/06/03/world/asia/canada -china-wang-yi.html

Bueger, C. (2014). Pathways to practice: Praxiography and international politics. *European Political Science Review, 6*(3), 383–406.

———. (2015). Making things known: Epistemic practices, the United Nations, and the translation of piracy. *International Political Sociology, 9*(1), 1–18.

Bueger, C., & Gadinger, F. (2014). *International practice theory: New perspectives*. Palgrave Macmillan.

———. (2015). The play of international practice. *International Studies Quarterly, 59*(3), 449–460.

Bueger, C., & Mireanu, M. (2014). Proximity. In C. Aradau, J. Huysmans, A. Neal, & N. Voelckner (Eds.), *Critical security methods: New frameworks for analysis* (pp. 118–141). Routledge.

Burke, C. T., Emmerich, N., & Ingram, N. (2013). Well founded social fictions: A defence of the concepts of institutional and familial habitus. *British Journal of Sociology of Education, 34*(2), 165–182.

Buszynski, L. (2012). China's naval strategy, the United States, ASEAN and the South China Sea. *Security Challenges, 8*(2), 19–32.

Buzan, B. (2010). China in international society: Is "peaceful rise" possible? *Chinese Journal of International Politics, 3*, 5–36.

Buzan, B., & Lawson, G. (2012). Rethinking benchmark dates in international relations. *European Journal of International Relations, 20*(2), 437–462.

Callaghan, G. (2005). Accessing habitus: Relating structure and agency through focus group research. *Sociological Research Online, 10*(3), 1–12.

Callahan, W. (2006). War, shame, and time: Pastoral governance and national identity in England and America. *International Studies Quarterly, 50*(2), 395–419.

———. (2012). China's strategic futures. *Asian Survey, 52*(4), 617–642.

———. (2016). China's "Asia dream": The Belt Road Initiative and the new regional order. *Asian Journal of Comparative Politics, 1*(3), 226–243.

Campbell, C. (2017, October 24). Xi Jinping becomes China's most powerful leader since Mao Zedong. *Time*. http://time.com/4994618/xi-jinping-china-19th-congress-ccp-mao -zedong-constitution/

Carlson, A. (2009). A flawed perspective: The limitations inherent within the study of Chinese nationalism. *Nations and Nationalism, 15*(1), 20–35.

Ceco, L. (2021). Chinese diplomat accuses Trudeau of making Canada "running dog of US." *The Guardian*. https://www.theguardian.com/world/2021/mar/29/china-canada-justin -trudeau-tensions-escalate

CGTN. (2020, May 24). *FM Wang Yi: China to showcase a new Hubei and Wuhan to the world*. https://news.cgtn.com/news/2020-05-24/FM-Wang-Yi-China-to-showcase-a-new-Hubei -and-Wuhan-to-the-world-QKSJrGcboA/index.html

Chan, G., Lee, K. P., & Chan, L.-H. (2012). *China engages global governance: A new world order in the making?* Routledge.

Chan, I., & Li, M. (2015). New Chinese leadership, new policy in the South China Sea dispute? *Journal of Chinese Political Science, 20*(1), 35–50.

Chang, R. (2014, June 17). ASEAN must speak out on territorial spats, says Singapore minister Shanmugam. *Straits Times*. http://www.straitstimes.com/asia/se-asia/asean-must-speak -out-on-territorial-spats-says-singapore-minister-shanmugam

Chappell, B. (2020, November 30). *China refuses to apologize to Australia over official's tweet of doctored image*. NPR. https://www.npr.org/2020/11/30/940155014/china-refuses-to -apologize-to-australia-over-officials-tweet-of-doctored-image

Chen, D., Pu, X., & Johnston, I., A. (2014). Debating China's assertiveness: Correspondence. *International Security, 38*(3), 176–183.

Chen, I., & Hao, A. (2013). A harmonized Southeast Asia? Explanatory typologies of ASEAN countries' strategies to the rise of China. *Pacific Review, 26*(3), 265–288.

Chen, S. (2018, July 30). Artificial intelligence, immune to fear or favour, is helping to make China's foreign policy. *South China Morning Post*. https://www.scmp.com/news/china /society/article/2157223/artificial-intelligence-immune-fear-or-favour-helping-make -chinas

Chen, Y. (2003). China's foreign policy making as seen through Tiananmen. *Journal of Contemporary China, 12*(37), 715–738.

Cheng, D., & Wang, J. (2011). Lying low no more? China's new thinking on the *tao guang yang hui* strategy. *China: An International Journal, 9*(2), 195–216.

Cheung, G., Cheung, T., & Mai, J. (2021, December 20). Beijing defends "democracy with Hong Kong characteristics" model as white paper released a day after Legco election cites end goal of universal suffrage. *South China Morning Post*. https://www.scmp.com/news /hong-kong/politics/article/3160358/democracy-hong-kong-characteristics-best-model -citys-future

Chhabra, T., & Haas, R. (2019). *Global China: Domestic politics and foreign policy*. Brookings Institute. https://www.brookings.edu/research/global-china-domestic-politics-and -foreign-policy/

Chi, D. (2018, January 8). *Chinese foreign ministry opens spokesperson WeChat account*. GBtimes. https://gbtimes.com/chinese-foreign-ministry-opens-spokesperson-wechat-account

Chin, G., & Thakur, R. (2010). Will China change the rules of global order? *Washington Quarterly, 33*(4), 119–138.

China Foreign Affairs University. (2018). *Leadership*. http://en.cfau.edu.cn/col/col2509/index .html

Chong, K. P. (2017, October 25). China's Xi Jinping stacks 25-member Politburo with loyalists. *Straits Times*. https://www.straitstimes.com/asia/east-asia/chinas-xi-stacks-25-member -politburo-with-loyalists

Chong, K. P., Chow, J., & Lim, J. (2016, November 25). China comments on SAF armoured vehicles and equipment seized, as SAF sends officers to Hong Kong. *Straits Times*. https: //www.straitstimes.com/asia/east-asia/saf-team-on-their-way-to-hong-kong-to-address -security-of-seized-equipment

Christiansen, T. (2016). A liberal institutionalist perspective on China-EU relations. In J. Wang & W. Song (Eds.), *China, the European Union, and the international politics of global governance* (pp. 29–50). Palgrave Macmillan.

Chua, A. (2017, January 25). *Terrex vehicles could be home by Feb 11: Ng Eng Hen*. Today. http://www.todayonline.com/singapore/saf-terrexes-hk-be-shipped-directly-singapore -hopefully-home-feb-11

Clausen, J. A. (1968). *Socialization and society*. Little, Brown.

Clinton, D. (2011). The distinction between foreign policy and diplomacy in American international thought and practice. *The Hague Journal of Diplomacy, 6*(3–4), 261–276.

Clover, C., & Cheung, G. (2017, January 10). China links seized vehicles to Singapore's ties with Taiwan. *Financial Times.* https://www.ft.com/content/9f424c24-d711-11e6-944b-e7eb37a6aa8e

Clover, C., & Ju, S. F. (2018, March 6). China's diplomacy budget doubles under Xi Jinping. *Financial Times.* https://www.ft.com/content/2c750f94-2123-11e8-a895-1ba1f72c2c11

Cohen, A. (2011). Bourdieu hits Brussels: The genesis and structure of the European field of power. *International Political Sociology, 5*(3), 335–339.

———. (2018). Pierre Bourdieu and international relations. In T. Medvetz & J. J. Sallaz (Eds.), *The Oxford handbook of Pierre Bourdieu* (pp. 200–248). Oxford University Press.

Cohen, R. (1998, May 4). Putting diplomatic studies on the map. *Diplomatic Studies Program Newsletter.* Centre for the Study of Diplomacy.

Coker, C. (2015). *The improbable war: China, the United States and logic of great power conflict.* Oxford University Press.

Cooper, F. A., & Cornut, J. (2018). The changing practices of frontline diplomacy: New directions for inquiry. *Review of International Studies, 45*(2), 300–319.

Cornut, J. (2015). To be a diplomat abroad: Diplomatic practice at embassies. *Cooperation and Conflict, 50*(3), 385–401.

———. (2018). Diplomacy, agency, and the logic of improvisation and virtuosity in practice. *European Journal of International Relations, 24*(3), 712–736.

Cui, T. [@AmbCuiTiankai]. (2019, July 12). #Taiwan is part of #China. [Tweet]. Twitter. https://twitter.com/AmbCuiTiankai/status/1149695176358715392

Dai, X. (2016, June 9). *Weibo* post. https://www.weibo.com/1571497285/DAVuAhodQ

Denyer, S. (2015, December 29). China's Xi tells grumbling party cadres: "Don't talk back." *Washington Post.* https://goo.gl/z8VOYk

Department of Policy Planning. Ministry of Foreign Affairs. People's Republic of China. (2018). *China's foreign affairs 2018.* World Affairs Press.

Der Derian, J. (1987). *On diplomacy: A genealogy of Western estrangement.* Blackwell.

Ding, I. (2022). *The performative state: Public scrutiny and environmental governance in China.* Cornell University Press.

Dittmer, J. (2016). Theorizing a more-than-human diplomacy: Assembling the British Foreign Office, 1839–1874. *The Hague Journal of Diplomacy, 11*(1), 78–104.

Doherty, B., & Davidson, H. (2018, September 5). Chinese envoy walks out of meeting after row with Nauru president amid "bullying" claims. *The Guardian.* https://www.theguardian.com/world/2018/sep/05/chinese-envoy-walks-out-of-meeting-after-row-with-nauru-president-amid-bullying-claims

Dreyer, J. T. (2006). *China's political system: Modernization and traditional.* Macmillan.

———. (2015). The "Tianxia trope": Will China change the international system? *Journal of Contemporary China, 24*(96), 1015–1031.

Dufort, P. (2013). Introduction: Experiences and knowledge of war. *Cambridge Review of International Affairs, 26*(4), 611–614.

Duncombe, C. (2017). Twitter and transformative diplomacy: Social media and Iran-US relations. *International Affairs, 93*(3), 545–562.

Duvall, R. D., & Chowdhury, A. (2011). Practices of theory. In E. Adler & V. Pouliot (Eds.), *International practices* (pp. 335–354). Cambridge University Press.

Eagleton-Pierce, M. (2013). *Symbolic power in the World Trade Organization.* Oxford University Press.

The Economist. (2020, February 20). China finds a use abroad for Twitter, a medium it fears at home. https://www.economist.com/china/2020/02/20/china-finds-a-use-abroad-for-twitter-a-medium-it-fears-at-home

Economy, E. C. (2014). China's imperial president: Xi Jinping tightens his grip. *Foreign Affairs, 93*(6), 80–91.

Emirbayer, M., & Johnson, V. (2008). Bourdieu and organizational analysis. *Theory and Society, 37*(1), 1–44.

Epstein, C. (2010). Who speaks? Discourse, the subject and the study of identity in international politics. *European Journal of International Relations, 17*(2), 327–350.

Eriksen, T. H., & Nielsen, F. S. (2001). *A history of anthropology.* Pluton Press.

Erlanger, S. (2020, May 3). Global backlash builds against China over coronavirus. *New York Times.* https://www.nytimes.com/2020/05/03/world/europe/backlash-china-coronavirus.html

Fairbank, J. (1983). *The United States and China* (4th ed.). Harvard University Press.

Farrow, L. (2016, July 26). ASEAN statement on South China Sea "shows weakness." *Sydney Morning Herald.* http://www.smh.com.au/world/asean-statement-on-south-china-sea-shows-weakness-20160726-gqdy5f.html

Feng, L. (2020). The recalibration of Chinese assertiveness: China's responses to the Indo-Pacific challenge. *International Affairs, 96*(1), 9–27.

Findlay, C., & Watson, A. (1997). Economic growth and trade dependency in China. In D. Goodman & G. Segal (Eds.), *China rising: Nationalism and interdependence* (pp. 107–133). Routledge.

Flyvbjerg, B. (2006). Five misunderstandings about case-study research. *Qualitative Inquiry, 12*(2): 219–245.

Foot, R. (2014). "Doing some things" in the Xi Jinping era: The United Nations as China's venue of choice. *International Affairs, 90*(5), 1085–1100.

Foreign and Commonwealth Office. United Kingdom. (2018, May 11). *Freedom of Information Act 2000 Request Ref: 0404–18.* https://assets.publishing.service.gov.uk/government/uploads/system/uploads/attachment_data/file/740897/FOI_0404-18_Letter_FCO_UK_staff.pdf

Fengling 峰岭. (2017, June 27). *Xiang dang waijiaoguan, gaokao zhiyuan zenme tian? Zhe shi yi fen jiyu 400 ming waijiaoguan de xiangxi shuju baogao [Calling all future diplomats: How should you best fill in the National College Entrance Examination? View this detailed analysis report of 400 diplomats for insights].* https://m.sohu.com/n/498909419/

Forsby, A. (2011). An end to harmony? The rise of a Sino-centric China. *Political Perspectives, 5*(3), 5–26.

Friedberg, A. L. (2014). The sources of Chinese conduct: Explaining Beijing's assertiveness. *Washington Quarterly, 37*(4), 133–150.

Fu, Y. (2018). *Kan shijie* [Seeing the world]. Zhongxin chuban jituan.

Fu, Z. (1993). *Autocratic tradition and Chinese politics.* Cambridge University Press.

Gan, N., & Liu, Z. (2016, November 28). Beijing demands Singapore abide by "one-China" principle after military vehicles seized in Hong Kong. *South China Morning Post.* http://www.scmp.com/news/china/diplomacy-defence/article/2049769/beijing-demands-singapore-abide-one-china-principle

Gherardi, S. (2017). Sociomateriality in posthuman practice theory. In A. Hui, T. Schatzki, & E. Shove (Eds.), *The nexus of practices: Connections, constellations, practitioners* (pp. 38–51). Routledge.

Glas, A. (2017). Habits of peace: Long-term regional cooperation in Southeast Asia. *European Journal of International Relations, 23*(4), 833–856.

———. (2022). *Practicing peace: Conflict management in Southeast Asia and South America.* Oxford University Press.

Glaser, B. S. (2012). Chinese foreign policy research institutes and the practice of influence. In G. Rozman (Ed.), *China's foreign policy: Who makes it and how is it made?* (pp. 87–124). Asan Institute for Policy Studies.

Glaser, B. S., & Saunders, P. C. (2002). Chinese civilian foreign policy research institutes: Evolving roles and increasing influence. *China Quarterly, 171,* 597–616.

Glasius, M. (2018). What authoritarianism is . . . and is not: A practice perspective. *International Affairs, 94*(3), 515–533.

Global Times. (2021, July 5). China urges global efforts to tackle "biggest" cybersecurity threat posed by the US. https://www.globaltimes.cn/page/202107/1227875.shtml

Go, J. (2008). Global fields and imperial forms: Field theory and the British and American empires. *Sociological Theory, 26*(3), 201–229.

Godement, F. (2012). How do monetary and financial issues interact with China's foreign policy making? In G. Rozman (Ed.), *China's foreign policy: Who makes it, and how is it made?* (pp. 229–250). Asan Institute for Policy Studies.

Goffman, E. (1959). *The presentation of self in everyday life.* Anchor Books.

Goh, S. N. (2018, March 19). NPC 2018: China's foreign minister Wang Yi promoted in move to boost diplomacy. *Straits Times.* https://www.straitstimes.com/asia/east-asia/npc-2018 -chinas-foreign-minister-wang-yi-promoted-to-state-councillor

Goldstein, A. (2001). The diplomatic face of China's grand strategy: A rising power's emerging choice. *China Quarterly, 168,* 835–865.

———. (2003). An emerging China's emerging grand strategy. In G. J. Ikenberry & M. Mastanduno (Eds.), *International relations theory and the Asia-Pacific* (pp. 57–106). Columbia University Press.

———. (2012). China's foreign policy and the leadership transition: Prospects for change under the "fifth generation." In G. Rozman (Ed.), *China's foreign policy: Who makes it, and how is it made?* (pp. 39–64). Asan Institute for Policy Studies.

Gregory, E. J. (2018, August 15). *Control issues are feeding China's "discourse power" project.* National Interest. https://nationalinterest.org/feature/control-issues-are-feeding-chinas -discourse-power-project-28862

Grenfell, M. (2008). *Pierre Bourdieu: Key concepts.* Acumen.

Gries, P. H. (2001, July). Tears of rage: Chinese nationalist reactions to the Belgrade embassy bombing. *China Journal, 46,* 25–43.

———. (2005). Social psychology and the identity-conflict debate: Is a "China threat" inevitable? *European Journal of International Relations, 11*(2): 235–263.

The Guardian. (2015, July 6). Malaysian taskforce investigates allegations $700M paid to PM Najib. https://www.theguardian.com/world/2015/jul/06/malaysian-task-force-investi gates-allegations-700m-paid-to-pm-najib

Guo, F. (2019, November 25). *Xinhua headlines: Defending multilateralism in challenging era.* Xinhua. http://www.xinhuanet.com/english/2019-11/26/c_138582709.htm

Gutierrez, N. (2017, April 28). *Indonesia's Jokowi: ASEAN must have common stand on South China Sea.* Rappler. https://www.rappler.com/world/regions/asia-pacific/indonesia/ bahasa/englishedition/168215-south-china-sea-jokowi-asean

Guzzini, S. (2013). *Power, realism and constructivism.* Routledge.

Hadano, T. (2020, April 8). Chinese diplomat backpedals on blaming US for coronavirus. *Nikkei Asian Review.* https://asia.nikkei.com/Spotlight/Coronavirus/Chinese-diplomat-backpedals-on-blaming-US-for-coronavirus

Hagström, L. (2015). The "abnormal" state: Identity, norm/exception and Japan. *European Journal of International Relations, 21*(1), 122–145.

Häkli, J. (2013). State space—Outlining a field theoretical approach. *Geopolitics, 18*(2), 343–355.

Hale, T., Liu, C., & Urpelainen, J. (2020). *Belt and Road decision-making in China and recipient countries: How and to what extent does sustainability matter?* ISEP, BSG, and Climate-Works Foundation. https://sais-isep.org/wp-content/uploads/2020/04/ISEP-BSG-BRI-Report-.pdf

Hameiri, S., & Jones, L. (2016). Rising powers and state transformation: The case of China. *European Journal of International Relations, 22*(1), 72–98.

Han, G. X. D. (2017). China's normative power in managing South China Sea disputes. *Chinese Journal of International Politics, 11*(3), 269–297.

Hansen, L. (2011). Performing practices: A post structuralist analysis of the Muhammad cartoon crisis. In E. Adler & V. Pouliot (Eds.), *International practices* (pp. 280–309). Cambridge University Press.

Harding, H. (1981). *Organizing China.* Stanford University Press.

Hardt, H. (2017). How NATO remembers: Explaining institutional memory in NATO crisis management. *European Security, 26*(1): 120–48.

Hatton, C. (2013, March 19). *Who makes China's foreign policy?* BBC. https://www.bbc.com/news/world-asia-china-21826852.

Hayton, B. (2020). *The invention of China.* Yale University Press.

He, K., & Feng, H. (2013). Xi Jinping's operational code beliefs and China's foreign policy. *Chinese Journal of International Politics, 6*(3), 209–231.

Hewitt, D. (2015, May 7). China's premier says some Chinese bureaucracy is a "big joke" as government seeks to streamline economy. *International Business Times.* http://www.ibtimes.com/chinas-premier-says-some-chinese-bureaucracy-big-joke-government-seeks-streamline-1911955

Hille, K. (2020a, May 12). "Wolf warrior" diplomats reveal China's ambitions. *Financial Times.* https://www.ft.com/content/7d500105-4349-4721-b4f5-179de6a58f08

———. (2020b, October 19). Taiwan accuses Chinese officials of beating up diplomat in Fiji. *Financial Times.* https://www.ft.com/content/53d687cc-f194-4a4e-b0c8-edd45dd293ad

Ho, W. F. (2018, March 25). China factor looms ahead of election. *The Nation.* https://www.thestar.com.my/news/nation/2018/03/25/china-factor-looms-ahead-of-election-the-china-card-was-flashed-in-almost-every-general-election-in/

Hocking, B., & Spence, D. (2002). *Foreign ministries in the European Union: Integrating diplomats.* Palgrave Macmillan.

Holslag, J. (2010). *Trapped giants: China's military rise.* Routledge.

Hopf, T. (2018). Change in international practices. *European Journal of International Relations, 24*(3), 687–711.

Hornby, L. (2018, August 2018). Mahathir Mohamad warns against "new colonialism" during China visit. *Financial Times.* https://www.ft.com/content/7566599e-a443-11e8-8ecf-a7ae1beff35b

Hu, W. (2019). Xi Jinping's "major country diplomacy": The role of leadership in foreign policy transformation. *Journal of Contemporary China, 28*(115), 1–14.

Hu, Z. [@SpokespersonHZM]. (2020, April 2). *Welcome to my Twitter account.* [Tweet]. Twitter. https://twitter.com/SpokespersonHZM/status/1245682456272891907

Hua, C. [@SpokespersonCHN]. (2020a, February 17). *Ambassador Richard Grenell tweeted on consequences of choosing an "untrustworthy" 5G vendor.* [Tweet]. Twitter. https://twitter .com/SpokespersonCHN/status/1229325922559348736

———. (2020b, February 20). *Worst selling fiction!* [Tweet]. Twitter. https://twitter.com/ SpokespersonCHN/status/1230344965659586560

———. (2020c, March 30). *China is practicing "mask propaganda"?* [Tweet]. Twitter. https:// twitter.com/spokespersonchn/status/1244628726232408065

———. [@SpokespersonCHN]. (2020d, May 8). *The #US keeps calling for transparency & investigation.* [Tweet]. Twitter. https://twitter.com/SpokespersonCHN/status/1258780531 707109377

Huang, A. Z., and Wang, R. (2019). Building a network to "tell China stories well": Chinese diplomatic communication strategies on Twitter. *International Journal of Communication, 13*, 2984–3007.

Huang, C. (2016, July 3). Why do so many countries have claims to territory in the South China Sea? *South China Morning Post.* http://www.scmp.com/news/china/diplomacy-de fence/article/1983481/why-do-so-many-countries-have-claims-territory-south

Hughes, C. R. (2005). Nationalism and multilateralism in Chinese foreign policy: Implications for Southeast Asia. *Pacific Review, 18*(1), 119–135.

Hughes, C. W. (2009). Japan's response to China's rise: Regional engagement, global containment, dangers of collision. *International Affairs, 85*(4), 837–856.

Ikenberry, G. J. (2008). The rise of China and the future of the West: Can the liberal system survive? *Foreign Affairs, 87*(1), 23–37.

———. (2011). The future of the liberal world order: Internationalism after America. *Foreign Affairs, 90*(3), 56–68.

Ingram, N. (2009). Working-class boys, educational success and the misrecognition of working-class culture. *British Journal of Sociology of Education, 30*(4), 421–434.

ISEAS-Yusof Ishak Institute. (2020, January 16). *State of Southeast Asia: 2020.* https://www .iseas.edu.sg/images/pdf/TheStateofSEASurveyReport_2020.pdf

———. (2021, February 10). *State of Southeast Asia: 2021.* https://www.iseas.edu.sg/wp-content /uploads/2021/01/The-State-of-SEA-2021-v2.pdf

———. (2022). *State of Southeast Asia: 2022.* https://www.iseas.edu.sg/articles-commentaries/ state-of-southeast-asia-survey/the-state-of-southeast-asia-2022-survey-report/

Ismail, S. (2016, April 25). *China's pact with Cambodia, Laos an interference in ASEAN's domestic affairs: Former sec-gen.* CNA. http://www.channelnewsasia.com/news/asiapacific/ china-s-pact-with/2729132.html

Jackson, P. (2008). Pierre Bourdieu, the "cultural turn" and the practice of international history. *Review of International Studies, 34*(1), 155–181.

———. (2011). *The conduct of inquiry in international relations: Philosophy of science and its implications for the study of world politics.* Routledge.

Jaipragas, B. (2017, January 22). Are China-Singapore relations about to thaw? *South China Morning Post.* http://www.scmp.com/week-asia/geopolitics/article/2063656/are-china -singapore-relations-about-thaw

Jakobson, L. (2016). Domestic actors and the fragmentation of China's foreign policy. In R. Ross & J. I. Bekkevold (Eds.), *China in the era of Xi Jinping* (pp. 137–164). Georgetown University Press.

Jakobson, L., & Knox, D. (2010). *New foreign policy actors in China* (SIPRI Policy Paper No. 26). Stockholm International Peace Research Institute. https://www.sipri.org/sites/ default/files/files/PP/SIPRIPP26.pdf

Jerdén, B. (2014). The assertive China narrative: Why it is wrong and how so many still bought into it. *Chinese Journal of International Politics, 7*(1), 47–88.

Jervis, R. (1976). *Perception and misperception in international relations* (new ed.). Princeton University Press.

Johnston, I. A. (1995). *Cultural realism: Strategic culture and grand strategy in Chinese history.* Princeton University Press.

———. (2008). *Social states: China in international institutions, 1980–2000.* Princeton University Press.

———. (2013). How new and assertive is China's new assertiveness? *International Security, 37*(4), 7–48.

Jones, A., & Clark, J. (2019). Performance, emotions, and diplomacy in the United Nations assemblage in New York. *Annals of the American Association of Geographers, 109*(4), 1262–1278.

Jones, L., & Zeng, J. (2019). Understanding China's "Belt and Road Initiative": Beyond "grand strategy" to a state transformation analysis. *Third World Quarterly, 40*(8), 1415–1439.

Jones, T. B., & Mattiacci, E. (2019). A manifesto, in 140 characters or fewer: Social media as a tool of rebel diplomacy. *British Journal of Political Science, 49*(2), 739–761.

Joseph, J., & Kurki, M. (2018). The limits of practice: Why realism can complement IR's practice turn. *International Theory, 10*(1), 71–97.

Kaneko, M. (2022, October 23). China's Xi starts rare 3rd term with allies dominating leadership. *Kyodo News.* https://english.kyodonews.net/news/2022/10/ed0340efbad6-chinas-xi-to-launch-new-leadership-filled-with-allies.html

Kang, D. C. (2003). Getting Asia wrong: The need for new analytical frameworks. *International Security, 27*(4), 57–85.

Kao, S. S. (2014). Scarborough Shoal dispute, China's assertiveness, and Taiwan's South China Sea policy. *International Journal of China Studies, 5*(1), 153–178.

Kauppi, N. (2018). Transnational social fields. In T. Medvetz & J. J. Sallaz (Eds.), *The Oxford handbook of Pierre Bourdieu* (pp. 183–199). Oxford University Press.

Kausikan, B. (2018, March 26). Bilahari Kausikan: Why small countries should not behave like a small country. *Para Limes.* https://blogs.ntu.edu.sg/paralimes/2018/03/26/bilahari-smallcountries/

Keohane, R. O. (1998). International institutions: Can interdependence work? *Foreign Policy, 110*, 82–96.

Keohane, R. O., & Martin, L. L. (2003). Institutional theory as a research program. In C. Elman & M. F. Elman (Eds.), *Progress in international relations theory: Appraising the field* (pp. 71–108). MIT Press.

Kerr, R., & Robinson, S. (2009). The hysteresis effect as creative adaptation of the habitus: Dissent and transition to the "corporate" in post-Soviet Ukraine. *Organization, 16*(6), 829–853.

Kirshner, J. (2010). The tragedy of offensive realism: Classical realism and the rise of China. *European Journal of International Relations, 18*(1), 53–75.

Kissinger, H. (2012). *On China.* Penguin Group.

Klare, M. (2001). *Resource wars: The new landscape of global conflict.* Owl Books.

Kleiner, J. (2008). The inertia of diplomacy. *Diplomacy and Statecraft, 19*(2), 321–349.

Kuo, L. (2018, July 10). Liu Xia: Widow of Nobel laureate arrives in Berlin after release from China. *The Guardian.* https://www.theguardian.com/world/2018/jul/10/liu-xia-nobel-laureates-widow-allowed-to-leave-china-for-europe

Kurlantzick, J. (2007). China's new diplomacy and its impact on the world. *Brown Journal of World Affairs, 14*(1), 221–235.

Kustermans, J. (2011). The state as citizen: State personhood and ideology. *Journal of International Relations and Development, 14*, 1–27.

Kwan, J. (2020). Chinese embassy distributes coronavirus "health packages" to Manchester students. *Mancunion*. https://mancunion.com/2020/04/15/chinese-embassy-distributes -coronavirus-health-packages-to-manchester-students/

Laffey, M. (2000). Locating identity: Performativity, foreign policy and state action. *Review of International Studies, 26*(3), 429–444.

Lahire, B. (2010). *The plural actor*. Cambridge: Polity Press.

Lam, W. (2016). Xi Jinping's ideology and statecraft. *Chinese Law and Government, 48*(6), 409–417.

———. (2018, August 1). *Xi's grip loosens amid trade war policy paralysis*. Jamestown Foundation. https://jamestown.org/program/xis-grip-on-authority-loosens-amid-trade-war -policy-paralysis/

Lampton, D. M. (1992). A plum for a peach: Bargaining, interest, and bureaucratic politics in China. In K. G. Lieberthal & D. M. Lampton (Eds.), *Bureaucracy, politics and decision making in post-Mao China* (pp. 34–58). University of California Press.

———. (2015). Xi Jinping and the National Security Commission: Policy coordination and political power. *Journal of Contemporary China, 24*(95), 759–777.

Landale, J. (2020, May 13). *Coronavirus: China's new army of tough-talking diplomats*. British Broadcasting Corporation. https://www.bbc.com/news/world-asia-china-52562549

Lanteigne, M. (2017). *China foreign policy: An introduction*. Routledge.

Latour, B. (1996). On actor-network theory: A few clarifications. *Soziale Welt, 47*(4), 369–381.

———. (2005). *Reassembling the social*. Oxford University Press.

Lau, M. (2015, May 20). Chinese president Xi Jinping demands loyalty from state security agencies. *South China Morning Post*. http://www.scmp.com/news/china/policies-politics /article/1804134/chinese-president-xi-jinping-demands-loyalty-state

Lau, S. (2020, April 27). Coronavirus: Germany "rejected China's bid for positive spin" on pandemic response. *South China Morning Post*. https://www.scmp.com/news/china/diploma cy/article/3081800/coronavirus-germany-rejected-chinas-bid-positive-spin-pandemic

Lee, J.-H. (2018, November 18). "Simply not true": China rejects claims APEC diplomats tried to "barge" in on PNG minister's office to influence communique. *South China Morning Post*. https://www.scmp.com/news/asia/australasia/article/2173782/police-called-chinese -diplomats-barging-png-foreign-minister

Leonard, V. W. (1989). A Heideggerian phenomenologic perspective on the concept of the person. *Advances in Nursing Science, (11)*4: 40–55.

Lequesne, C. (2020). Ministries of foreign affairs: A crucial institution revisited. *The Hague Journal of Diplomacy, 15*(1–2), 1–12.

Lesch, M., & Loh, D. M. H. (2022). Field overlaps, normativity and the contestation of practices in China's Belt and Road Initiative. *Global Studies Quarterly, 2*(4):1–12.

Levy, J. (2008). Case studies: Types, designs, and logics of inference. *Conflict Management and Peace Science, 25*(1), 1–18.

Lew, L. (2019, November 27). China overtakes United States to boast world's biggest diplomatic network, think tank says. *South China Morning Post*. https://www.scmp.com/news /china/diplomacy/article/3039640/china-overtakes-united-states-boast-worlds-biggest -diplomatic

Li, C. (2016). *Chinese politics in the Xi Jinping era: Reassessing collective leadership.* Brookings Institute.

———. (2017). *The Power of Ideas.* World Scientific Publishing.

Li, J. (2019a, January 1). Waijiao bu fayan ren zhidu shi zenyang jianli de. *The Paper.* https://www.thepaper.cn/newsDetail_forward_2897667

Li, Jason (2019b, August 27). *Conflict mediation with Chinese characteristics: How China justifies its non-interference policy.* Stimson Center. https://www.stimson.org/2019/conflict-mediation-chinese-characteristics-how-china-justifies-its-non-interference-policy/

Li, M. (2011). Rising from within: China's search for a multilateral world and its implications for Sino-US relations. *Global Governance: A Review of Multilateralism and International Organizations, 17*(3), 331–351.

Li, M., & Loh, D. M. H. (2015). China's fluid assertiveness in the South China Sea dispute. In A. Tan (Ed.), *Security and conflict in East Asia* (pp. 91–101). Routledge.

Li, Z. (2017, May 18). *Li Zhaoxing zhuanwen daonian Qian Qichen: Cong ta shenshang xuedao shu bujin de diandi [Li Zhaoxing on former top diplomat Qian Qichen: I learnt a great deal from him].* Ifeng News. http://news.ifeng.com/a/20170518/51118543_0.shtml

Lieberthal, K., & Oksenberg, M. (1988). *Policy making in China.* Princeton University Press.

Lin, X. (2017, July 9). *We have "zero contact" with North Korea, senior Chinese military officer tells Conversation.* CNA. https://www.channelnewsasia.com/news/cnainsider/we-have-zero-contact-with-north-korea-senior-chinese-military-9016132

Lin, Y. (2019, July 31). The Trojan Horse: How WeChat infiltrates Western politics, part 2. *Epoch Times.* https://www.theepochtimes.com/the-trojan-horse-how-wechat-infiltrates-western-politics-part-2_3025237.html

Lipsky, M. (1980). *Street-level bureaucracy: Dilemmas of the individual in public services.* Russell Sage Foundation.

Liu, Xiaohong (2001). *Chinese ambassadors.* University of Washington Press.

Liu, X. (2008). *Zhongguo zhu chaoxian dashi Liu Xiaoming zai jinian Zhou Enlai zongli danchen 110 zhounian ji fang chao 50 zhounian zhaodai hui shang de Jianghua [Speech by Chinese ambassador to the DPRK Liu Xiaoming at the reception to commemorate the 110th birth anniversary of Premier Zhou Enlai and the 50th anniversary of DPRK-China diplomat ties].* Waijiao Bu, February 19. http://www3.fmprc.gov.cn/web/dszlsjt_673036/ds_673038/t430614.shtml.

Liu, Z. (2016, July 12). What's China's "nine-dash line" and why has it created so much tension in the South China Sea? *South China Morning Post.* https://www.scmp.com/news/china/diplomacy-defence/article/1988596/whats-chinas-nine-dash-line-and-why-has-it-created-so

Lloyd-Damnjanovic, A. (2018). *A preliminary study of PRC political influence and interference activities in American higher education.* Wilson Center. https://www.wilsoncenter.org/sites/default/files/media/documents/publication/prc_political_influence_full_report.pdf

Loh, A. A. (2008). Deconstructing cultural realism. In G. Wang & Y. Zheng (Eds.), *China and the new international order* (281–290). Routledge.

Loh, D. M. H. (2015, December). *Hong Kong's political future after the "umbrella revolution."* RSIS Policy Report. https://goo.gl/fND5Us

———. (2016, August 5). What price ASEAN unity? *RSIS Commentary.* https://www.rsis.edu.sg/wp-content/uploads/2016/08/CO16200.pdf

———. (2017). Defending China's national image and "defensive soft power": The case of Hong Kong's "umbrella revolution." *Chinese Journal of Political Science, 22*(1), 117–134.

———. (2018a). Diplomatic control, foreign policy, and change under Xi Jinping: A field-theoretic account. *Journal of Current Chinese Affairs, 47*(3), 111–145. https://doi.org/10.1177/186810261804700305.

———. (2018b). The disturbance and endurance of norms in ASEAN: Peaceful but stressful. *Australian Journal of International Affairs, 72*(5), 385–402.

———. (2020a, May 22). *The power and limits of China's "mask diplomacy."* East Asia Forum. https://www.eastasiaforum.org/2020/05/22/the-power-and-limits-of-chinas-mask-diplomacy/

———. (2020b, June 12). *Over here, overbearing: The origins of China's "wolf warrior" style diplomacy.* Hong Kong Free Press. https://hongkongfp.com/2020/06/12/over-here-overbearing-the-origins-of-chinas-wolf-warrior-style-diplomacy/

———. (2023, April 19). *Very interesting speech by Singapore's minister of state for foreign affairs* [post]. LinkedIn. https://www.linkedin.com/posts/dylanloh_parliament-sitting-19-april-2023-activity-7054636107992346626-84ih

Loh, D. M. H., & Loke, B. (2023, July 20). COVID-19 and the international politics of blame: Assessing China's crisis (mis)management practices. *China Quarterly, 1–17,* https://doi.org/10.1017/S0305741023000796.

Lok, J., & de Rond, M. (2013). On the plasticity of institutions: Containing and restoring practice breakdowns at the Cambridge University Boat Club. *Academy of Management Journal 56*(1), 185–207.

Lu, N. (2000). *The dynamics of foreign-policy decision making in China* (2nd ed.). Westview Press.

Luo, Z. (2016, June 15). Canada should not be "blinded" over human rights differences with China. *Globe and Mail.* http://www.theglobeandmail.com/opinion/canada-should-not-be-blinded-over-human-rights-differences-with-china/article30282085

Lynch, D. (2009). Chinese thinking on the future of international relations: Realism as the *Ti*, rationalism as the *Yong*? *China Quarterly, 192,* 87–107.

———. (2013). Securitizing culture in Chinese foreign policy debates: Implications for interpreting China's rise. *Asian Survey, 54*(4), 629–652.

Ma, L., & Zhou, W. (2011, April 28). China's defense policy "ensures national security." *China Daily.* http://www.chinadaily.com.cn/china/2011-04/28/content_12408739.htm

Madsen, R. M. (2016). Transnational fields and power elites: Reassembling the international with Bourdieu and practice theory. In T. Basaran, D. Bigo, E.-P. Guittet, & R. B. J. Walker (Eds.), *International political sociology: Transversal lines* (pp. 106–125). Routledge.

Mahler, S. J. (2000). Constructing international relations: The role of transnational migrants and other non-state actors. *Identities: Global Studies in Culture and Power, 7*(2), 197–232.

Manor, I., & Crilley, R. (2019). The mediatisation of MFAS: Diplomacy in the new media ecology. *The Hague Journal of Diplomacy, 15*(1–2), 66–92.

Manor, I., & Pamment, J. (2019). Towards prestige mobility? Diplomatic prestige and digital diplomacy. *Cambridge Review of International Affairs, 32*(2), 93–131.

Mapendere, J. (2005). Track one and a half diplomacy and the complementarity of tracks. *Culture of Peace Online Journal, 2*(1), 66–81.

Marlow, I., & Li, D. (2019). *Chinese diplomat deletes tweet that angered Susan Rice.* Bloomberg. https://www.bloomberg.com/news/articles/2019-07-16/chinese-diplomat-deletes-tweet-on-race-that-angered-susan-rice

Martin, P., & Li, J. (2020, March 23). *Rare spat between Chinese diplomats signals split over Trump.* Bloomberg. https://www.bloomberg.com/news/articles/2020-03-23/china-s-top-envoy-to-u-s-breaks-with-foreign-ministry-on-virus

Martina, M., Blanchard, B., & Birsel, R. (2017, September 1). *China says Xi transcends West as a diplomatic "pioneer."* Reuters. https://www.reuters.com/article/us-china-congress -diplomacy/china-says-xi-transcends-west-as-a-diplomatic-pioneer-idUSKCN1BC4KQ

Martin-Mazé, M. (2017). Returning struggles to the practice turn: How were Bourdieu and Boltanski lost in (some) translations and what to do about it? *International Political Sociology, 11*(2), 203–220.

Mastro, O. S. (2015). Why Chinese assertiveness is here to stay. *Washington Quarterly, 37*(4), 151–170.

Mattern, J. B. (2011). A practice theory of emotion for international relations. In E. Adler & V. Pouliot (Eds.), *International practices* (pp. 63–86). Cambridge University Press.

McConnell, F. (2018). Performing diplomatic decorum: Repertoires of "appropriate" behavior in the margins of international diplomacy. *International Political Sociology, 12*(4), 362–381.

McConnell, F., & Dittmer J. (2017). Liminality and the diplomacy of the British Overseas Territories: An assemblage approach. *Society and Space, 36*(1), 139–158.

McDonough, P. M. (1997). *Choosing colleges: How social class and schools structure opportunity.* SUNY Press.

McMillan, K. (2018). *The constitution of social practices.* Routledge.

Mearsheimer, J. J. (2006). China's unpeaceful rise. *Current History, 105*(690), 160–162.

———. (2010). The gathering storm: China's challenge to US power in Asia. *Chinese Journal of International Politics, 3*(4), 381–396.

Mérand, F. (2010). Pierre Bourdieu and the birth of European defense. *Security Studies, 19*(2), 342–374.

Mérand, F., & Forget, A. (2013). Strategy. In R. Adler-Nissen (Ed.), *Bourdieu in international relations* (pp. 93–113). Routledge.

Mercer, J. (1995). Anarchy and identity. *International Organization, 49*(2), 229–252.

Meredith, S. (2019, November 27). *China has overtaken the US to have the world's largest diplomatic network, think tank says.* CNBC. https://www.cnbc.com/2019/11/27/china-has -overtaken-the-us-to-have-the-worlds-largest-diplomatic-network.html

Ministry of Foreign Affairs [外交部]. PRC. (2000). *Ministry of Foreign Affairs headquarters.* https://www.fmprc.gov.cn/chn/other/premade/6360/main.html

———. (2011, August 29). *Waijiaobu xinwen fabu zhidu "shengji" [Ministry of Foreign Affairs' press release system receives an upgrade].* State Council Information Office. http://www .scio.gov.cn/xwfbh/zdjs/document/994161/994161.htm

———. (2013, July 13). *Waijiaobu [Ministry of Foreign Affairs].* Suowen Civil Service Information Network. http://www.chinagwyw.org/hao/zhongyang/xzjg/113672.html

———. (2017). *The facts and China's position concerning the Indian border troops' crossing of the China-India boundary in the Sikkim sector into the Chinese territory.* China's Ministry of Foreign Affairs. https://www.fmprc.gov.cn/mfa_eng/wjdt_665385/2649_665393/ P020170802542676636134.pdf

———. (n.d.). *Chinese embassies.* https://www.fmprc.gov.cn/mfa_eng/wjb_663304/zwjg_66 5342/2490_665344

Ministry of Foreign Affairs. Singapore. (2018, August 2). *Joint Communiqué of the 51st ASEAN Foreign Ministers' Meeting Singapore, 2 August 2018.* https://www.mfa.gov.sg/Newsroom/ Press-Statements-Transcripts-and-Photos/2018/08/communique

Moorman, C., & Miner, A. S. (1997). The impact of organizational memory on new product performance and creativity. *Journal of Marketing Research, 34*(1), 91–106.

Morozov, V., & Rumelili, B. (2012). The external constitution of European identity: Russia and Turkey as Europe-makers. *Cooperation and Conflict, 47*(1), 28–48.

Myanmar Times. (2017, June 19). ASEAN centrality must be earned: Experts. https://www
.mmtimes.com/asean-focus/26451-asean-centrality-must-be-earned-experts.html

Nan, A. S. (2005). Track one-and-a-half diplomacy: Contributions to Georgia-South Ossetian peacemaking. In R. J. Fisher (Ed.), *Paving the way* (pp. 161–173). Lexington Books.

Nathan, A. J., & Scobell, A. (2012). *China's search for security.* Columbia University Press.

Nathan, A. J., & Tsai, K. S. (1995). Factionalism: A new institutionalist restatement. *China Journal, 34,* 157–192.

Needle, D. (2004). *Business in context.* Thomson Learning.

Neumann, I. B. (2002). Returning practice to the linguistic turn: The case of diplomacy. *Millennium: Journal of International Studies, 31*(3), 627–651.

———. (2012). *At home with the diplomats: Inside a European foreign ministry.* Cornell University Press.

———. (2013). *Diplomatic sites: A critical enquiry.* C. Hurst.

Neumann, I. B., & Pouliot, V. (2011). Untimely Russia: Hysteresis in Russian-Western relations over the past millennium. *Security Studies, 20*(1), 105–137.

Nexon, D. H., & Neumann, I. B. (2018). Hegemonic-order theory: A field-theoretic account. *European Journal of International Relations, 24*(3), 662–686.

Ng, E. H. (2016, November 25). *A friendly round of golf. Enjoyed a round of golf this evening at Marina Bay Golf Course with Chinese Ambassador Chen Xiaodong, food tycoon Sam Goi and my fellow Grassroots Adviser Chong Kee Hiong.* [Image attached] [Status update]. Facebook. https://www.facebook.com/ngenghen/posts/1178739108886013

Ng, J. (2017, July 8). Beijing says Sino-British treaty on Hong Kong handover still binding but does not allow UK to interfere. *South China Morning Post.* http://www.scmp.com/news/hong-kong/politics/article/2101823/we-still-recognise-sino-british-joint-declaration-legally

Nicolini, D. (2012). *Practice theory, work, and organization.* Oxford University Press.

Nordin, A. H., & Smith, G. M. (2018). Reintroducing friendship to international relations: Relational ontologies from China to the West. *International Relations of Asia Pacific, 18*(3), 369–396.

Oberfield, Z. W. (2010). Rule following and discretion at government's frontlines: Continuity and change during organization socialization. *Journal of Public Administration Research and Theory, 20*(4), 735–755.

Office of the Historian. US Department of State. (1971, June 30). *Conversation between President Nixon and the ambassador to the Republic of China (McConaughy).* https://history .state.gov/historicaldocuments/frus1969-76v17/d136.

Orlikowski, W. J. (2007). Sociomaterial practices: Exploring technology at work. *Organization Studies, 28*(9), 1435–1448.

O'Brien, K., & Li, L. (2006). *Rightful resistance in rural China.* Cambridge University Press.

O'Tuathail, G. (2003). "Just out looking for a fight": American affect and the invasion of Iraq. *Antipode, 35*(5), 219–236.

Özbilgin, M., & Tatli, A. (2005). Book review essay: Understanding Bourdieu's contribution to organization and management studies. *Academy of Management Review, 30*(4), 855–869.

Pan, C., & Kavalski, E. (2018). Theorizing China's rise in and beyond international relations. *International Relations of the Asia-Pacific, 18*(3), 289–311.

Parameswaran, P. (2015, October 2). The truth about China's "interference" in Malaysia's politics. *The Diplomat.* https://thediplomat.com/2015/10/the-truth-about-chinas-interference -in-malaysias-politics

———. (2016, June 21). What really happened at the ASEAN-China Special Kunming meet-

ing. *The Diplomat.* https://thediplomat.com/2016/06/what-really-happened-at-the-asean
-china-special-kunming-meeting

Pieke, N. F. (2009). *The good communist.* Cambridge University Press.

Pillsbury, M. (2015). *The hundred year marathon: China's secret strategy to replace the America as the global superpower.* Henry Holt.

Pop, L. (2009). Strategic action is not enough: A Bourdieuian approach to EU enlargement. *Perspectives on European Politics and Society, 10*(2), 253–266.

Porter, T. (2013). Tracing associations in global finance. *International Political Sociology, 7*(3), 334–338.

Pouliot, V. (2008). The logic of practicality: A theory of practice of security communities. *International Organization, 62*(2), 257–288.

———. (2010a). *International security in practice: The politics of NATO-Russia diplomacy.* Cambridge University Press.

———. (2010b). The materials of practice: Nuclear warheads, rhetorical commonplaces and committee meetings in Russian-Atlantic relations. *Cooperation and Conflict, 45*(3), 294–311.

———. (2011). Diplomats as permanent representatives: The practical logics of the multilateral pecking order. *International Journal, 66*(3), 543–561.

———. (2013). Methodology: Putting practice theory into practice. In R. Adler-Nissen (Ed.), *Bourdieu in international relations: Rethinking key concepts in IR* (pp. 45–77). Routledge.

———. (2016). *International pecking orders: The politics and practice of multilateral diplomacy.* Cambridge University Press.

Pouliot, V., & Cornut, J. (2015). Practice theory and the study of diplomacy: A research agenda. *Cooperation and Conflict, 50*(3), 297–315.

Pouliot, V., & Mérand, F. (2013). Bourdieu's concepts. In R. Adler-Nissen (Ed.), *Bourdieu in international relations: Rethinking key concepts in IR* (pp. 24–44). Routledge.

Pouliot, V., & Therien, J.-P. (2017). Global governance in practice. *Global Policy, 9*(2), 163–172.

Prime Minister's Office Singapore. (2016, August 22). *National Day Rally 2016 English Speech (Part 1)* [Video]. YouTube. https://www.youtube.com/watch?v=4b6ovLL3iEE

Pugliese, G. (2015). The China challenge, Abe Shinzo's realism, and the limits of Japanese nationalism. *SAIS Review of International Affairs, 35*(2), 45–55.

Pu, X. (2019). *Rebranding China: Contested status signalling in the changing global order.* Stanford University Press.

Pye, L. W. (1995). Factions and the politics of guanxi: Paradoxes in Chinese administrative and political behaviour. *China Journal, 34*, 35–53.

Qi, H. (2019). Joint development in the South China Sea: China's incentives and policy choices. *Journal of Contemporary East Asia Studies, 8*(2), 220–239.

Qin, Y. (2007). Why is there no Chinese international relations theory? *International Relations of the Asia-Pacific, 7*(3), 313–340.

———. (2010). International society as a process: Institutions, identities, and China's peaceful rise. *Chinese Journal of International Politics, 3*(2), 129–153.

Qiu, Z. (2017, January 23). China's outdated foreign service needs rebooting for the age of Trump. *Foreign Policy.* https://foreignpolicy.com/2017/01/23/reboot-chinas-foreign-service-for-the-age-of-trump/

———. (2018, May 9). How PRC diplomatic messaging impedes its foreign policy objectives. *China Brief, 18*(8). https://jamestown.org/program/how-prc-diplomatic-messaging-impedes-its-foreign-policy-objectives/

Raymond, C. (2019). Committed knowledge: Autonomy and politicization of research institutions and practices in wartime Lebanon (1975–1990). In R. Jacquemond & F. Lang (Eds.), *Culture and crisis in the Arab world: Art, practice and production in spaces of conflict* (pp. 73–102). I. B. Tauris.

Reckwitz, A. (2002). Toward a theory of social practices: A development in culturalist theorizing. *European Journal of Social Theory, 5*(2), 243–263.

———. (2017). Practices and their affects. In A. Hui, T. Schatzki, & E. Shove (Eds.), *The nexus of practices: Connections, constellations, practitioners* (pp. 115–125). Routledge.

Rees, E. (2018, July 9). *China's unlikely weapon: Tourists.* Stratfor. https://worldview.stratfor .com/article/chinas-unlikely-weapon-tourists

Reuters. (2018, August 21). *Malaysia's Mahathir cancels China-backed rail, pipeline projects.* https://www.reuters.com/article/us-china-malaysia/malaysias-mahathir-cancels-china -backed-rail-pipeline-projects-idUSKCN1L60DQ

———. (2020, December 4). *Canada condemns China for doctored tweet of Australian soldier.* https://www.reuters.com/article/uk-australia-china-tweet-canada-idUKKBN28D307

Rice, S. [@AmbassadorRice]. (2019, July 15). *You are a racist disgrace* [Tweet]. Twitter. https:// twitter.com/AmbassadorRice/status/1150584069354414080

Ringmar, E. (1996). On the ontological status of the state. *European Journal of International Relations, 2*(4), 439–466.

Rogowski, R. (1999). Institutions as constraints on strategic choice. In D. A. Lake & R. Powell (Eds.), *Strategic choice and international relations* (pp. 115–136). Princeton University Press.

Rosecrance, R. (1973). *International relations: Peace or war?* McGraw-Hill.

Ross, R. S. (2013). The domestic sources of China's "assertive diplomacy," 2009–10. In R. Foot (Ed.), *China across the divide: The domestic and global in politics and society* (pp. 72–96). Oxford University Press.

Rozman, G. (2012). Chinese national identity and foreign policy: Linkages between the two. In G. Rozman (Ed.), *China's foreign policy: Who makes it, and how is it made?* (pp. 153–184). Asan Institute for Policy Studies.

Rudd, K. (2018). *Xi Jinping, China and the global order.* Asia Society. https://asiasociety.org /sites/default/files/2019-01/Xi%20Jinping_China%20and%20the%20Global%20Order .pdf

Ruggie, G. (1998). *Constructing the world polity: Essays on international institutionalism.* Routledge.

Ruwitch, J. (2019, December 4). *China demands "fighting spirit" from diplomats as trade war, Hong Kong protests simmer.* Reuters. https://www.reuters.com/article/us-china-diplomacy /china-demands-fighting-spirit-from-diplomats-as-trade-war-hong-kong-protests-simmer -idUSKBN1Y80R8

Rühlig, N. T. (2022). *China's foreign policy contradictions.* Oxford University Press.

Saich, T. (2001). *Governance and politics of China.* Palgrave.

Santos, M. (2016, July 12). *Philippines wins arbitration case vs. China over South China Sea.* Inquirer.net. https://globalnation.inquirer.net/140358/philippines-arbitration-decision -maritime-dispute-south-china-sea-arbitral-tribunal-unclos-itlos

Satow, E. (1979). *Satow's guide to diplomatic practice.* London: Longmans.

Schatzki, T. (1996). *Social practices: A Wittgensteinian approach to human activity and the social.* Cambridge University Press.

———. (1997). Practices and actions: A Wittgensteinian critique of Bourdieu and Giddens. *Philosophy of the Social Sciences, 27*(3), 283–308.

———. (2001). Introduction: practice theory. In T. R. Schatzki, K. K. Cetina, & E. V. Savigny (Eds.), *The practice turn in contemporary theory* (pp. 10–23). Routledge.

———. (2010). *The timespace of human activity: On performance, society, and history as indeterminate teleological events*. Lexington Books.

———. (2011). *Where the action is (on large social phenomena such as sociotechnical regimes)* (Sustainable Practices Research Group, Working Paper 1). University of Manchester. http://www.sprg.ac.uk/publications-amp-presentations/discussion-papers/schatzki-practice-theory-macro-phenomena-sociotechnical-regimes

Schmidt, R. (2017). Reflexive knowledges in practices. In A. Hui, T. Schatzki, & E. Shove (Eds.), *The nexus of practices: Connections, constellations, practitioners* (pp. 141–155). Routledge.

Schurmann, F. (1968). *Ideology and organization in communist China* (2nd ed.). University of California Press.

Seib, P. (2012). *Real-time diplomacy*. Palgrave Macmillan.

Senn, M., & Elhardt, C. (2014). Bourdieu and the bomb: Power, language and the doxic battle over the value of nuclear weapons. *European Journal of International Relations, 20*(2), 316–340.

Sevastopulo, D. (2021, July 16). China snubs senior US official in worsening diplomatic standoff. *Financial Times*. https://www.ft.com/content/2d034271-fcd7-4977-9d50-13bc048e6084

Shambaugh, D. (2011). Coping with a conflicted China. *Washington Quarterly, 34*(1), 7–27.

———. (2013). *China goes global: The partial power*. Oxford University Press.

———. (2015). China's soft-power push: The search for respect. *Foreign Affairs, 94*(4), 99–107.

Sharma, M. (2020, April 27). *Diplomacy is another victim of the virus*. Bloomberg. https://www.bloomberg.com/opinion/articles/2020-04-26/china-s-wolf-warrior-officials-herald-the-end-of-diplomacy

Sharp, P. (1999). For diplomacy: Representation and the study of international relations. *International Studies Review, 1*(1), 33–57.

Shindo, R. (2018). Resistance beyond sovereign politics: Petty sovereigns' disappearance into the world of fiction in post-Fukushima Japan. *Security Dialogue, 49*(3), 183–199.

Shi, J. (2020). China wants its diplomats to show more fighting spirit. It may not be intended to win over the rest of the world. *South China Morning Post*. https://www.scmp.com/news/china/diplomacy/article/3079493/china-wants-its-diplomats-show-more-fighting-spirit-it-may-not.

Shi, Y. (2013). "Triumphalism" and decision making in China's Asia policy. *Economic and Political Studies, 1*(1), 107–119.

Shirk, S. L. (1990). "Playing to the provinces": Deng Xiaoping's political strategy of economic reform. *Studies in Comparative Communism, 23*(3–4), 227–258.

Shove, E. (2017, February 2). Elizabeth Shove—practice theory methodologies do not exist. *Practice Theory Methodology* [blog]. https://practicetheorymethodologies.wordpress.com/2017/02/15/elizabeth-shove-practice-theory-methodologies-do-not-exist/

Shove, E., Watson, M., & Spurling, N. (2015). Conceptualizing connections: Energy demand, infrastructures and social practices. *European Journal of Social Theory, 18*(3), 274–287.

Si, C. (2018, April 12). ASEAN-China innovation year, forum opens in Beijing. *China Daily*. http://www.chinadaily.com.cn/a/201804/12/WS5acf477aa3105cdcf6517ebe.html

Silver, L., Devlin, K., & Huang, C. (2021, June 30). *Large majorities say China does not respect the personal freedoms of its people*. Pew Research Center. https://www.pewresearch.org/global/2021/06/30/large-majorities-say-china-does-not-respect-the-personal-freedoms-of-its-people/

Sina News. (2016, June 24). *Wu Jianmin zhui daohui juxing Zhao Qizheng zhuiyi waishi diandi zan zhishuai [Wu Jianmin memorial service held, diplomat remembered by Zhao Qizheng as a straightforward person]*. Sina News. http://news.sina.com.cn/o/2016-06-24/doc-ifxtmwri4375947.shtml

Siow, M. (2016, August 22). There may be more trouble ahead for China and Singapore. *South China Morning Post*. http://www.scmp.com/week-asia/politics/article/2006266/there-may-be-trouble-ahead-china-and-singapore

Smith, B. (2019, December 2). *Meet the Chinese diplomat who got promoted for trolling the US on Twitter*. Buzzfeed. https://www.buzzfeednews.com/article/bensmith/zhao-lijian-china-twitter

Smith, G. (2014, November 8). The top four myths about China in the Pacific. *The Interpreter*. https://www.lowyinstitute.org/the-interpreter/top-four-myths-about-china-pacific

Sociopolítica de Asia Pacífico. (2018, August 25). China's embassy in Spain coerced the university of Salamanca regarding Taiwan. https://deasiapacifico.wordpress.com/2018/08/25/chinas-embassy-in-spain-coerced-the-university-of-salamanca-regarding-taiwan/

Solomon, T., & Steele, Brent J. (2017). Micro-moves in international relations theory. *European Journal of International Relations, 23*(2), 267–291.

Song, H. L., & Gao, L. (2017). *Yang Jiechi tongzhi jianli [Résumé of Comrade Yang Jiechi]*. Chinese Communist Party News. http://cpc.people.com.cn/19th/n1/2017/1025/c414305-29608918.html

South China Morning Post. (2018a, August 9). Chinese officials remember diplomat who helped shape "Law of the Sea." https://www.scmp.com/news/china/diplomacy-defence/article/2159035/chinese-officials-remember-diplomat-who-helped-shape

———. (2018b, September 6). China must apologise for "arrogance" at Pacific summit, says Nauru president. https://www.scmp.com/news/china/diplomacy/article/2163002/china-must-apologise-arrogance-pacific-summit-says-nauru

Spies, Y. K. (2019). *Global diplomacy and international society*. Palgrave Macmillan.

Spokesperson. [@MFA_China]. (2019, December 12). *Appreciate #JamesCurran & @FareedZakaria vision & objectiveness*. [Tweet]. Twitter. https://twitter.com/MFA_China/status/1205138247510192134

Spry, D. (2019). From Delhi to Dili: Facebook diplomacy by ministries of foreign affairs in the Asia-Pacific. *The Hague Journal of Diplomacy, 15*(1–2), 93–125.

Stein, J. G. (2011). Background knowledge in the foreground. In E. Adler & V. Pouliot (Eds.), *International practices* (pp. 87–107). Cambridge University Press.

Steinmetz, G. (2004). Odious comparisons: Incommensurability, the case study, and "small N's" in sociology. *Sociological Theory, 22*(3), 371–400.

Stenslie, S., & Gang, C. (2016). Xi Jinping's grand strategy from vision to implementation. In R. Ross & J. I. Bekkevold (Eds.), *China in the era of Xi Jinping* (pp. 117–136). Georgetown University Press.

Stephens, H. (2016, June 16). Wang Yi's "temper tantrum" in Canada. *The Diplomat*. http://thediplomat.com/2016/06/wang-yis-temper-tantrum-in-canada

Stern, R., & O'Brien, K. (2012). Politics at the boundary: Mixed signals and the Chinese state. *Modern China, 38*(2), 174-198.

Storey, J. I. (1999). Creeping assertiveness: China, the Philippines and the South China Sea dispute. *Contemporary Southeast Asia, 21*(1), 95–118.

Straits Times. (2017, January 17). China-Singapore joint council for bilateral cooperation slated for next month. http://www.straitstimes.com/politics/singapolitics/china-singapore-joint-council-for-bilateral-cooperation-slated-for-next-month

———. (2020a, March 31). In China, diplomat Zhao Lijian rises as aggressive foreign policy

takes root. https://www.straitstimes.com/asia/east-asia/in-china-diplomat-zhao-lijian
-rises-as-aggressive-foreign-policy-takes-root

———. (2020b, April 7). China spokesman Zhao Lijian defends coronavirus tweets criticised
by Trump. https://www.straitstimes.com/asia/east-asia/china-spokesman-zhao-lijian-de
fends-coronavirus-tweets-criticised-by-trump

Subotic, J., & Zarakol, A. (2012). Cultural intimacy in international relations. *European Journal of International Relations, 19*(4), 915–938.

Sun, J. (2016). Growing diplomacy, retreating diplomats—how the Chinese foreign ministry
has been marginalized in foreign policymaking. *Journal of Contemporary China, 26*(105),
419–433.

Sun, Y. (2014). *Africa in China's foreign policy.* Brookings Institute. https://www.brookings
.edu/research/africa-in-chinas-foreign-policy/

Sutter, R. (2012). *Chinese foreign relations: Power and policy since the cold war.* Rowman and
Littlefield.

Swaine, D. M. (2010). Perceptions of an assertive China. *China Leadership Monitor, 32,* 1–19.
https://carnegieendowment.org/files/CLM32MS1.pdf

Swan, J., & Allen-Ebrahimian, B. (2020, March 22). *Top Chinese official disowns U.S. military
lab coronavirus conspiracy.* Axios. https://www.axios.com/china-coronavirus-ambassador
-cui-tiankai-1b0404e8-026d-4b7d-8290-98076f95df14.html

Swartz, D. (1997). *Culture and power: The sociology of Pierre Bourdieu.* University of Chicago
Press.

Taber, N. (2018, August 10). How Xi Jinping is shaping China's universities. *The Diplomat.*
https://thediplomat.com/2018/08/how-xi-jinping-is-shaping-chinas-universities/

Taipei Times. (2019, July 18). China's tweeting diplomats open new front in tensions. http://
www.taipeitimes.com/News/world/archives/2019/07/18/2003718901

Tang, S. (2008). From offensive to defensive realism: A social evolutionary interpretation of
China's security strategy. In R. Ross, S. Ross, & F. Zhu (Eds.), *China's ascent: Power, security and the future of international politics* (pp. 141–162). Cornell University Press.

Tariq, Q., & Chan, A. (2015, September 25). Envoy: China against terrorism, discrimination
and extremism. *The Star.* https://www.thestar.com.my/news/nation/2015/09/25/china
-ambassador-petaling-street/

Thayer, C. (2011). Chinese assertiveness in the South China Sea and Southeast Asian responses.
Journal of Current South East Asian Affairs, 30(2), 77–104.

———. (2013). ASEAN, China and the Code of Conduct in the South China Sea. *SAIS Review
of International Affairs, 33*(2), 75–84.

Thomas, N. (2021, July 28). Far more world leaders visit China than America. *The Interpreter.* https://www.lowyinstitute.org/the-interpreter/far-more-world-leaders-visit-china
-america

Tilley, V. Q. (2003). Emancipating cultural pluralism. In C. E. Toffolo (Ed.), *Emancipating
cultural pluralism* (pp. 37–54). State University of New York Press.

Today. (2017, January 9). *PM Lee has asked HK leader for immediate return of Terrexes.* http://
www.todayonline.com/singapore/pm-lee-writes-hk-chief-exec-requesting-return-terrexes
-defence-minister-urges-compliance

Toh, W. L. (2016, December 14). Exhibition to mark ASEAN-China ties. *Straits Times.* https:
//www.straitstimes.com/singapore/exhibition-to-mark-asean-china-ties

Toosi, N. (2019, December 8). In response to Trump, China gets mean. *Politico.* https://www
.politico.com/news/2019/12/08/china-trump-twitter-077767

Vanderklippe, N., & Fife, R. (2016, June 2). China's foreign minister demanded meeting with

Trudeau. *Globe and Mail*. http://www.theglobeandmail.com/news/world/chinas-foreign
-minister-demanded-meeting-with-justin-trudeau/article30256455

Vauchez, A. (2011). Interstitial power in fields of limited statehood: Introducing a "weak field"
approach to the study of transnational settings. *International Political Sociology, 5*(3), 340–
345.

Vaughan, D. (2002). Signals and interpretive work: The role of culture in a theory of practical
action. In K. A. Cerulo (Ed.), *Culture in mind: Toward a sociology of culture and cognition*
(pp. 28–54). Routledge.

Vennesson, P. (2008). Case studies and process tracing: Theories and practices. In D. D. Porta
& M. Keating (Eds.), *Approaches and methodologies in the social sciences* (pp. 223–239).
Cambridge University Press.

Visoka, G. (2018). Metis diplomacy: The everyday politics of becoming a sovereign state.
Journal of Cooperation and Conflict. https://journals.sagepub.com/doi/abs/10.1177/
0010836718807503

Voeten, E. (2011). The practice of political manipulation. In E. Adler & V. Pouliot (Eds.), *International
practices* (pp. 255–279). Cambridge University Press.

Wacquant, L. J. (1989). Towards a reflexive sociology: A workshop with Pierre Bourdieu. *Sociological
Theory, 7*(1), 26–63.

———. (2011). Habitus as topic and tool: Reflections on becoming a prizefighter. *Qualitative
Research in Psychology, 8*(1), 81–92.

Wæver, O., Buzan, B., Kelstrup, M., & Lemaitre, P. (1993). *Identity, migration and the new
security agenda in Europe*. St. Martin's Press.

Walther, M. (2014). *Repatriation to France and Germany: A comparative study based on Bourdieu's
theory of practice*. Springer.

Waltz, K. N. (1959). *Man, the state and war*. Columbia University Press.

———. (1979). *Theory of international politics*. McGraw-Hill.

Wang, C. (2022, June 30). *Xin zhongguo waijiao guan xuanba luyong zhidu de fa zhan yu
biange*. Aisixiang. http://www.aisixiang.com/data/135020.html

Wang, G., & Zheng, Y. (Eds.). (2008). *China and the new international order*. Routledge.

Wang, Hongying (2000). Multilateralism in Chinese foreign policy: The limits of socialization. *Asian Survey, 40*(3), 475–491.

Wang (2003, September 10). Gongwuyuan liushi baogao: Zhongyang buwei san nian liushi
rencai [Civil servant turnover report: 1039 talents left Chinese central government ministries
and agencies in the past 3 years]. *People's Daily*. http://www1.people.com.cn/GB/
jingji/1037/2081317.html

Wang, J. (2011). China's search for a grand strategy: A rising great power finds its way. *Foreign
Affairs, 90*(2), 68–79.

Wang, X. (2012). *The civil servant's notebook*. Penguin China Library.

Wang, Y. (2016). Offensive for defensive: The Belt and Road Initiative and China's new grand
strategy. *Pacific Review, 29*(3): 455–463.

———. (2017). Yang Jiechi: Xi's top diplomat back in his element. *China Brief, 17*(16), 1–19.

Wang, Yi (n.d.). *Follow the guidance of Xi Jinping thought on socialism with Chinese characteristics
for a new era to break new ground in China's foreign relations*. Chinese People's Institute
of Foreign Affairs. http://www.cpifa.org/en/cms/book/232

Wang, Z., & Zeng, J. (2016). Xi Jinping: The game changer of Chinese elite politics? *Contemporary
Politics, 22*(3), 469–486.

Wanous, J. P. (1992). *Organizational entry: Recruitment, selection, orientation and socialization
of newcomers* (2nd ed.). Addison-Wesley.

Weeden, L. (2010). Reflections on ethnographic work in political science. *Annual Review of Political Science, 13,* 255–272.

Weiss, J. C. (2014). *Powerful patriots: Nationalist protest in China's foreign relations.* Oxford University Press.

Wendt, A. (2004). The state as person in international theory. *Review of International Studies, 30*(2), 289–316.

———. (2015). *Quantum mind and social science.* Cambridge University Press.

Wenger, E. C. (1998). *Communities of practice: Learning, meaning, and identity.* Cambridge University Press.

———. (n.d.). Communities of practice: A brief introduction. https://scholarsbank.uoregon .edu/xmlui/bitstream/handle/1794/11736/A%20brief%20introduction%20to%20CoP .pdf?sequence=1&isAllowed=y

Wenger, E. C., & Snyder, W. M. (2000). Communities of practice: The organizational frontier. *Harvard Business Review, 78*(1), 139–145.

Whiting, S. A. (1995, June). National identity emerges in how the policy-making elite perceives and articulates the image of China in its relationship with the outside world. *China Quarterly, 144,* 295–316.

Wilkinson, T. (2017, September 14). Tillerson trims State Department staff and vows to make diplomacy more efficient. *Los Angeles Times.* https://www.latimes.com/nation/la-fg-pol -state-department-plan-20170915-story.html

Wintour, P. (2020, April 15). France summons Chinese envoy after coronavirus "slur." *The Guardian.* https://www.theguardian.com/world/2020/apr/15/france-summons-chinese -envoy-after-coronavirus-slur

Wu, H. (2019). *Move over Trump: China's tweeting diplomats open fresh front in propaganda fight.* Reuters. https://www.reuters.com/article/us-china-diplomacy-internet/move-over -trump-chinas-tweeting-diplomats-open-fresh-front-in-propaganda-fight-idUSKCN1UB oMQ

Wu, W. (2017, December 22). German ambassador Michael Clauss on relations with China, the challenges and potential. *South China Morning Post.* https://www.scmp.com/news/ china/diplomacy-defence/article/2125328/german-ambassador-michael-clauss-relations -china

———. (2020, May 24). Chinese foreign minister Wang Yi defends "wolf warrior" diplomats for standing up to "smears." *South China Morning Post.* https://www.scmp.com/news/ china/diplomacy/article/3085856/chinese-foreign-minister-wang-yi-defends-wolf-warrior

Wu, X. (2001). Four contradictions constraining China's foreign policy behaviour. *Journal of Contemporary China, 10*(27), 293–301.

Wuthnow, J. (2017). Chinese perspectives on the Belt and Road Initiative: Strategic rationales, risks, and implications. *China Strategic Perspectives, 12,* 1–45. https://inss.ndu.edu/Portals /68/Documents/stratperspective/china/ChinaPerspectives-12.pdf

Xi, J (2018, March 1). *Xi Jinping: Zai jinian Zhou Enlai tongzhi danchen 120 zounian zhuotan-hui shang jianghua [Xi Jinping: Speech commemorating Zhou Enlai's 120 birth anniversary].* Xinhua. http://www.xinhuanet.com/2018-03/01/c_1122473470.htm.

———. (2020, October 28). *Xi jinping xinshi dai zhongguo tese shehui zhuyi sixiang yu zhong-guo huayu jianggou.* Xinhuanet. http://www.xinhuanet.com/politics/2020-10/28/c_ 1126666536.htm

Xinhua. (2018, March 21). *Zhonguo Zhongyang yinfa Shenhua dang he guojia jigou gaige fangan.* http://www.xinhuanet.com/2018-03/21/c_1122570517.htm

———. (2021, July 22). *Meiguo changwu fu guowu qing she man jiang fang hua.* http://www
.xinhuanet.com/english/2018-03/21/c_137055471.htm.

Yahuda, M. (2013). China's new assertiveness in the South China Sea. *Journal of Contemporary China, 22*(81), 446–459.

Yan, X. (2014). From keeping a low profile to striving for achievement. *Chinese Journal of International Politics, 7*(2), 153–184.

Yang, H. (2022, August 5). Officials, experts across Asia reiterate support for one-China principle. *China Daily.* https://www.chinadaily.com.cn/a/202208/05/WS62ec117ca310fd2b29e705c4.html

Yang, X. (2016, November 3). *Remarks by ACC secretary-general H. E. Yang Xiuping at the reception marking the 5th anniversary of the ASEAN-China Centre.* ASEAN-China Centre. http://www.asean-china-center.org/english/2016-11/03/c_136748391.htm

Yeo, A. (2019). China's rising assertiveness and the decline in the East Asian regionalism narrative. *International Relations of the Asia-Pacific, 40*(3), 445–475.

Yi, W. (2009, October 31). *Zhuwai waijiao renyuan jiehun yao rushi baogao yu jiehunfa bing bu maodun [Chinese diplomatic envoys stationed abroad must truthfully report marital status and ensure its consistency with Marriage Law].* News 163. http://news.163.com/09/1031/16/5MVGM91S000120GU.html

You, J. (2014). The PLA and diplomacy: Unraveling myths about the military role in foreign policy making. *Journal of Contemporary China, 23*(86), 236–254.

———. (2017). Xi Jinping and PLA centrality in Beijing's South China Sea dispute management. *China: An International Journal, 15*(2), 1–21.

Yu, J. (2018). The Belt and Road Initiative: Domestic interests, bureaucratic politics and the EU-China relations. *Asia Europe Journal, 16*(3), 223–236.

Yu, Z. (2018, April 15). Zhongguo tegao: Wang Qishan dazao Zhongguo waijiao xin geju [China feature: Wang Qishan charts new direction and structure for Chinese diplomacy]. *Lianhe Zaobao.* http://www.zaobao.com.sg/znews/greater-china/story20180415-850883

Yun, S. (2014, April 14). *Africa in China's foreign policy.* Brookings Institute. https://www.brookings.edu/articles/africa-in-chinas-foreign-policy/

Zarakol, A. (2011). *After defeat.* Cambridge University Press.

Zeng, J., Xiao, Y., & Breslin, S. (2015). Securing China's core interests: The state of the debate in China. *International Affairs, 91*(2), 245–266.

Zhongguo Xinwen. (2009a, October 31). *Guanyuan: Zhu wai waijiao renyuan nianling tiaojian shengzhi 23 sui you san dian kaolu [Official: There are three considerations for raising the age for overseas-based diplomats to 23].* http://www.chinanews.com/gn/news/2009/10-31/1940774.shtml

———. (2009b, October 31). *Waijiao guanyuan cheng, zhonguo jiang zengjia zhu wai waijiao renyuan rensu [The foreign ministry will increase the number of overseas diplomats].* http://www.chinanews.com/gn/news/2009/10-31/1940850.shtml

———. (2009c, October 31). *Zhongguo zhuwaiwaijiao jigou da 254 ge zhuwaiwaijiao renyuan jinwu qian ren [There are 254 overseas missions with around 5000 personnel in total].* http://www.chinanews.com/gn/news/2009/10-31/1940791.shtml

Zha, L. [@ZhaLiyou]. (2019, December 20). *We have requested personnels to assist.* [Tweet]. Twitter. https://twitter.com/ZhaLiyou/status/1207961589460004870

———. (2020a, February 9). *You very cold blooded.* [Tweet]. Twitter. https://twitter.com/ZhaLiyou/status/1226313231511089152

———. (2020b, February 16). *You speak in such a way that you look like part of the virus and you will be eradicated just like virus.* [Tweet]. Twitter. https://twitter.com/ZhaLiyou/status/1228923041297551360

Zhai, K., & Yew, L. T. (2020, March 31). *In China, a young diplomat rises as aggressive foreign policy takes root.* Reuters. reuters.com/article/amp/idUSKBN21I0F8

Zhang, A. H. (2014). Bureaucratic politics and China's anti-monopoly law. *Cornell International Law Journal, 47*(3), 671–707.

Zhang, D. (2017, July 19). *Full text of Chinese state councilor's article on Xi Jinping's diplomacy thought.* Xinhua. http://news.xinhuanet.com/english/2017-07/19/c_136455986.htm

Zhang, G. (2011, December 27). *Guanyu huayu quan de jidian sikao.* Xuanjiang Jia wang. http://www.71.cn/2011/1227/656723.shtml

Zhang, J. (2003). Chinese nationalism and its foreign policy implications. In David W. Lovell (Ed.), *Asia-Pacific security: Policy challenges* (chap. 9). Singapore: Institute of Southeast Asian Studies.

———. (2013). China's growing assertiveness in the South China Sea: A strategic shift? In *The South China Sea and Australia's regional security environment* (National Security College Occasional Paper No. 5). http://nghiencuuquocte.org/wp-content/uploads/2014/10/The-South-China-Sea-and-Australia%E2%80%99s-regional-security-environment.pdf

Zhang, Y. (2008). Understanding Chinese views of the emerging world order. In G. Wang & Y. Zheng (Eds.), *China and the new international order* (pp. 149–167). Routledge.

Zhao, K. (2016, April 19). China's rise and its discursive power strategy. *Chinese Political Science Review, 1*(3)1–25.

Zhao, L. [@zlj517]. (2019, November 30). *Out of respect for President Trump, US & its people, on the occasion of thanksgiving day, I pay special thanks to US for squandering trillions of dollars in Afghanistan, Iraq, Libya, Syria . . .* [Tweet]. Twitter. https://twitter.com/zlj517/status/1200504907503030273

———. (2020, March 12). *2/2 CDC was caught on the spot.* [Tweet]. Twitter. https://twitter.com/zlj517/status/1238111898828066823

Zhao, Q. (1992). Domestic factors of Chinese foreign policy: From vertical to horizontal authoritarianism. *Annals of the American Academy of Political and Social Science, 519*, 158–175.

Zhao, S. (2013a). Chinese foreign policy as a rising power to find its rightful place. *Perceptions, 18*(1), 101–128.

———. (2013b). Foreign policy implications of Chinese nationalism revisited: The strident turn. *Journal of Contemporary China, 22*(82), 535–553.

———. (2015). Rethinking the Chinese world order: The imperial cycle and the rise of China. *Journal of Contemporary China, 24*(96), 961–982.

Zheng, S. (2018, September 5). Beijing accused of pressuring Spanish university to drop Taiwanese cultural event. *South China Morning Post.* https://www.scmp.com/news/china/diplomacy/article/2162875/beijing-accused-pressuring-spanish-university-drop-taiwanese

Zheng, Y., Lye, L. F., & Chen, G. (2010). *China's foreign policy in 2009: Shouldering greater responsibilities and building stronger partnerships?* China Policy Institute. https://www.nottingham.ac.uk/iaps/documents/cpi/briefings/briefing-58-foreign-affairs-2009.pdf

Zhou, L., & Jun, M. (2021, July 21). China promises US a "tutorial" in how to treat other countries equally ahead of deputy secretary of state Wendy Sherman's visit. *South China Morning Post.* https://www.scmp.com/news/china/diplomacy/article/3142438/china-promises-us-tutorial-how-treat-other-countries-equally

Zhu, Z. (2011). Chinese foreign policy: External and internal factors. *China: An International Journal, 9*(2), 185–194.

———. (2020, May 15). Interpreting China's "wolf-warrior diplomacy." *The Diplomat*. https://thediplomat.com/2020/05/interpreting-chinas-wolf-warrior-diplomacy/

Zhuang, P. (2018, September 15). China joins row over tourists' complaint of ill-treatment by Swedish police after hostel booking confusion. *South China Morning Post*. https://www.scmp.com/news/china/diplomacy/article/2164381/china-joins-row-over-tourists-complaint-ill-treatment-swedish

Zulfakar, M. (2016, June 15). After Kunming, ASEAN must be united on South China Sea at Laos meeting. *The Star*. https://www.thestar.com.my/opinion/columnists/mergawati/2016/06/15/after-kunming-asean-must-be-united/

Index

actor-network theory (ANT), 29–30

actors: diplomatic actors, 36, 67–69, 77, 174, 182, 184–89; primary actors, 73–75, 174, 184; secondary actors, 73–75, 174, 184, 186; substate actors, 18, 25, 117

Adler, Emanuel, 27, 29–32, 60–61, 65, 137–8, 183

agency, 9, 25–26, 30, 33, 65, 142, 191

Alder-Nissen, Rebecca, 2, 69, 76, 85, 149–150, 153, 180

anticorruption, 19, 77, 81, 83, 185

artifacts, 28, 87, 105, 151

artificial intelligence (AI), 154

Asian Infrastructure Investment Bank (AIIB), 11, 19

assertiveness: "Assertive China," 15–16; "assertiveness," 16, 41, 46, 63–65, 180; Chinese assertiveness, 2–6, 50–54, 63–64, 113–14, 137–39, 181–82, 190; diplomatic assertiveness, 5–7, 9, 13, 16, 41, 67, 110, 119–21, 131, 139, 149, 153; embodied assertiveness, 46, 51, 53, 65, 67

Association of Southeast Asian Nations (ASEAN): and China, 6, 9, 40–43, 46, 52–61, 69, 87, 89–92, 94–95, 140, 142, 147, 183, 186, 190; ASEAN chair, 52, 61, 91; ASEAN elites, 53; ASEAN

Foreign Ministers' Meeting, 52, 89–90, 190; ASEAN norms, 54–55, 90, 92, 147; ASEAN statements, 6, 40, 46, 52–56, 90–91, 147; consensus norm, 186; South China Sea (SCS), 3, 6, 9, 43, 52–56, 183; Special ASEAN-China Foreign Ministers' Meeting, 41, 52, 90

Australia, 8, 84

background knowledge, 27–28, 31, 37, 60, 102, 108, 113,

Bai, Tian, 93

bargaining, 16–18

Beijing Foreign Studies University (BFSU), 75, 78–79

Belt and Road Initiative (BRI), 4, 11, 15–16, 19, 58, 65, 139

biao tai, 83, 153

Bicchi, Federica, 2, 29, 82

bilateral, 13, 22, 50, 55–57, 86–87, 93–95

birth anniversaries, 33

Bjola, Corneliu, 73, 120–121

Bourdieu, Pierre, 10–11, 17–18, 26–29, 32–35, 46–47, 51, 67–80, 86–87, 99–103, 123–24, 182, 184–85, 187–88, 191

Breslin, Shaun, 4–5

Brown, Kerry, 7, 26, 42, 68, 75, 95, 102, 115, 185

Printed in the USA
CPSIA information can be obtained
at www.ICGtesting.com
JSHW080242110224
57013JS00001B/1